Pro MEAN Stack Development

Elad Elrom

Apress®

Pro MEAN Stack Development

Elad Elrom
New York
USA

ISBN-13 (pbk): 978-1-4842-2043-6   ISBN-13 (electronic): 978-1-4842-2044-3
DOI 10.1007/978-1-4842-2044-3

Library of Congress Control Number: 2016960665

Managing Director: Welmoed Spahr
Acquisitions Editor: Louise Corrigan
Development Editor: James Markham
Technical Reviewer: Anselm Bradford
Editorial Board: Steve Anglin, Pramila Balan, Laura Berendson, Aaron Black, Louise Corrigan,
    Jonathan Gennick, Todd Green, Robert Hutchinson, Celestin Suresh John, Nikhil Karkal,
    James Markham, Susan McDermott, Matthew Moodie, Natalie Pao, Gwenan Spearing
Coordinating Editor: Nancy Chen
Copy Editor: Lauren Marten Parker
Compositor: SPi Global
Indexer: SPi Global
Artist: SPi Global

Distributed to the book trade worldwide by Springer Science+Business Media New York, 233 Spring Street, 6th Floor, New York, NY 10013. Phone 1-800-SPRINGER, fax (201) 348-4505, e-mail orders-ny@springer-sbm.com, or visit www.springer.com. Apress Media, LLC is a California LLC and the sole member (owner) is Springer Science + Business Media Finance Inc (SSBM Finance Inc). SSBM Finance Inc is a **Delaware** corporation.

For information on translations, please e-mail rights@apress.com, or visit www.apress.com.

Apress and friends of ED books may be purchased in bulk for academic, corporate, or promotional use. eBook versions and licenses are also available for most titles. For more information, reference our Special Bulk Sales–eBook Licensing web page at www.apress.com/bulk-sales.

Any source code or other supplementary materials referenced by the author in this text are available to readers at www.apress.com. For detailed information about how to locate your book's source code, go to www.apress.com/source-code/. Readers can also access source code at SpringerLink in the Supplementary Material section for each chapter.

Printed on acid-free paper

Contents at a Glance

Contents

About the Author

Elad Elrom is a coder, technical lead, and technical writer. He has co-authored four technical books. Elad has consulted for a variety of clients in different fields, from large corporations such as HBO, Viacom, NBC Universal, and Weight Watchers to smaller startups. Elad is also a certified PADI dive instructor, a motorcycle enthusiast, and a certified pilot.

About the Technical Reviewer

Anselm Bradford is a front-end web developer passionate about open source projects for government, non-profits, and higher education.

Currently, he's developing tools to help protect consumers from misleading and illegal financial practices. He has experience working on social services discovery for Code for America, user research at Imgur, and digital media curriculum development at AUT University.

He's the lead author on the book *HTML5 Mastery* (Apress).

Acknowledgments

I would like to thank Jessica Wendle for proofreading each chapter before it was sent back for the Editor's Review phase—your contribution is invaluable.

Additionally, I would like to express my gratitude to the coordinating editor, Nancy Chen, for her superb professionalism and constant encouragement. Many thanks to Akshat Paul for his on-point reviews and to the technical reviewer, Anselm Bradford, who has provided valuable comments and useful insights. I would also like to acknowledge the Apress editors, Ben Renow-Clarke and Louise Corrigan. Without them, this book would not have been possible.

Last but surely not least, I would like to thank the entire production team at Apress, who have labored to have this book published on time, and you, the reader, for purchasing a copy of this book and putting in the time and effort to better yourself.

CHAPTER 1

■ ■ ■

Code Dependencies

In this chapter, we will be installing tools, customizing and setting our development workarea on a Mac for developing applications on all devices. We will be installing tools such as integrated development environment (IDE), Git, node.js, npm, Grunt, Gulp, Bower, and Xcode.

These tools are not only necessary so we can hit the ground running in the following chapters, but having access to node.js, Grunt, Gulp, Bower, and Git will also give us access to millions of free open source libraries. Keep in mind that each tool we will discuss in this chapter has many features and can be used in many different ways—in fact, there are entire books covering each tool. Once you become equipped with basic knowelege, feel free to explore and broaden your personal knowledge on each individual tool. Even if you are already familiar with the some or all of the tools covered in this chapter, we encourage you to take a look at this chapter anyway, since there will be additional configuration and customization that will help make using these tools easier.

Git Version Control

We'll start off by installing Git. What is Git? It is a free open source distributed version control system. If you have previously been using other version control systems such as SVN or CVS, we would still encourage you to install Git. Git is great tool to have, considering many open source libraries are only available on Git. In fact, there are millions of open source Git libraries, so this is a cruicial piece of software to have in your arsenal of tools. It gives you access to free software you can use rather than rushing to develop a solution on your own.

The easiest way to install Git is to simply download and install the latest version from the following link :

```
http://git-scm.com/download/mac
```

Before you begin downloading and installing using their installer, we recommend installing an additional package manager that can be used to install other Unix tools and open source software on a Mac. This will come handy when you begin to need additional tools. There are very few package managers on the market for Mac—Homebrew, Fink, and Macports are the most popular ones. Homebrew is the newest and most well liked package manager of these three.

To install Homebrew, open Terminal by typing "terminal" in the Spotlight search box (right top corner) (see Figure 1-1).

© Elad Elrom 2016
E. Elrom, *Pro MEAN Stack Development*, DOI 10.1007/978-1-4842-2044-3_1

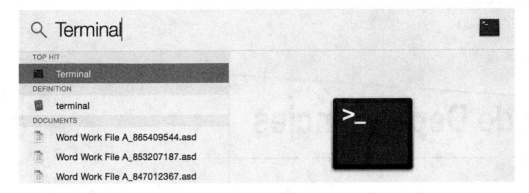

Figure 1-1. *Terminal search in Spotlight*

Before rushing to install Homebrew and Git, check to ensure you don't already have them installed on your machine. Once Terminal opens, up type in:

```
$ git
$ brew
```

Typing "git" in Terminal will give you a printout example of usage and commands. Similarly, Brew will print out example usage, troubleshooting, and commands. If they are already installed, feel free to skip this step.

Type in the following command, as shown in Figure 1-2:

```
$ ruby -e "$(curl -fsSL https://raw.githubusercontent.com/Homebrew/install/master/install)"
(See Figure 1-2).
```

```
● ● ●                    ⌂ eli — bash — 80×24
Last login: Sat Feb 20 18:39:26 on ttys000
eli@Elis-MBP-6 ~ $ ruby -e "$(curl -fsSL https://raw.githubusercontent.com/Homeb
rew/install/master/install)"
```

Figure 1-2. *Install Homebrew using terminal*

The default Terminal color scheme is "basic"— a white background with black text color—but you can easily change it by typing "command" + "," when the Terminal window is focused, under the "Profiles" ➤ "Text" options. I selected the "Homebrew" color scheme.

After Brew installation is completed, you can start using Brew and use it to install Git. In Terminal, type:

```
$ brew install git bash-completion
```

That's it! Once you're done, confirm Git has been installed by typing in Terminal:

```
$ git
```

Typing "git" in Terminal will give you a printout example of usage and commands.

Customize Git

We recommend bookmarking this URL: https://git-scm.com/. It is a great source to use if you need to find documents, the latest available version of Git, and much more.

Next, we want to configure and customize Git. We will start with entering your personal information. To do so, type in Terminal:

```
$ git config --global user.name "Your Name"
$ git config --global user.email "you-email@email-address.com"
$ git config --global apply.whitespace nowarn
```

Git Customization and Configuration

The following site is a great resource for Git customization and configuration:

```
https://git-scm.com/book/en/v2/Customizing-Git-Git-Configuration
```

In terms of customization, we recommend customizing colors for Git so it will appear more "readable" once you begin to work in a command line. The default Git settings will color output your list of files when you are in Terminal. However, we will customize it a bit more and select the appropriate colors for the type of repositories (repos) that we will be using. To do so, type into Terminal:

```
$ vim ~/.gitconfig
```

This will open the Git configuration file in a text editor and allow you to make changes. If you have previously used different text editors such vi, feel free to do so here.

Paste the following into a Git config file, below the existing settings:

```
[color]
    branch = auto
    diff = auto
    status = auto
[color "branch"]
    current = yellow reverse
    local = yellow
    remote = green
[color "diff"]
    meta = yellow bold
    frag = magenta bold
    old = red bold
    new = green bold
[color "status"]
    added = yellow
    changed = green
    untracked = cyan
```

If you are not familiar with vim, or maybe just a bit rusty, use the following instructions to edit and save the Git config file:

1. To open the file, type: "vim ~/.gitconfig".

2. Next, insert content; type "i" on your keyboard.

3. Continue by pasting code using "command + v", just like in any other text editor.

4. Lastly, to save, press the escape key on your keyboard and type ":wq" and press enter. Note: if you are unhappy with the changes and you want to just quit, type ":q!", which will revert the changes and quit.

You can confirm that your changes have been made by typing:

```
$ cat ~/.gitconfig
```

Adding gitexcludes

Now let's add the "gitexcludes" file. This file will instruct Git to ignore specific files. For now, let's just tell Git to ignore Mac famouse "DS_Store" file:

```
$ vim ~/.gitexcludes
```

Then, type in a list of files you would like to ignore:

```
.DS_Store
```

This file can be very useful. Let's say you work on a large team, and each developer wants to keep their own IDE settings. You can use this file to ignore an entire folder.

Adding the Repo Branch

Next on the list is branches. Branches are a staging environment. When you don't want to make changes in the working directory, you can request a copy from Git and make changes on that branch, then integrate the branch into the working environment when you are ready to commit the changes. Git records these commits and they show as a fork of the project. Git allows you to add, delete, and rename these branches, so it's helpful know what branch you're working are on without having to ask Git to tell you.

We'll add some magic to your Bash prompt so that it will include your branch information. Doing this will add the repo branch. Figure 1-3 shows the folder name along with the branch name in brackets "(master)".

```
eli@Elis-MBP-6 theluxurygame-app (master) $ ls
total 216
drwxr-xr-x     3 eli    admin      102 Oct 20   2014 hooks
drwxr-xr-x     3 eli    admin      102 Oct 20   2014 .cordova
drwxr-xr-x     6 eli    admin      204 Oct 20   2014 test
drwxr-xr-x     5 eli    admin      170 Oct 21   2014 ..
-rw-r--r--     1 eli    admin      180 Oct 21   2014 README.md
drwxr-xr-x     9 eli    admin      306 Dec 15   2014 plugins
-rw-r--r--     1 eli    admin       32 May  7   2015 .gitignore
drwxr-xr-x     4 eli    admin      136 May  7   2015 platforms
drwxr-xr-x     5 eli    admin      170 May  7   2015 res
drwxr-xr-x    17 eli    admin      578 Nov 30 20:24 www
drwxr-xr-x    13 eli    admin      442 Dec 21 15:07 certificates
drwxr-xr-x    16 eli    admin      544 Jan 25 21:35 docs
drwxr-xr-x   122 eli    admin     4148 Jan 26 06:53 node_modules
-rw-r--r--@    1 eli    admin    10244 Jan 26 07:12 .DS_Store
-rw-r--r--     1 eli    admin     1688 Jan 26 07:12 package.json
-rw-r--r--     1 eli    admin    85969 Jan 26 07:13 Gruntfile.js
drwxr-xr-x    15 eli    admin      510 Jan 26 07:31 .git
drwxr-xr-x    13 eli    admin      442 Jan 26 07:31 .idea
drwxr-xr-x    19 eli    admin      646 Feb 21 10:04 .
eli@Elis-MBP-6 theluxurygame-app (master) $ █
```

Figure 1-3. *Command line showing branch name*

This setting will be very useful when you switch between branches following the Gitflow process (discussed later in this chapter).

Configure bash_profile

To configure these options, we will be editing the Bash profile file. Bash profile is used to set PATH and other shell environmental variables. There are two type of bash profile files: .bash_profile and .bashrc. bash_profile excutes login shell commands, while bashrc excutes non-login shell commands. In our case, we want the changes to be reflected in all directories and all users, so we will be using bash_profile.

To edit, open the bash_profile file in a vim editor by typing in Terminal:

```
$ vim ~/.bash_profile
```

Then add the following code to your Bash file:

```
parse_git_branch() {
    git branch 2> /dev/null | sed -e '/^[^*]/d' -e 's/* \(.*\)/ (\1)/'
}
source /usr/local/etc/bash_completion.d/git-completion.bash
GIT_PS1_SHOWDIRTYSTATE=true
export PS1="\u@\h \W\[\033[32m\]\$(parse_git_branch)\[\033[00m\] $ "
```

Lastly, remember to run the Bash profile file to allow these changes to take effect:

```
$ . ~/.bash_profile
```

Figure 1-4 shows the command line with the repo branch name and colors:

By the way, in Figure 1-4, we are using a "git status" command, which shows you the changes in your Git directory in comparison to the remote server. In your directory, this command won't work until you set an actual Git project and will create a "fatal" error message if you type "git status", but we wanted to show you what it looks like on a working Git direcctory.

```
eli@Elis-MBP-6 theluxurygame-app (master) $ git status
On branch master
Your branch is up-to-date with 'origin/master'.

Changes not staged for commit:
  (use "git add <file>..." to update what will be committed)
  (use "git checkout -- <file>..." to discard changes in working directory)

        modified:   .idea/workspace.xml
        modified:   platforms/ios/TheLuxuryGame.xcodeproj/project.xcworkspace/:
te.xcuserstate
        modified:   www/index.html
        modified:   www/partials/about.html

no changes added to commit (use "git add" and/or "git commit -a")
eli@Elis-MBP-6 theluxurygame-app (master) $ █
```

Figure 1-4. *Command line with adjusted colors and branch name prompt*

Additionally, you can add extra commands to a Bash profile to ajust your working environment to your liking. For instance, the code below sets custom colors for list view, shortcuts to edit Bash profile, change directory to locations and reload Bash profile automatically with one command: "bash". See below:

```
alias ls='ls -ltra'
export CLICOLOR=1
export LSCOLORS=ExFxCxDxBxegedabagacad
export ANDROID_HOME=/usr/local/opt/android-sdk

alias vimb='vim ~/.bash_profile'
alias runb='. ~/.bash_profile'
alias cdr='cd /Applications/XAMPP/xamppfiles/htdocs/'
alias bash='. ~/.bash_profile'
```

Download Git Libraries

There are millions of open source Git repos, and now that you have installed Git, you can start taking advantage of these libraries. As an example, we will be downloading the following repository:

```
https://github.com/pilwon/ultimate-seed
```

First, we want to create a directory and change it into the newly created directory:

```
$ mkdir ultimate-seed && cd $_
```

Then you can clone the repository from the hosting server:

```
$ git clone https://github.com/pilwon/ultimate-seed
```

Git "Hello World"

Now you are ready to set up your first project, and since we are starting from scratch, we will be creating your Git-hosted project.

First, create a directory where your project will reside. To do so, type into the terminal:

```
$ mkdir [/path/to/your/project] && cd $_
```

This will create the directory and change the current working directory into the newly created directory. Then, initiate Git by typing in the following command line:

```
$ git init
```

Here are the complete commands to create a "test" folder and init git on your desktop:

```
$ cd ~/Desktop
$ mkdir test && cd $_
$ git init
$ git status
```

That's it! You've created your project and intiated a Git.

Now, you can create a repo on GitHub, Bitbucket, AWS CodeCommit, or your favorite hosting solution and upload your code.

Need help deciding which hosting solution you should be using? we believe that it boils down to factors such as how many members are on your team, the repo size, the number of repo you need, and your budget. To make it easy to select your version control remote hosting solution, we have created a quick comparison between GitHub, Bitbucket, and AWS CodeCommit (Table 1-1).

Table 1-1. *Git showdown*

	GitHub	Bitbucket	AWS CodeCommit
Filesize limit	1GB	1GB	10GB
Free Repo	Free Unlimited users	Free for unlimited users	Free for up to 5 active users
Private Repo	Starts at $7/month	Free for up to 5 users	Free for up to 5 active users
Web Visual	GitHub Flow	Not available	Not available
3rd Party Integration	Integration with many 3rd party tools.	Integrate via Plugins	Integrates well with AWS services.
Pricing	Private repo $7/month	Free for up to 5 users	$1 per active user per month

Visit the following link, which will provide more information on these three types of hosted Git solutions: http://stackshare.io/stackups/github-vs-bitbucket-vs-aws-codecommit

As you can see from Table 1-1, GitHub is great for publishing free open source libraries and would be our primary choice. It's great for open source projects and provides easy-to-use UI and integration with many tools, however it does not offer free private repos. That feature alone makes Bitbucket and AWS CodeCommit good tools to add to your arsenal. Not having to pay an additional fee for source control adds great value in my opinion, especially when it's your personal repo.

To upload a repo to Bitbucket, start by creating a free account by going to https://bitbucket.org and signing up. Then, create a new repository by selecting "Create a repository" or going to "Create" ➤ "Create Repository" in your dashboard (Figure 1-5).

Figure 1-5. *Creating a new repository on BitBucket*

Next, select the repository owner, name, description, and other settings. Notice that you have an option to set the access level as private (Figure 1-6).

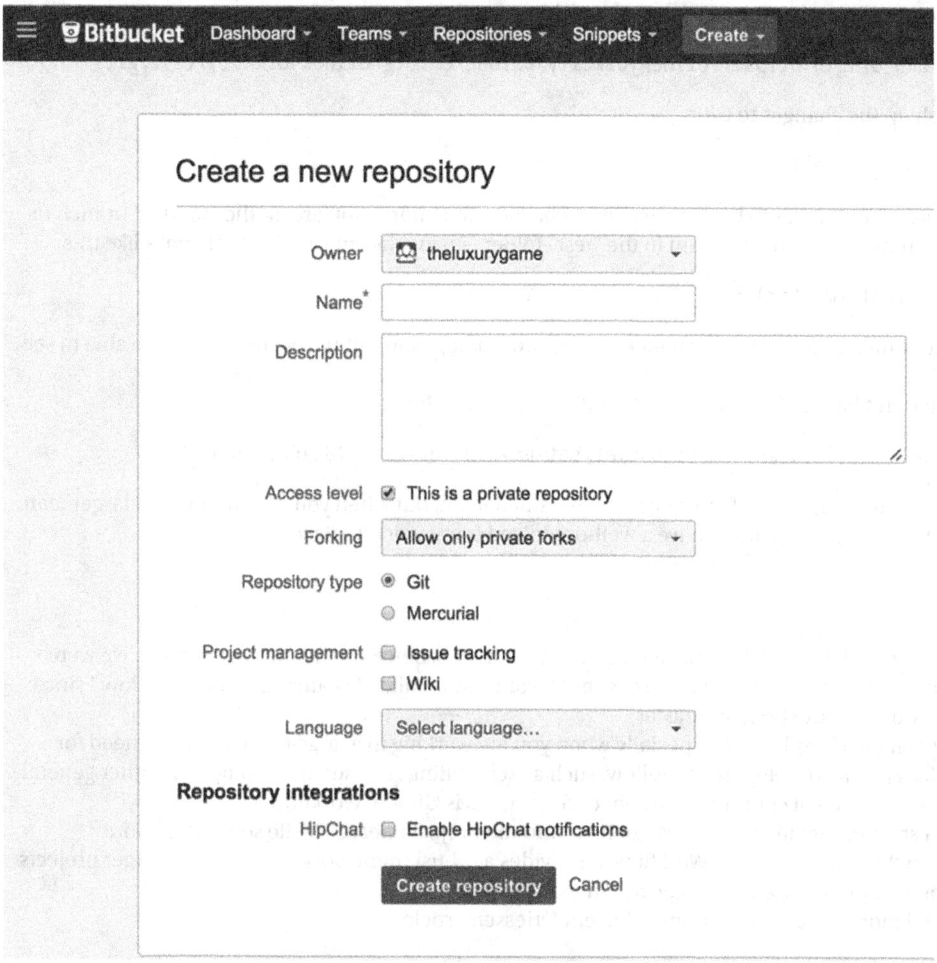

Figure 1-6. *Create a new repository settings window on Bitbucket*

Next, change the directory (cd) to where your project resides, in case you are not there, and add a file. For instance you can just add a markdown readme file (we'll talk more about markdown in later chapters):

```
$ vim readme.md
```

Inside of "vim", press "i" to insert any text and ":wq" to save and quit. Now we can commit our changes:

```
$ git add .
$ git commit -m 'first commit'
```

Now we are ready to commit our project. To add a remote origin location, change to your username and repo name and then type the following into the command line:

```
$ git remote add origin ssh://git@bitbucket.org/[username]/[repo-name].git
```

Here's an example of what the code should look like:

```
$ git remote add origin https://elinewyorkcity@bitbucket.org/elinewyorkcity/test.git
```

Lastly, push up the changes to Git:

```
$ git push -u origin –all
```

This will push the changes to the "master" branch. You can confirm you are on the "master" branch in terminal. My terminal shows me that I am in the "test" folder—using the "master" branch looks like this:

```
eli@Elis-MBP-6 test (master) $
```

This will commit and upload your changes. Now, you can log in to Bitbucket and you will be able to see your files.

In case you don't have SSH set up yet, follow the instructions here:

```
https://confluence.atlassian.com/bitbucket/set-up-ssh-for-git-728138079.html
```

This simple setup works great for a project with a small team, but when you're working with larger team it can become a challenge if you don't have a well-organized framework in place.

Gitflow

So far we've created and uploaded a repo and downloaded a repo. Since we did not set a branch, we were working with the "master" branch. This type of simple workflow is called "Feature Branch Workflow," since we are using only one feature branch (master).

As things get more complicated, especially when you are working in a large team, there is a need for standard practices that all developers can follow, such as scheduling releases, fixing bugs, and other general development tasks. The most common solution for these tasks is Gitflow Workflow.

Gitflow is a strict branching model designed around the project release. While somewhat more complicated than the Feature Branch Workflow, it provides a robust framework for managing larger projects and has been proven to work well on projects with many members.

You can read more about it here, from a Vincent Driessen article:

```
http://nvie.com/posts/a-successful-git-branching-model/
```

We will not be explaining the entire Gitflow model since it's beyond the scope of this book, but we would like to point out a couple of tools that will make using Gitflow much easier and reduce the boilerplate code needed to follow the Gitflow practice.

Take a look at the following repository:

```
https://github.com/nvie/gitflow
```

As we mentioned earlier, to download this tool, all you have to do is type into the command line:

```
$ git clone https://github.com/nvie/gitflow
```

Installing Gitflow is simple with Brew:

```
$ brew install git-flow
```

Next, to initialize a new repository with the basic Gitflow branch structure, use the following command:

```
$ git flow init [-d]
```

Using the "-d" flag will accept all default settings. Then you can implement operations such as list, start, finish, and publish a branch.

Gitflow on GitHub

As you become more comfortable with Git, and specifically if you are using GitHub as your Git remote server provider, you will find GitHub to be a friendly environment. In fact, it has a built-in user interface (UI) to make pull requests, merge branches, and perform all Gitflow and other structure operations.

Nevertheless, for programmers, using a UI can take longer than a command line operation. Luckily, there is an open source tool called "node-gh" that allow us to perform the commands via Terminal instead of GitHub UI. Check it out here: `https://github.com/node-gh/gh`

In addition to this, I have forked and cloned gh repository and added commands to match Gitflow so you can also make a pull request in the command line, in addition to following Gitflow methodology:

```
git clone https://github.com/eladelrom/node-gh
```

Node.js

Node.js is a fast, lightweight JavaScript runtime built on Chrome's V8 JavaScript engine, and uses an event-driven, non-blocking I/O model. It includes the npm package ecosystem, with access to hundreds of thousands of packages.

You can install node via Brew:

```
$ brew install node
```

However, for Mac, the safest way is to install Node.js is using the installer available here: `http://nodejs.org`. See Figure 1-7:

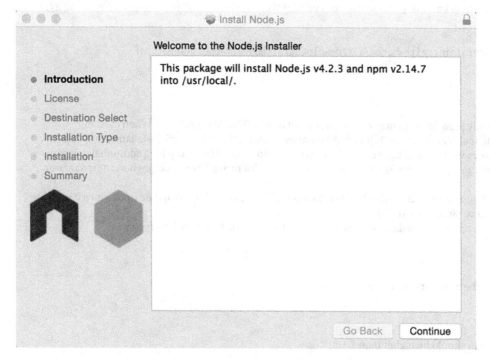

Figure 1-7. Node.js Mac installer

To check that the installation was successful, type into the command line terminal:

```
$ node
```

Typing "node." will kick off the interactive shell (AKA "REPL"). Next, type:

```
> console.log('Hello World');
```

Node.js replies with "Hello World". See Figure 1-8.

```
eli@Elis-MBP-6 theluxurygame-app (master) $ node
> console.log('Hello World');
Hello World
undefined
>
(^C again to quit)
>
eli@Elis-MBP-6 theluxurygame-app (master) $
```

Figure 1-8. *Node.js Hello World example*

This interactive shell is great for testing one-liners. To exit out of it, press Ctrl + C twice.

Do you want to know more about Git commands? You can visit the following page to download a Git cheat sheet:

```
https://training.github.com/kit/downloads/github-git-cheat-sheet.pdf
```

npm

npm is the Node.js package manager. It's mainly used to install Node.js packages. When used in development, it allows you to easily link dependencies to your project for quick installation and updates.

npm comes with Node.js right out of the box, so you don't need to do anything additional to install it. You can now install any package for your project. See the list of available packages here: https://www.npmjs.com/

Although npm does comes with Node.js, it's a good idea to know how to update npm, since it needs to be updated more often than Node.js.

To update, open Terminal and ensure node.js is at least v0.10.32. Check it by typing:

```
$ node -v
```

To check the npm version, type:

```
$ npm -v
```

The version should be higher than 2.1.8.

To update npm, type the following:

```
$ [sudo] npm install npm -g
```

See Figure 1-9 for the complete commands.

```
eli@Elis-MBP-6 theluxurygame-app (master) $ node -v
v0.10.32
eli@Elis-MBP-6 theluxurygame-app (master) $ npm -v
1.4.28
eli@Elis-MBP-6 theluxurygame-app (master) $ sudo npm install npm -g
Password:
/usr/local/bin/npm -> /usr/local/lib/node_modules/npm/bin/npm-cli.js
npm@3.5.1 /usr/local/lib/node_modules/npm
eli@Elis-MBP-6 theluxurygame-app (master) $
```

Figure 1-9. *Installing npm and checking Node.js and npm versions*

Grunt

Next on our list is Grunt. Grunt is a JS-based task runner. It provides easy automation using JavaScript, with access to thousands of plugins to choose from to automate just about anything you can think of. Additionally, publishing your own Grunt plugin to npm is easy to do.

■ **Note**   A task runner is automation. We developers are known to be "lazy" and prefer to create an automated task when doing repetitive work.

Now that we have Node.js and npm, you can install Grunt. Install Grunt by using command line interface (CLI) globally:

```
$ [sudo] npm install -g grunt-cli
```

If you want to install Grunt on a local project, the npm init command will create a basic package.json file and add Grunt to the "devDependencies" section, using a tilde version range. Type the following:

```
$ npm install grunt --save-dev
```

There are thousands of plugins available for Grunt. These plugins are what really make Grunt great. They give you access to community open-source projects that will help you to easily automate your tasks. You can see a list here: http://gruntjs.com/plugins. Anytime you need anything that Grunt doesn't offer out of the box, you can simply search the Grunt plugin directory and see if there is a plugin available.

Installing a Grunt plugin is just like installing any of the other node modules. For example, to install the grunt-nglue plugin, type this:

```
$ npm install grunt-nglue --save-dev
```

See more details here: http://gruntjs.com/getting-started

Gulp

Another JS-based task runner is Gulp. Gulp emerged after Grunt and was quickly adopted by a large portion of the JS community. Gulp is a streaming build system. When you think of Gulp, imagine Grunt, but faster and less work for your config boilerplate code.

In a nutshell, Grunt focuses on configuration, while Gulp focuses on gluing community-developed micro-tasks to one another.

Each Gulp module is a streaming node, which has nothing to do with Gulp except for the module name. Gulp runs on its own, while Grunt plugins only work inside of Grunt.

Many consider Gulp to be better. Most developers choose one or the other, but they can be used together for different tasks.

To install, in Terminal, type:

```
$ [sudo] npm install --g gulp
```

To install Gulp on a local project, the npm init command will create a basic package.json file (if you don't already have one) and will add Gulp to the devDependencies section. Using a tilde version range, type the following;

```
$ npm install --save-dev gulp
```

Now you can browse through the Gulp plugin list, located here: `http://gulpjs.com/plugins/`
To create your first Gulp file, check the GitHub project here:

```
https://github.com/gulpjs/gulp/blob/master/docs/getting-started.md
```

Bower

Last but not least is the Bower package manager. Bower helps keep track of your project's packages as well as making sure they are up to date. See: `http://bower.io/`

You can install Bower easily with npm:

```
$ [sudo] npm install -g bower
```

To install locally, use the following command:

```
$ npm install --save-dev bower
```

Now you can search for packages here: `http://bower.io/search/`
To install a package, simply type into the Terminal:

```
$ bower install some-package
```

Bower is used together with many other tools and can be integrated with all sorts of setups and workflows to your liking.

Check the Bower tools page, which includes tons of links to many tools you can integrate:

```
http://bower.io/docs/tools/
```

Having Node.js, npm, Grunt, Gulp, and Bower will give you instant access to about half a million free open source community projects, and I personally believe that they're essential to have before starting any JavaScript project.

Integrated Development Environment

The first thing we will do with an integrated development environment (IDE) is set our developer environment. WebStorm (https://www.jetbrains.com/webstorm/) by Jetbrains would be our first pick for the best type of app/site we will be building. It combines the entire "MEAN" stack development into one easy-to-use IDE.

You will be able to easily develop MongoDB, Express.js, AngularJS, and Node.js using WebStorm. It also includes integration with everything else that we will be using in this book. The only caveat is that their pricing model has changed, and they are now charging a yearly subscription, which can be a big turnoff for large businesses. At the time of this writing, the cost is $649 per year for a business license. However, for individual customers, the price is as low as $59 for the first year and free for students and and open source contributors.

Of course, there are many other free alternatives to WebStorm, especially if you are comfortable with command line. For instance, Sublime Text (https://www.sublimetext.com/), Notepad++ (https://notepad-plus-plus.org/) and brackets.io (http://brackets.io/) can be great alternatives.

Keep in mind that this is based entirely on personal preference, and you will have no problem working with whatever IDE you prefer, whether your main choice is listed here or not.

Now, let's install and configure the WebStorm IDE. Go to the download page and begin downloading:

https://www.jetbrains.com/webstorm/download/

At the time of writing, the current version of WebStorm is Version 2016.1.3. Once the download is completed, start WebStorm. The first message will request the type of license. If you don't have a license, you can use the "evaluate for free for 30 days" option. See Figure 1-10:

Figure 1-10. *WebStorm license activation window*

In the initial WebStorm configuration window, the Keymap scheme has plenty of options in case you are used to other IDEs, such as Visual Studio or Eclipse. For color scheme, "Darcula" is the default, but feel free to select a different one. You can view a preview of the theme (see Figure 1-11).

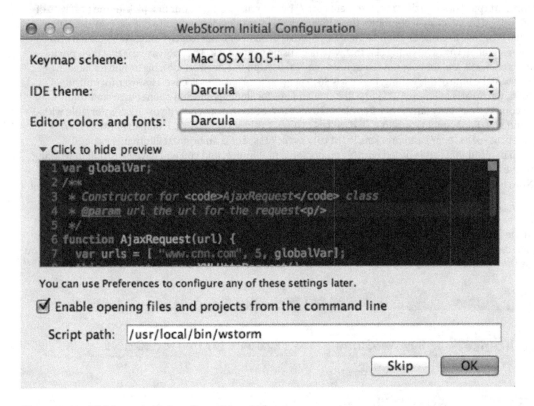

Figure 1-11. *WebStorm initial configuration window*

Once you click "OK," WebStorm 11 restarts and gives you the option to create a new project, open, or check out from Version Control, as shown in Figure 1-12. Select "Create New Project."

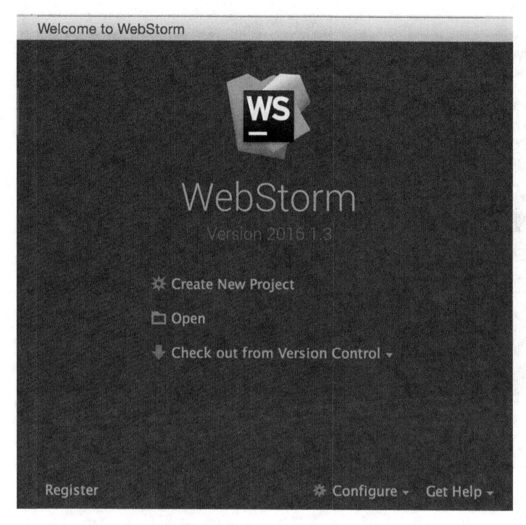

Figure 1-12. *WebStorm welcome window*

We will be creating two projects: an AngularJS project and a Node.js project.

Let's start with the AngularJS app. Select "Create New Project," select "AngularJS," and then "Create." See Figure 1-13.

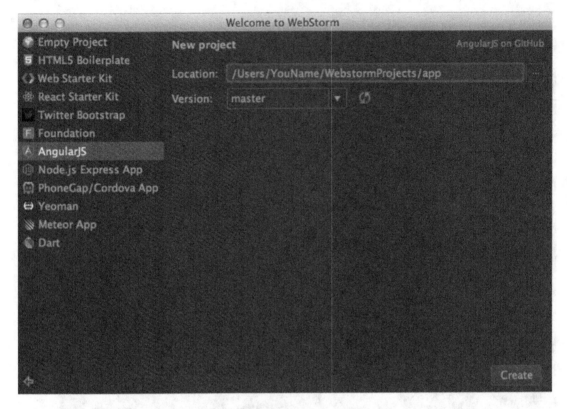

Figure 1-13. *WebStorm welcome window.*

As you can see, WebStorm automatically downloads the AngularJS seed project, so you can get started right away. See Figure 1-14.

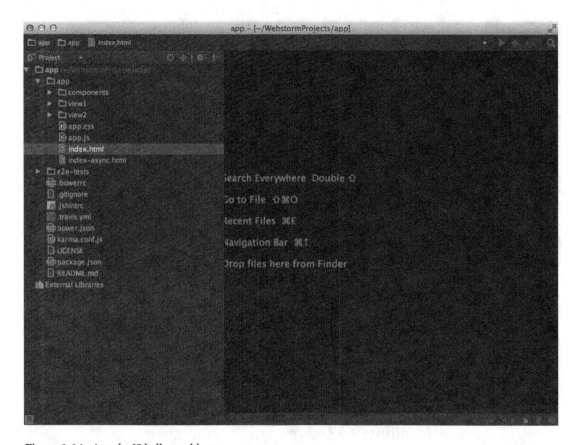

Figure 1-14. *AngularJS hello world app*

All you have to do now is double click "index.html" (see Figure 1-15). Once you hover over the page, the browsers' icons will show up.

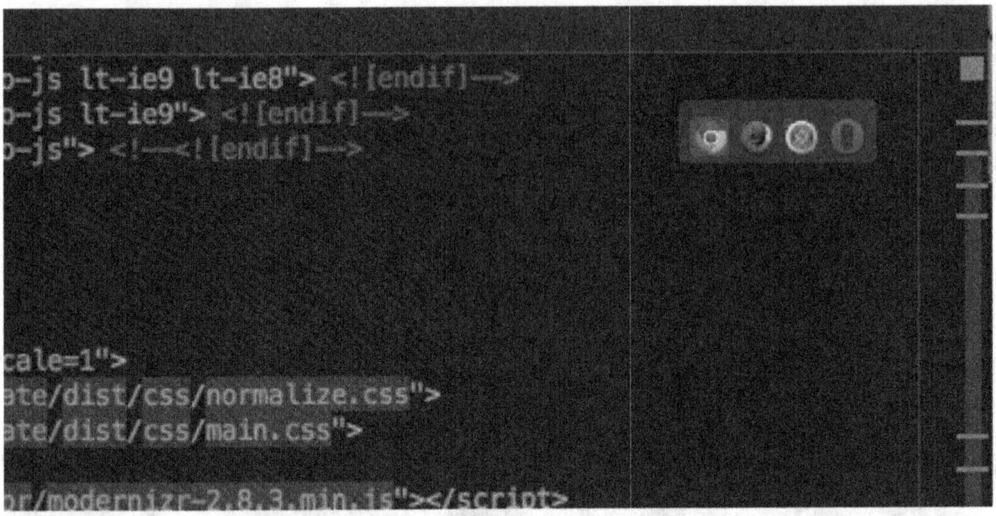

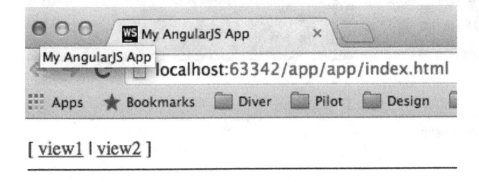

Figure 1-15. *Index.html browser icons*

Select the browser of your choice and the "Hello World" app will open up in your browser (see Figure 1-16).

[view1 | view2]

Angular seed app: v

Figure 1-16. *Angular seed app running in the browser*

The same process will work for the Node.js app. Select "Create New Project," then select "Node.js Express App" and finally "Create" (see Figure 1-17).

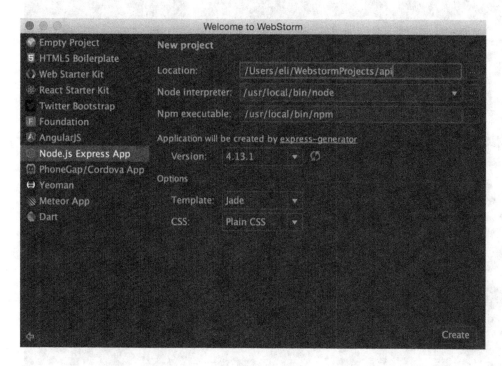

Figure 1-17. *Creating a Node.js express app in WebStorm*

Next, your work environment will open up and you can begin working on your Node.js project right away. See Figure 1-18.

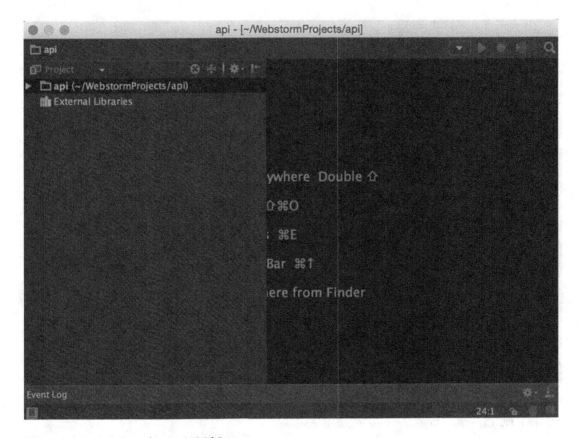

Figure 1-18. *Node.js workspace in WebStorm*

Installing a Free Open Source IDE

Installing and setting WebStorm was a breeze, but it's not completely necessary, and you can perform your entire development using free, open source tools. Sublime Text can be used to view files in any development language; in fact, you can create your entire development directory on your own and simply view and edit the contents of your files with the Sublime Text editor. Download Sublime Text here:

http://www.sublimetext.com/

Now all you have to do is add a folder (Figure 1-19). To do so, follow these steps:

1. Select top menu, then: "Project" ➤ "Add Folder to Project..."

2. Browse to the folder where your files are located and select that folder.

Figure 1-19. Sublime Text select a project folder menu

You can now select and edit files (Figure 1-20).

Figure 1-20. *Edit an HTML file in Sublime Text*

Installing Xcode

Lastly, another great set of tools that we would recommend installing would be Apple "Xcode" (see Figure 1-21). This includes an IDE for developing iOS apps, a compiler, instruments, a simulator and SDKs. We will need these once we start to develop apps that will be deployed for iOS.

Visit the following link to download:

```
https://developer.apple.com/xcode/download/
```

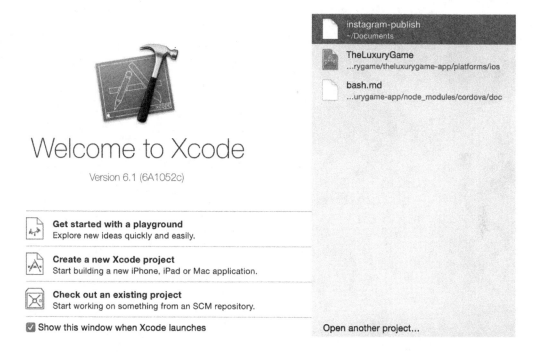

Figure 1-21. *Xcode welcome screen*

Summary

In this chapter, we covered installing, customizing, and configuating tools such as integrated development environments (IDEs), and we installed Brew, Git, Node.js, npm, Grunt, Gulp, Bower, WebStorm, Sublime Text and Xcode. These tools will come handy in the following chapters as we start to develop and deploy applications. Keep in mind that there are entire books and much more information online for each of the tools we discussed. We have only scratched the surface in this regard, but feel free to acquire more information on your own; the more you know about these tools, the easier it will be to develop your applications quickly and efficiently in the future. In the next chapter, we will be rolling out servers, customizing them, and configuring them so we can deploy our code and see it work.

CHAPTER 2

■ ■ ■

Rollout Servers

In the previous chapter, we learned to install and configure our personal work environment so that we would be able to hit the ground running. In this chapter we are going to put on our administrative hats and roll out the servers that we can then use to deploy our MEAN stack apps. We will roll out Ubuntu and Linux servers and install both MongoDB and MySQL databases. These servers can be used to deploy MEAN stack-type applications, as well as to deployment of a Linux server will be helpful in the future, as we will be using it to deploy our app, as well as connecting to the database and running cron jobs. With these servers deployed and configured, we will be able to tackle just about anything that comes our way and see the code in action.

Ubuntu Server

There once was a time when deploying servers was expensive; in the past, a dedicated server could easily cost over $1,000 per month. All of this changed with the delivery of cloud computing. In fact, we can now deploy servers for free under low resource configurations, and scale up as needed. In this chapter, we will be rolling out an Ubuntu server; SSH connecting to the server; installing and updating software such as Git, Node.js, and npm; and creating a web folder we can deploy our code into.

MEAN stack-type applications can be deployed in many different ways, including Heroku or Cloud9 which enable deployment straight to a cloud server or a $5 Node.js Cloud Server on Ubuntu using digitalocean.com. Another solution is utilizing Vagrant VM, which we will be covering in Chapter 9 of this book in more detial.

In this book specifically, we've chosen to deploy using Amazon EC2 and Vagrant VM, since we want to give you the tools to be able to deploy and administrate the server yourself. If you decide to go with a solution that provides automation, it will be easier, but you will have the tools in your arsenal and will not be forced to depend on one particular service or another. The benefit of having these servers at our disposol early is that we're able to deploy the examples from this book, or any other code you would like to deploy.

We highly recommend keeping track of the steps you take as you set your environment to ensure you will always be able to easily replicate it, in case you want to switch providers or you experience a server collapse. Ubuntu is a widely used OS (Operating System), popular for the Node.js application. It's easy to deploy, configure, and scale.

■ **Note**   Ubuntu is a free and widely used Linux-based OS available for all type of devices and is a popular server OS to deploy Node.js-type applications.

When using Amazon EC2 on a low-resource bandwidth, you can deploy your server easily, freely, and effortlessly. According to Amazon, "Amazon Elastic Compute Cloud (EC2) provides scalable computing capacity in the Amazon Web Services (AWS) cloud." They promise, "You can develop and deploy applications faster and use Amazon EC2 to launch as many or as few virtual servers as you need."

With that being said, it takes some knowledge and dodging some minefields to be able to roll servers on EC2 free of cost for a year. Amazon EC2 specifically designed their forms so that any misstep could end in hundreds of dollars in fees if you are not careful or you don't know exactly what you are being asked. Although it's easy to make a slip-up and end up receiving a bill from Amazon, their customer support will allow you to change your settings and they will then remove the charge.

In this article, we will help you navigate through some of the more confusing forms and install all the basic software necessary to be able to run the servers you need to deploy MEAN stack (MongoDB, Express.js, AngularJS, Node.js) apps, and more.

To begin, you may read and reference the Amazon Free tier article here: `http://aws.amazon.com/free/`

This article gives Amazon's definition of what their free tier includes. It can change, so be sure to pay close attention to what they offer to continue using the free tier.

At the time of writing, Amazon EC2's free tier includes:

- 750 hours per month of t2.micro instance usage
- For example, run one instance for one month or two instances for half a month.

Amazon's Relational Database Service (RDS) includes:

- 750 hours of Amazon RDS Single-AZ db.t2.micro instance
- 30 GB of database storage
- 15 million I/Os

Keep in mind:

- Free services will expire 12 months after signup.
- They are available to new AWS customers.
- You can check the latest pricing information for the free and paid accounts here: `https://aws.amazon.com/ec2/pricing/`.

To get started, sign up for Amazon Web Services, then sign into AWS using the following URL to create an EC2 instance: `https://us-west-2.console.aws.amazon.com/ec2/v2`

To launch a new server, select "Create Instance" ➤ "Launch Instance" from the bottom of the page (Figure 2-1).

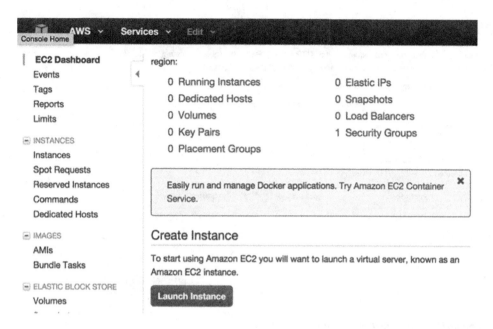

Figure 2-1. *Launch an instance on Amazon EC2*

Next, select: "Ubuntu Server 14.04 LTS" under "Free tier eligible", and hit "Select". see Figure 2-2 below:

Figure 2-2. *Select Ubuntu image from Amazon EC2 options*

■ **Note** Keep in mind that 14.04 LTS is the latest Ubuntu version number available on Amazon. That may change, but the instructions here will stay relevant as long as Amazon provide this service with its interface.

After you select the server type, the next screen will read "Step 2: Choose an Instance Type," the Amazon wizard will start, and you can now configure the server:

1. Ensure you select a server under the "Free tier eligible" again.

2. On the next screen, select: "t2.micro Free tier eligible."

3. Select "Review and Launch."

4. In the preview screen, choose "Edit security groups." Important: For HTTP and HTTPS, you want to open it to the world (0.0.0.0/0), but SSH limit to "My IP" so that no one else can SSH your server. See Figure 2-3 below:

29

Step 6: Configure Security Group

specific traffic to reach your instance. For example, if you want to set up a web server and allow Internet traffic to reach your instance, add rules that allow unrestricted access to the HTTP and HTTPS ports. You can create a new security group or select from an existing one below. Learn more about Amazon EC2 security groups.

Figure 2-3. *Configuring your security group in Amazon AWS*

5. Next, select "Review and Launch."

6. A screen will open reading "Step 7: Review Instance Launch. Click "Launch."

7. Select "Create a new key pair" ➤ [Your key name] ➤ "Download Key Pair" and save it somewhere safe. These keys encrypt and decrypt your login information, ensuring you can log in to your account using SSH.

8. Lastly, "Launch Instances."

And that is all there is to it. It's pretty simple and straightforward, and now you have a server to work with.

To ensure your account won't be charged, there are two options:

1. The safest way to avoid billing is to disable your server after you are done using it. That's a good option if your server is just staging for you to experiment. To do so, follow these steps:

    a. In AWS home, select "EC2."

    b. Select "Instances" under the "EC2 Dashboard" left menu pane.

    c. Right click the server. Under "Instance State" select "Stop."

    d. That will ensure the instance is not using any additinoal resources.

    e. You can also right click the server and, under "Instace State," select "Terminate" to completely remove the server and ensure you won't get billed.

2. The other option is to set a billing alert.

    a. Go to this URL : https://console.aws.amazon.com/billing/

b. Start by enabling the feature that monitors estimated charges. Click "Enable Now" at the bottom of the screen.

c. The preferences page will come up. Select "Receive Billing Alerts" and select "Save preferences."

d. Now you can create a billing alert. Open the SNS Home page: `https://console.aws.amazon.com/sns/`

e. Click "Get started" and select "Create topic."

f. The topic popup will open up. Select a name (for instance, you can use "email_billing_notification") and a display name (such as "billing.") Then, click "Create topic."

g. Next, open "Cloud watch": `https://console.aws.amazon.com/cloudwatch/`.

h. From the left menu under "Alarms," select "Billing" and choose the region your EC2 was deployed in.

i. Select "Create Alarm."

j. In the "Create Alarm" popup, select "When my total AWS charges for the month exceed," select "$0.1" and enter your email address, then click "Create Alarm."

k. Confirm your email address, and that's it. You will get an email if you are being billed.

SSH Connection and Upgrade Servers

Now that we have created the server, downloaded an SSH key, and set the security level, the next step is to connect and configure the server with all the software we will need. We will be using this server for our API / Services, so this step involves SSH, the Ubuntu server, and beginning to install our software.

First, we will create an IP address and associate the server, so that our server have an actual IP address instead of the tag ID Amazon assigns to a server.

To do this, select "NETWORK & SECURITY" ➤ "Elastic IPs" ➤ "Allocate New Address" on the AWS left side menu. A popup will appear asking "Are you sure you want to allocate a new IP address?" Select "Yes Allocate".

Next, right click and select "Associate Address" ➤ "instance" ➤ "select instance ID" (you should only have one option, since we have only launched one server) and then select "associate." Now we will create an SSH shortcut to access the servers. Configurating the SSH in the config file will allow us to easily access the new server that we just set up.

To edit the SSH config file, return to the Mac OSX Terminal and type:

```
vim ~/.ssh/config
```

Next, insert the new server information:

```
Host api
HostName [elastic ip address]
User ubuntu
IdentityFile /[location to API key]/[api key name].pem
```

You will need to set the permission of the server key:

```
$ chmod 400 /[location to API key]/[api key name].pem
```

Lastly, try to SSH the server; in the command line, type:

```
$ ssh api
```

When the command line asks, "Are you sure you want to continue connecting (yes/no)?" reply "yes" and you should then be able to log in. See Figure 2-4.

```
eli@Elis-MacBook-Pro-6 certificates (master) $ chmod 400 theluxurygame-amazon-api-key.pem
eli@Elis-MacBook-Pro-6 certificates (master) $ ssh tlg-api-new
The authenticity of host '52.88.75.138 (52.88.75.138)' can't be established.
RSA key fingerprint is 87:53:7e:1c:b9:ff:00:32:4b:21:ea:83:20:c2:d9:6a.
Are you sure you want to continue connecting (yes/no)? yes
Warning: Permanently added '52.88.75.138' (RSA) to the list of known hosts.
Welcome to Ubuntu 14.04.2 LTS (GNU/Linux 3.13.0-48-generic x86_64)

 * Documentation:  https://help.ubuntu.com/

  System information as of Sat Dec 19 22:54:50 UTC 2015

  System load: 0.0              Memory usage: 5%   Processes:         82
  Usage of /:  9.8% of 7.74GB   Swap usage:   0%   Users logged in:  0

  Graph this data and manage this system at:
    https://landscape.canonical.com/

  Get cloud support with Ubuntu Advantage Cloud Guest:
    http://www.ubuntu.com/business/services/cloud

0 packages can be updated.
0 updates are security updates.



The programs included with the Ubuntu system are free software;
the exact distribution terms for each program are described in the
individual files in /usr/share/doc/*/copyright.

Ubuntu comes with ABSOLUTELY NO WARRANTY, to the extent permitted by
applicable law.

ubuntu@ip-172-31-19-240:~$ 
```

Figure 2-4. SSH server via command line

Now that we are logged in to the new Ubuntu server we have launched, the next step is to set the Bash profile file with shortcuts to make our lives easier. In the command line, while SSH is logged in to the server, type:

```
$ vim ~/.bash_profile
```

Paste the code shown in Listing 2-1.

Listing 2-1. Bash profile shortcuts

```
alias stopnode='sudo forever stop 0'
alias startnode='sudo forever start server.js'
alias cdr='cd /home/ubuntu/www'
```

```
alias vimb='vim ~/.bashrc'
alias runb='. ~/.bashrc'
alias taillog='tail -f /home/ubuntu/www/data/eventslogs'

alias l='ls -ltra'
alias c='clear'
alias cls='clear'
alias ll='ls -ltra'
alias killnode='sudo killall -2 node'

export PORT=8081
sudo iptables -A PREROUTING -t nat -i eth0 -p tcp --dport 80 -j REDIRECT --to-port 8081
sudo iptables -A PREROUTING -t nat -i eth0 -p tcp --dport 443 -j REDIRECT --to-port 8000
```

Save and close the file, but remember to run the following code to reload the Bash settings:

```
$ . ~/.bash_profile
```

Notice that we have been settings two aliases to clear the screen: "c" and "cls". This is personal preference; you can set it however you want.

You can test that everything is working by typing "c", which should clear the screen. Notice that we have already placed shortcuts to start and stop the node service we will be creating (startnode, stopnode); edit and run this Bash profile (vimb, runb); kill all node services (killnode); and even redirect to port 80, so we will be able to view our node services in the browser.

We will explain more about these shortcuts once we create our first Node.js services in the following chapters.

Install and Update Software

We first want to upgrade and ensure that we have the latest software available. It's always a good idea to do the upgrade first to ensure that any software we install next will be based on the latest update. It would be a shame to spend the time installing everything only to find an issue with the server and services once we do the upgrade.

Start off by downloading the package lists from the repositories and "update" them to get information on the newest versions of packages available. To do so, type in command line, while still SSH to the server, the following command:

```
$ sudo apt-get update
```

Once the newest versions of the packages have been updated, we can update the server:

```
$ sudo apt-get -y upgrade
```

Afterward, install rcconf, a Debian Runlevel configuration tool, which will allow you to control which services are opened when the server starts or restarts:

```
$ sudo apt-get install rcconf
```

Next, install the "build-essential," which will gather an informational list of packages:

```
$ sudo apt-get install build-essential
```

And now we can actually install what we really need:

```
$ sudo apt-get install libssl-dev
```

Installing Git

As you may recall, in Chapter 1, we installed and configured Git on our local box. It's useful to install Git on the server for few reasons, including that we can use Git to deploy our scripts. Usually, when you upload Node.js apps, it is common to not install the entire library that the project uses, since this can be installed with one command. To install Git on Ubuntu, all we have to do is type the following command:

```
$ sudo apt-get install git-core
```

Installing Node.js

Next, we will install Node.js. As you may also recall, we installed and configured Node.js on our local box, and now we need to do the same on the server so we can run Node.js for the apps we will be creating. To install Node.js, follow Listing 2-2.

Listing 2-2. Installing Node.js on Ubuntu server

```
$ sudo wget http://nodejs.org/dist/v0.10.7/node-v0.10.7.tar.gz
$ sudo tar xzf node-v0.10.7.tar.gz
$ cd node-v0.10.7
$ sudo ./configure --prefix=/usr
$ sudo make
$ sudo make install
```

Notice that we have selected to install Node.js version 0.10.7, because the services we will be using play nicely with that version. It is important to know which Node.js you're running, since many times Node.js is not backwards compatible, and a change in Node.js may break your apps.

Installing npm

Now that we have Git, we can easily install the npm package manager on Ubuntu. npm package manager is an essential tool used to install all of the libraries we will need. To do so, follow the following code sequence in Listing 2-3.

Listing 2-3. Installing npm on Ubuntu

```
$ cd ~
$ git clone git://github.com/isaacs/npm.git
$ cd npm/scripts
$ chmod +x install.sh
$ sudo ./install.sh
```

Creating Our Web Folder

In our next step, we want to create a web folder. Remember that the Amazon Ubuntu server comes stripped right out of the box, and we will have to install everything we need. To create the folder, type in the command line:

```
$ cd ~
$ mkdir ~/www
$ cd ~/www
```

Equipped with npm, we can now install "forever" service globally. Forever service (`https://www.npmjs.com/package/forever`) is a simple command line tool that will help us ensure the Node.js script is running continuously, even after we close our command line. We can install it easily with npm. In the command line, type:

```
$ cd ~
$ sudo npm install -g forever
```

Now that the "forever" tool is installed, we can forward the port from 8081 to 80:

```
$ export PORT=8081
$ sudo iptables -A PREROUTING -t nat -i eth0 -p tcp --dport 80 -j REDIRECT --to-port 8081
```

The command above is for illustration purposes. We do not need to run that command since we have already completed the port redirect in the Bash profile file, so everytime we restart the server, the port forward will be completed automatically.

Lastly, just to make sure, you can ensure your account falls under the free tier once again by going to Amazon's EC2 billing home: `https://console.aws.amazon.com/billing/home`

And that's it—you now have a free AWS Ubuntu server for the year that you can use to install Node.js services. We also installed upgrades, essential software including node, npm and the "forever" tool.

We configured the Bash profile for simple commands on the server and set up an easy way to connect to the new server. In future chapters, we will learn to install services that can be run on any devices and configure the server to include SSH and other essential tools.

Linux Server

In this section, we will roll out a free Linux.

Now, why do we even need a Linux server if the core focus of this book is MEAN stack? Linux servers come in handy in the following scenarios:

- Hosting your AngularJS app on Linux instead of Express server

- Hosting your WordPress blog

- Automating tasks

Just as setting Ubuntu, Amazon EC2 offers free service for a year for Linux servers. In this section, we will start a Linux server and configure the server, install software, and update and connect to the new server.

Since we have already created an Ubuntu server under our current account, you will need to create this second server under a separate email account, since Amazon provides only one server per email. The other alternative is to terminate the Ubuntu server with servers provided at the Ubuntu server sub chapter.

Start a Linux server

1. Login in to Amazon: https://us-west-2.console.aws.amazon.com/console/home

2. Next, select "EC2" ➤ "Launch Instance," just as we have done in Ubuntu.

3. Choose "Amazon Linux" ➤ "Select" (see Figure 2-5 below).

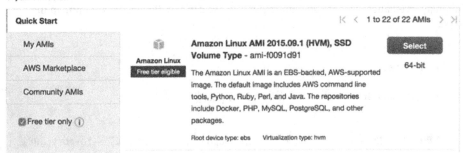

Figure 2-5. *Selecting a Linux Amazon Machine Image*

On the next page, select: "General purpose" ➤ "t2.micro Free tier eligible" ➤ "Review and Launch." On the preview screen, select "Edit security groups." Important: For HTTP and HTTPS, we want to open it to the world (0.0.0.0/0), but SSH limit to "My IP" so that no one else can SSH your server. See Figure 2-6.

Figure 2-6. *Configure Linux security group*

Note that the security group name doesn't matter. We selected "API," but you can leave it as the default "launch-wizard-1." Now that we have completed the configuration of our server, select "Review and Launch" ➤ "Launch."

Before the server launches, you will be asked about a key pair. Select "Create a new key pair" ➤ [Your key name] ➤ "Download Key Pair" and save it somewhere safe. Lastly, launch instances by clicking "View instances" button.

All of this should be somewhat familiar, since we completed the same steps previously when we rolled out the Ubuntu server. Once again, you can ensure your account falls under the free tier by going to the Amazon EC2 billing home:

```
https://console.aws.amazon.com/billing/home
```

Create IPs and Associate Servers

Now that our server has started, we want to associate it with an IP address, just as we've done with the Ubuntu server. To do so, on the AWS Left side menu, select "NETWORK & SECURITY" ➤ "Elastic IPs" ➤ "Allocate New Address."

Right click and select "Associate Address" ➤ "instance" ➤ "select instance ID" (you should only have one option) ➤ "associate."

All of these steps are exactly the same as the steps we used with the Ubuntu server.

Next, we also want to create an SSH shortcut to access the servers. As you may have noticed, setting up the shortcut is very useful and allows us to easily access the new Ubuntu server; we will edit the SSH config file and add the Linux server. In the command line, type:

```
$ vim ~/.ssh/config
```

Insert the new server information as follows:

```
Host app
HostName [elastic ip address]
User ec2-user
IdentityFile /[location to key]/[api key name].pem
```

Next, set the permission of the server key, which is necessary in order to connect to the server:

```
$ chmod 400 /[location to key]/[api key name].pem
```

Lastly, try to SSH the server. In the command line, type:

```
$ ssh app
```

Just as before, when it asks "Are you sure you want to continue connecting (yes/no)?" Reply "yes" and you should then be logged in.

Set Bash Profile

Now that we're logged in to the server, our next step, just as in setting the Ubuntu server, is setting up the Bash profile file for easy shortcuts. See Listing 2-4:

Listing 2-4. Linux Bash file.

```
$ vim ~/.bashrc

alias cdr='cd /var/www/html/'
alias vimb='vim ~/.bashrc'
alias runb='. ~/.bashrc'
alias l='ls -ltra'
alias c='clear'
alias cls='clear'
alias ll='ls -ltra'
```

Once you're finished, run the Bash file:

```
$ . ~/.bashrc
```

Notice that the shortcuts are a bit different. We have "cdr" to change the directory to the server home directory, we no longer need all the shortcuts for Node.js, and we kept the shortcuts for "l," "c," "cls," and "ll."

Update Software

Just as we've previously done for Ubuntu, we want to update the software and install some additional basic software that will help us to maintain the server. We will install Linux, Apache, MySQL, and PHP ("LAMP") software bundles, but first, we may find it useful to have a FTP installed so we can easily connect and distribute our files.

Set Up FTP

In order to set up the FTP client, we first need to SSH the server. We should already be in the server, since we ran this command:

```
$ ssh app
```

We will be using the free Very Secure FTP ("vsftpd") client. To install this software, type the following in the Linux command line:

```
$ sudo yum install vsftpd
```

To connect to the EC2 console, open security group and set a Custom TCP rule for ports 20-21 and ports 1024-1048. Without opening these ports, we will not be able to connect the FTP.

The next step is to update the "vsftpd.conf" file:

```
$ sudo vi /etc/vsftpd/vsftpd.conf
```

We want to set: "anonymous_enable=NO", and also add the following:

```
pasv_enable=YES
pasv_min_port=1024
pasv_max_port=1048
pasv_address=
```

Setting the "anonymous" enable to "NO" in "vsftpd.conf" file is important because we don't want random users to be able to access the FTP client. Lastly, you should also uncomment the following line in "vsftpd.conf" file:

```
"chroot_local_user=YES"
```

Save vi changes by clicking "escape" + ":" + "wq"
Next, restart the "vsftpd" client to apply these changes:

```
$ sudo /etc/init.d/vsftpd restart
```

Now that the client is installed and configured, we can create an FTP user:

```
$ sudo adduser eli
$ sudo passwd eli
```

Then you will be prompted to enter a new password:

```
[your password]
```

What we have done, as an example, is created a username "eli" and set a password.

That's it; we are now finished and can connect to FTP. The preferred FTP software is FileZilla, and it can be downloaded here:

```
https://filezilla-project.org/
```

However, feel free to use your preferred FTP client.

Install LAMP

To install LAMP, simply follow this Amazon blog post:

```
http://docs.aws.amazon.com/AWSEC2/latest/UserGuide/install-LAMP.html
```

Once LAMP is running, you should see the welcome page at the Amazon public IP address that we linked to this server. That's it—we have completed starting and setting up the Linux server, as well as upgrading software, setting up FTP, installing LAMP, and setting up shortcuts.

MongoDB Database

To start, exit the Linux server by typing in the command line:

```
$ exit
```

That will log you out and close the connection with the following output:

```
logout
```

Connection to your elastic IP address is now closed.

Next, we will install MongoDB. MongoDB is the "M" in the "MEAN" stack and often a faster and easier way to connect to certain types of applications. As you can see, MongoDB is not a replacement for the traditional NoSQL; we have still installed a MySQL database, which has its own good practices.

■ **Note**   MongoDB is one of the most popular NoSQL databases. NoSQLs were created to provide scaling support for increasing numbers of users that run the app on different devices. The old SQL database architecture failed since it was meant to be built on one database—the bigger, the better. Scaling is not easy under the old architecture. MongoDB allows to easily be scaled from a database servicing a mere few hundred to millions of users on all platforms.

The Ubuntu server we have created is a good place to install the MongoDB database, and with "apt-get," it will be a breeze.

Connect to Ubuntu Server

As you recall, we have a handy shortcut to the SSH the server; open the command line and type:

```
$ ssh api
```

Install and Configure MongoDB Database

The Ubuntu out-of-the-box package management tools (such as dpkg and apt) ensure package consistency and authenticity by requiring that distributors sign packages with GPG keys. To start, type the following into the command line to import the MongoDB public GPG key:

```
$ sudo apt-key adv --keyserver hkp://keyserver.ubuntu.com:80 --recv EA312927
```

Create a List File for MongoDB

Now, we want to create the "/etc/apt/sources.list.d/mongodb-org-3.2.list" file, which holds the sources list so we can update the MongoDB. Since we installed Ubuntu 14.04, we will use the command:

```
$ echo "deb http://repo.mongodb.org/apt/ubuntu trusty/mongodb-org/3.2 multiverse" | sudo tee
/etc/apt/sources.list.d/mongodb-org-3.2.list
```

Next, reload the local package database. Type in the following command:

```
$ sudo apt-get update
```

After that, install the MongoDB packages.

You can either install the latest stable version of MongoDB or a specific version of MongoDB. We will be installing the latest stable version of MongoDB.

In the Ubuntu command line, type:

```
$ sudo apt-get install -y mongodb-org
```

We have now installed MongoDB and, it's running. At any time, you can stop or restart the MongoDB database by typing the following commands:

```
$ sudo service mongod stop
$ sudo service mongod start
```

Or just run the restart command:

```
$ sudo service mongod restart
```

Now, to verify that MongoDB has restarted successfully, we can check the contents of the log file at "/var/log/mongodb/mongod.log" for a line reading:

```
$ cat /var/log/mongodb/mongod.log
```

MongoDB Hello World

After we have MongoDB installed and working, we can login in to MongoDB. To login in to the Ubuntu terminal, type:

```
$ mongo
```

■ **Note**   If you are getting memory warnings or any other warnings after starting the server, such as "transparent_hugepage," don't be too concerned at this point, since our MongoDB database is for testing purposes and not a production-grade database.

Next, switch to the database you want to use:

```
> use mydatabase
```

The database will reply with a confirmation:

```
switched to db mydatabase
```

Then, create a user object and insert the content of a user object:

```
> db.users.insert({username:"someuser",password:"password"})
```

MongoDB should reply with the following confirmation:

```
WriteResult({ "nInserted" : 1 })
```

Next, use the "find" MongoDB command to view a list of users:

```
> db.users.find()
```

Mongo will reply with a list of users:

```
{ "_id" : ObjectId("56cfd879edcf4111efe8f016"), "username" : "someuser", "password" :
"password" }
```

You can see the command we have typed into MongoDB in Ubuntu Command line in Figure 2-7:

```
MongoDB shell version: 3.2.1
connecting to: test
Server has startup warnings:
2016-01-29T05:19:36.927+0000 I CONTROL  [initandlisten]
2016-01-29T05:19:36.927+0000 I CONTROL  [initandlisten] ** WARNING: /sys/kernel/mm/transparent_hugepage/enabled is 'always'.
2016-01-29T05:19:36.927+0000 I CONTROL  [initandlisten] **        We suggest setting it to 'never'
2016-01-29T05:19:36.927+0000 I CONTROL  [initandlisten]
2016-01-29T05:19:36.927+0000 I CONTROL  [initandlisten] ** WARNING: /sys/kernel/mm/transparent_hugepage/defrag is 'always'.
2016-01-29T05:19:36.927+0000 I CONTROL  [initandlisten] **        We suggest setting it to 'never'
2016-01-29T05:19:36.927+0000 I CONTROL  [initandlisten]
> use mydatabase
switched to db mydatabase
> db.users.insert({username:"someuser",password:"password"})
WriteResult({ "nInserted" : 1 })
> db.users.find()
{ "_id" : ObjectId("56cfd879edcf4111efe8f016"), "username" : "someuser", "password" : "password" }
```

Figure 2-7. *MongoDB Hello World*

MySQL Database

As mentioned before, the MongoDB NoSQL database has its own usage, but it's always a good idea to also have a MySQL database ready in case we need a SQL database. To do this, sign into Amazon: `https://console.aws.amazon.com/console/home` using the Linux account.

1. After you log in, select "RDS" from the list of available services.

2. Next, select "Launch a MySQL DB Instance" or just "Launch" (depending on your welcome screen).

3. For the free tier database, select "MySQL MySQL Community Edition" and hit "Select." See Figure 2-8.

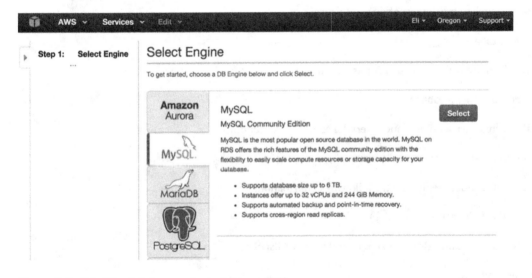

Figure 2-8. *Select the database engine in Amazon AWS*

4. In the next window, you will be asked whether you plan to use the database for "production purposes." Select "Dev/Test MySQL," then select "Next Step." See Figure 2-9.

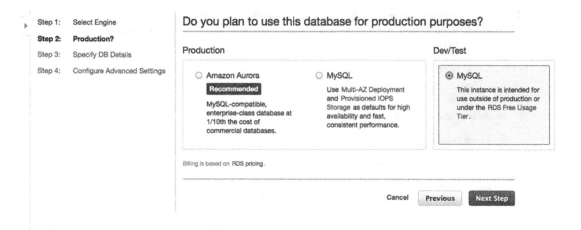

Figure 2-9. *Set database purpose in Amazon AWS*

5. Now we can select settings regarding our database. See Figure 2-10.

   a. Select the "Only show options that are eligible for RDS Free Tier" check box.

   b. Select "db.t2.micro" as the "DB Instance Class."

   c. Leave the remaining options as their default settings.

☑ Only show options that are eligible for RDS Free Tier

Instance Specifications

DB Engine	mysql	
License Model	general-public-license	↕
DB Engine Version	5.6.27	↕

💬 Review the **Known Issues/Limitations** to learn about potential compatibility issues with specific database versions.

DB Instance Class	db.t2.micro — 1 vCPU, 1 GiB RAM	↕
Multi-AZ Deployment	No	↕
Storage Type	General Purpose (SSD)	↕
Allocated Storage*	5 GB	

Select the DB instance class that allocates the computational, network, and memory capacity required by planned workload of DB instance. Learn More.

Details:db.t2.micro

Type	Micro Instan Currer Gener
vCPU	1 vCP
Memory	1 GiB
EBS Optimized	No

Settings

Figure 2-10. *MySQL instance specification window options*

6. On the next page, "Specify DB Details," set your user name and master password. Be sure to note these settings, as you'll need them later, and then select "Next Step" (see Figure 2-11).

Settings

DB Instance Identifier*	api
Master Username*	MyUserName
Master Password*	••••••••
Confirm Password*	••••••••

Retype the value you specified for Master Password.

* Required   Cancel   Previous   Next Step

Figure 2-11. Set your user name and passwrod setttings

7. The "Configure Advanced Settings" page will open. In the network and security section, select "Default VPC" with "VPC Security Group(s)" as "rds-launch-wizard (VPC)."

   a. Under "Database Options," select the DB Instance Identifier. In Figure 2-11, we are using "mydatabase" (choose your own name).

   b. Under "Database port," leave default port 3306.

8. Lastly, select "Launch DB Instance."

We are now done with this setup and have a MySQL database available at our disposal.

Connect to Database and Dump MySQL Database

The next step is to connect to the new database and create a MySQL "Hello World" database.

There are a few popular, free, and open source GUI tools used to connect to a MySQL database and make our lives easier—for instance, the popular phpMyAdmin (https://www.phpmyadmin.net/) web tool MySQL Workbench (https://dev.mysql.com/downloads/workbench/), which is most popular tool, and Sequel Pro (http://www.sequelpro.com/) make administrating a MySQL database a breeze.

Additionally, Navicat (http://www.navicat.com/) is another popular tool that allows for syncing larger databases as well as easily reverse-engineering an existing database for a Unified Modeling Language (UML) diagram, but it is not free. At the time of this writing, the starting cost is $19.99—see "Navicat for MySQL (iOS)" at the bottom of the price page (https://www.navicat.com/store/navicat-for-mysql).

Before we start connecting, we want to configure Amazon RDS to allow our IP address to connect to the database, as well as store the database information.

Log in to Amazon AWS (https://console.aws.amazon.com) and navigate to the EC2 server security group by clicking "NETWORK & SECURITY" at the bottom left pane menu. That will open the security group menu. See Figure 2-12.

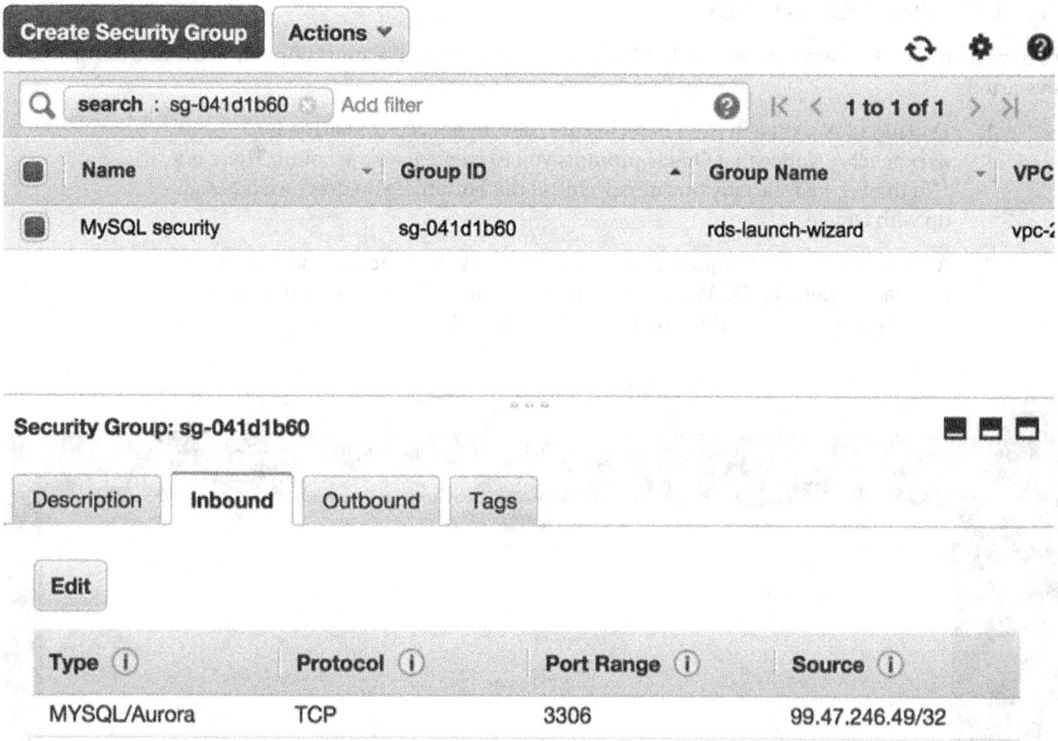

Create Security Group **Actions** ▾

Q search : sg-041d1b60 ○ Add filter ❓ |< < 1 to 1 of 1 > >|

	Name ▾	Group ID ▲	Group Name ▾	VPC
■	MySQL security	sg-041d1b60	rds-launch-wizard	vpc-2

Security Group: sg-041d1b60

Description	**Inbound**	Outbound	Tags

Edit

Type ⓘ	Protocol ⓘ	Port Range ⓘ	Source ⓘ
MYSQL/Aurora	TCP	3306	99.47.246.49/32

Figure 2-12. Setting MySQL security group in Amazon AWS

You will have an RDS security group created automatically for you. Next, click the "Inbound" tab and "Edit" button, so you can add "My IP" address and open port 3306 (see Figure 2-13) to allow our local machine IP address to be able to connect to the MySQL server. Remember that we are opening the port for our IP address only. In case you plan to work remotely or your IP address changes, you will need to update these settings.

However, it's highly recommended to simply open your IP addresss and keep this port closed to the outside world, since it's a major security risk and there isn't an administrator working full time; it's better to be safe than sorry.

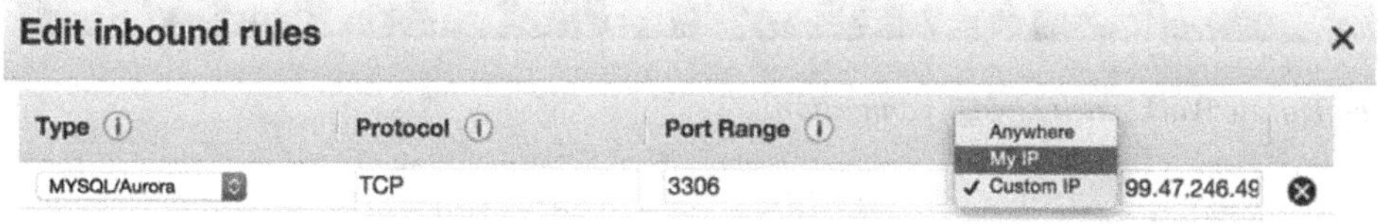

Edit inbound rules   ✕

Type ⓘ	Protocol ⓘ	Port Range ⓘ		
MYSQL/Aurora ⬍	TCP	3306	Anywhere My IP ✓ Custom IP	99.47.246.49 ✖

Figure 2-13. Opening port 3306 for machine local IP address

MySQL Workbench tool

We have mentioned a few tools thus far, but Workbench is probably the most popular of the free tools, so let's get started:

1. Download Workbench from here: `http://dev.mysql.com/downloads/workbench/`. Notice that Oracle prompts you to create a web account. There is a "No thanks, just start my download" link at the bottom if you don't wish to sign up with Oracle.

2. After installation is completed, we can configure Workbench to connect to our database. Open MySQL Workbench and select the "+" sign next to the "MySQL Connections" label on the top left side. See Figure 2-14.

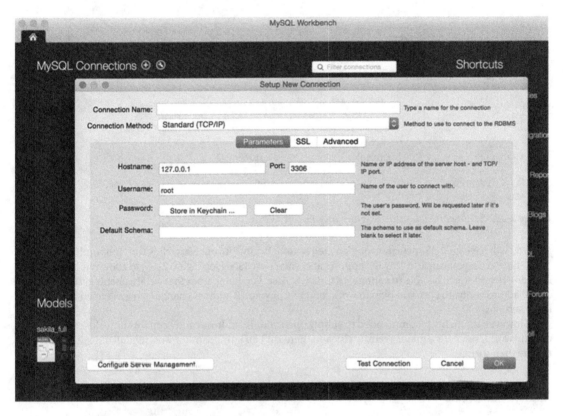

Figure 2-14. *Configurate Workbench MySQL connection*

3. The "Set Up New Connection" wizard will open. Set your Amazon RDS settings we configured earlier.

4. Next, select "Test Connection" (Figure 2-15).

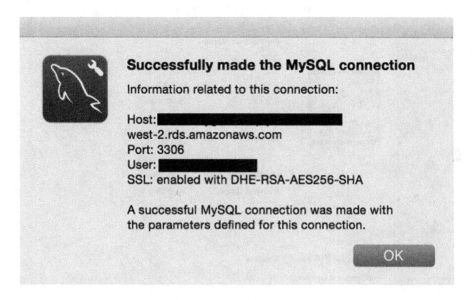

Figure 2-15. Test connection alert message

That's it! You are now connected to the database.

Create Your First Database and Table

To create your first table, right click on the left "schemas" area (see Figure 2-16) and select "Create Database." Enter the database name you want—the example name created for the table is "theluxurygame." Next, follow the same steps to create a table. Right click and then select "Create a table..." (Figure 2-16).

Figure 2-16. *Create a new database and table*

Now we can enter the table columns we want. For our example, we will add two columns: "user_id" and "user_name." For the "user_id," we set the column as an integer, as our primary key, and for the "user_name" we set this column as varchar type with a 45-character limit. See Figure 2-17.

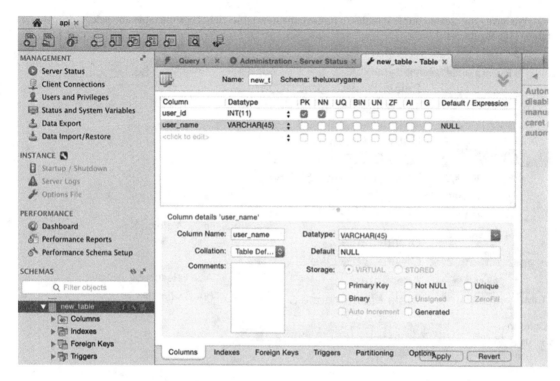

Figure 2-17. *Setting up a new table with columns*

Hit "apply" and the SQL will allow you to review the SQL statement. See Figure 2-18.

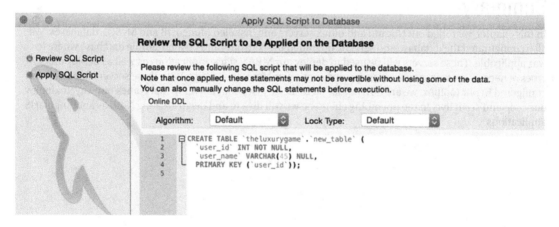

Figure 2-18. *SQL script review*

We have now created our first table. To remove the new table, right click the table and select "drop table" (See Figure 2-19).

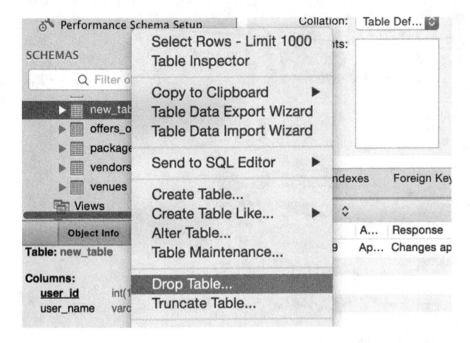

Figure 2-19. *Drop table from databse*

Summary

In this chapter, we rolled out Ubuntu and Linux servers and installed MongoDB and MySQL databases. We also configured the database and servers, upgraded the software, and created simple database where it was applicable. These servers will be used to deploy our MEAN stack applications as well as deploy other types of neccessary software, such as app automation or Linux shell script. With these servers deployed and configured in our toolbox, we are now equipped to tackle just about anything that comes our way, to deploy our code and see it live. In the upcoming chapters, we will dive in and begin creating Node.js and AngularJS applications.

CHAPTER 3

Node Modules

A typical MEAN application can often depend on up to hundreds of packages. These modules are often small and consist of both Node.js and Bower libraries. By combining libraries, you are able to create a mashup of small-shared building blocks and custom apps for the purpose of solving a larger problem.

The ability to harness node is powerful, not just for node-based applications, but for just about any task, regardless of the platform or language you might be using. In this chapter, we will be utilizing npm to install popular node modules, learning how to deploy a Node.js project, and setting up a config file for easy future updates. We will create our first node module and learn how to submit it to npm as an open source project.

npm Node Packages

npm (htttp://npm.com) is the premier location to search for modules. The source code for many of these libraries will usually live on GitHub (`http://github.com`). In fact, as you may recall from Chapter 1, we have already installed a few npm modules, such as Grunt, Gulp, and Bower. Also, we already have Git installed on our local and server environments, so you actually already have everything you will need to install and set your node modules. In this section, we will expand on this subject, help you find what you need, and provide a better understanding of how to install these packages.

npm began as the free and open source node package manager—it eventually became more than that. In fact, it's been used as package manager for Node.js, JavaScript, Grunt, Gulp, Bower, AngularJS, and much more. These days, npm allows holding private modules and makes it easy to share, update, and reuse code.

Note Notice that the words "module," "library," and "packages" are interchangeable and all mean the same thing: a directory of files with reusable code, capable of solving a specific targeted problem or set of problems.

At the time of this writing, there are over 250,000 open source packages on npm (Figure 3-1). npm has a URL listing the most starred packages:

```
https://www.npmjs.com/browse/star
```

© Elad Elrom 2016

E. Elrom, *Pro MEAN Stack Development*, DOI 10.1007/978-1-4842-2044-3_3

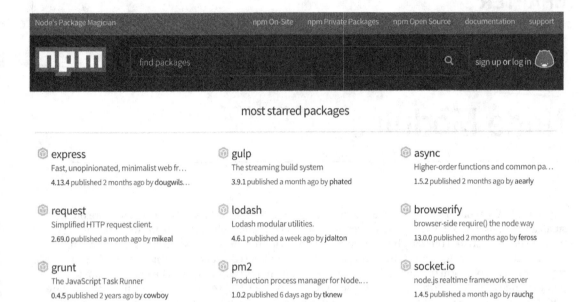

Figure 3-1. *npm most popular packages*

Additionally, npm lists stats for downloads in the last day, week, and month, so picking a node module can be based on useful information. In fact, we encourage you to visit the GitHub location of the code and check for the latest update, known errors, and other information to make sure you're picking a module that can do what you need.

Generally, node packages are one of two types:

1. **Server side modules**: as mentioned, npm originated as the node package manager, so you will find many server side packages to support the writing of your node app.

2. **Command line packages**: these packages can enhance the capability of the local environment or our server/s. Some notable examples: Grunt and Gulp packages, which we installed back in Chapter 1.

Once you've found the npm package you would like to install, all you have to do is open Terminal, and in the command line, simply type:

```
$ [sudo] npm install [modules]
```

Beside npm, you may search through this link farm and discover some usefull Node.js: `https://github.com/sindresorhus/awesome-nodejs`

You will learn a lot just looking at other people's code and seeing how they do a particular thing, so go ahead and explore.

Install Node.js Modules

Although it is simple to install node modules, we should be strategic about how we do so to global or local locations. The versions of libraries and the management of updates should all be taken into consideration before we begin installing.

To better understand the different types of installations, we'll create a dummy project and install few modules. In your favorite IDE, such as WebStorm or Sublime (see Chapter 1 if you haven't installed any), create a project and name it "Tester."

Here, we are using WebStorm IDE. From the top menu, select "File" ➤ "New Project…" and set the project name as "Tester," then select "Empty project" (Figure 3-2).

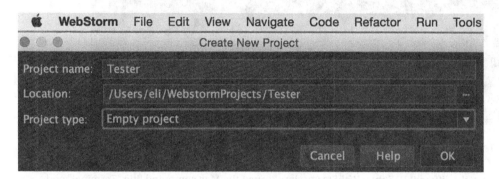

Figure 3-2. *Create tester project in WebStorm*

Hit "OK," and now you should have an empty shell project that we can start working with; see Figure 3-3.

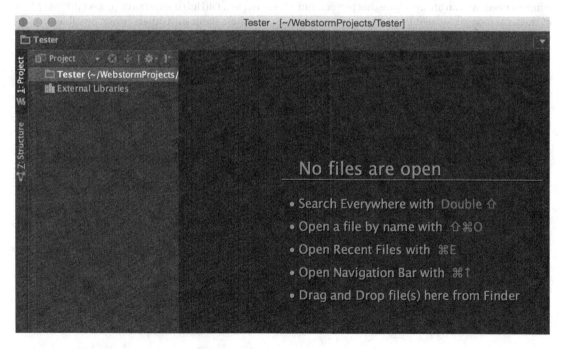

Figure 3-3. *Tester window project in WebStorm*

Notice that at the bottom of the project, there is an icon of a command line next to the word "Terminal." Click that and a Terminal will open up. We can use that Terminal to work in, just as Mac builds in a Terminal—see Figure 3-4.

53

Figure 3-4. *Terminal window in WebStorm*

If you selected a different IDE than WebStorm, simply open the Mac command line "Terminal" and navigate to the project root directory.

Let's say we need to manipulate dates and convert them from one format to another. We can create our own daunting library, but there's no need—npm lists a library called "moment" (https://www.npmjs.com/package/moment) that will allow us to parse, validate, and manipulate dates easily. If that library is missing what we need, we can always clone that project, since it's listed as a GitHub open source project (https://github.com/moment/moment), or create our own modules and share them with others (when possible) in case we cannot find what we need at all.

As mentioned, all you have to do is type into the command line Terminal:

```
$ npm install moment
```

If you type this command, it will create a "node_modules" directory in our project and add a "moment" library. Then, we are ready to continue; see Figure 3-5.

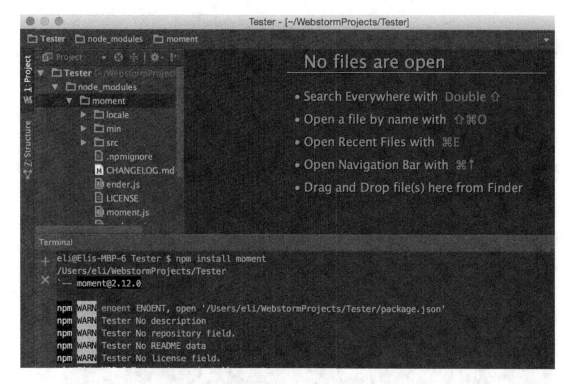

Figure 3-5. *Installing moment library command line output and project window*

npm has installed the library moment at version 2.12.0 locally. However, npm has spit out a warning message: "enoent ENOENT, open '/Users/eli/WebstormProjects/Tester/package.json'" (see Figure 3-5).

What is that all about? npm expects to have a package.json file in order to be able to manage and keep track of locally installed libraries. You can create this on your own; the most minimalistic "JASON" code is this name and version:

```
{ "name": "tester", "version": "1.0.0" }
```

The easiest way to create the package JSON file is to simply type into the command line:

```
$ npm init
```

You may also use the –yes flag to accept all of the default settings:

```
$ npm init --yes
```

We have selected the option without the –yes flag checked. It opens with a quick questionnaire and eventually creates the package JSON file. We have accepted the default settings we want by hitting the "enter" key—see Figure 3-6.

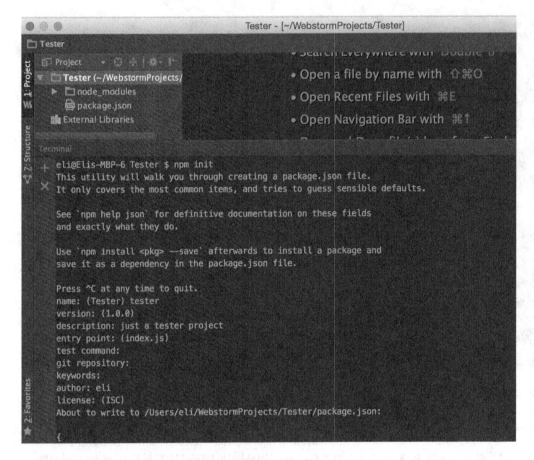

Figure 3-6. *npm init walk through to create package.json file*

The npm init command has generated the package.json file for us automatically in Listing 3-1.

Listing 3-1. Content of package.json file

```
{
  "name": "Tester",
  "version": "1.0.0",
  "description": "just a tester project",
  "main": "index.js",
  "dependencies": {
    "moment": "^2.12.0"
  },
  "devDependencies": {},
  "scripts": {
    "test": "echo \"Error: no test specified\" && exit 1"
  },
  "keywords": [],
  "author": "eli",
  "license": "ISC"
}
```

The file includes the name, version, description, author, and license, which you can edit at any time on your own.

Notice that this package.json file includes the following code:

```
test": "echo \"Error: no test specified\" && exit 1"
```

npm encourages developers to set a test file to ensure changes don't break the code, which is crucial when you have a project with many contributors. Later on in this chapter, we will show you how to set up a test through npm.

Additionally, sub-objects called "devDependencies" and "dependencies" have been created. It is also presumed that we installed moment and has added it to the "dependencies" library.

There are two types of packages: "dependencies" and "devDependencies":

- "Dependencies" are packages that are required by your application to work in production.

- "DevDependencies" are packages that are only necessary for development and testing.

An application can consist of hundreds of small modules, so managing your dependencies efficiently will help a lot in organizing your library and will eventually decrease deployment time, so it's a good practice to begin doing right away. The following sections discuss the four best options.

Caret Version Option

Notice that "moment" was installed as "^2.12.0". The "^" caret or circumflex symbol means that it will update to the most recent major version (the first number). ^2.12.0 will match any 2.x.x release, but will hold off on 3.x.x; this is the default setting, but it could potentially cause problems.

If "moment" updated their libraries and had broken previous code and you then fail to update your code, when you do an npm update or deploy, the code will break. Additionally, it is recommended to inspect the script before updating. npm includes security vulnerability scanning, but it is still possible for a package to include worms or unwanted scripts, so in addition to the possibility of breaking a script, it is also a security concern.

Tilde Version Option

In case you want to be more specific, use the tilde version option, which will match the most recent minor version (the middle number). ~2.12.0 will match all 2.12.x versions but will skip 2.2.x versions. This can help ensure that you only upgrade middle versions; the type will change, but you will bypass major changes.

```
"moment": "~2.12.x"
```

Latest Version Option

You are also able to update to the latest version, but as I said earlier, it may break your library if changes in code were made that were not backward compatible.

```
"moment": "latest"
```

Specific Version Option

Lastly, you can specify an exact version, such as "2.12.0," to ensure nothing breaks. You can limit the version with ">=", "<=", ">", "<", and so on.

```
"moment": "2.12.0"
```

Install Save Flag

Now that we have the package.json file, moving forward we can use the --save install flag to allow us to add any libraries to the package.json file. If we only want to save to the "devDependency" object, we will need to use the --save-dev install flag.

For instance, the command in Listing 3-2 will grant npm as root/Administrator (sudo) in case it needs to update any files or install and save Grunt as a devDependency.

Listing 3-2. Content of package.json file includes Grunt

```
sudo npm install grunt --save-dev
{
  "name": "tester",
  "version": "1.0.0",
  "description": "just a tester project",
  "main": "index.js",
  "dependencies": {
    "moment": "^2.12.0"
  },
  "devDependencies": {
    "grunt": "^1.0.1"
  },
  "scripts": {
    "test": "echo \"Error: no test specified\" && exit 1"
  },
  "author": "eli",
  "license": "ISC"
}
```

Global Installation

Another option is installing libraries globally. As we have mentioned, there are two ways to install npm packages: "locally" or "globally." In order to choose which type of installation is right for you, you will need to think about how you will want to use the package.

If you need the package for more than just your specific project, use the global flag:

```
$ sudo npm install -g epress
```

This command will install the Express library globally. Notice that we used "sudo" to allow administration rights and avoid errors, but it's not always necessary.

npm offers a large collection of docs covering just about anything to do with npm, from getting started to usage to configuration and everything in between. See: https://docs.npmjs.com/

Create Your Own First Node Modules

As I pointed out, there are more than 250,000 modules on npm alone. Creating a module is easy—in this section we will walk you through the process. We recommend that you follow this section as a guideline and create your own unique module so that you fully understand this process.

We chose a simple and minimalistic example so that you can easily grasp the idea. We've created a module to log messages in Node.js, but unlike "console.log," this one will use colors, allowing you to log different types of messages. You can set the type of function you want to log, which allows you to disable the messages from being logged all together.

Create a GitHub Project Repository

We are starting off by creating a Git repository. Log in to GitHub and select the top "+" sign and hit "new repository," which opens up the "create new repository" page: https://github.com/new and allows us to select the "repository name," owner, and other settings. Once the repo (repository) has been created, we will be given the Git location and command line instructions—see Figure 3-7:

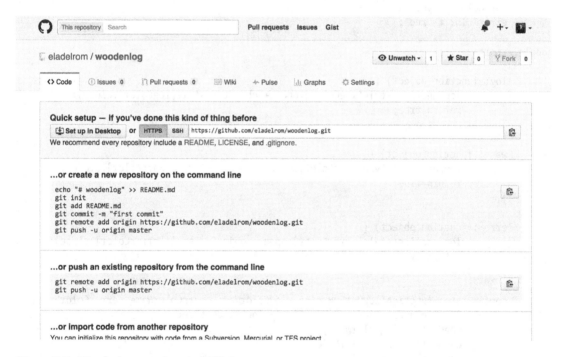

Figure 3-7. *Woodenlog repository in GitHub*

Notice we have created the repo name "woodenlog" as an example—you can create any name you want to practice publishing a project.

Create a Module Project

To continue, we will create a new project in WebStorm from the "Empty Project" template, following the same process as before:

"File" ➤ "New Project." For the project name, we'll be using "woodenlog." We already checked with npm (https://www.npmjs.com/) to ensure there isn't already a project with that name; it's not always easy to find a unique name these days.

Write Your Module Code

Next, we need to create an "index.js" file in the root directory. To create a new file in WebStorm, use the top menu "File" ➤ "New" ➤ "File," or right click the project and choose "File" ➤ "New."

The "index.js" file will be the entry point of the library.

We will be using the code in Listing 3-3.

Listing 3-3. Woodenlog index.js file

```
const style = require('ansi-styles');

var logFunction = console.log,
        logColor = 'green',
        warnColor = 'yellow',
        errorColor = 'red';

module.exports = {

        log: function(object) {
                logFunction(style[logColor].open + object + style[logColor].close);
                return true;
        },

        warn: function(object) {
                logFunction(style[warnColor].open + object + style[warnColor].close);
                return true;
        },

        error: function(object) {
                logFunction(style[errorColor].open + object + style[errorColor].close);
                return true;
        },

        configurate: function(logOutFunction, logColorName, warnColorName, errorColorName) {
                if (logOutFunction) logFunction = logOutFunction;
                logColor = logColorName;
                warnColor = warnColorName;
                errorColor = errorColorName;
                return true;
        }
};
```

We will be using the "ansi-styles" module. This is a library that uses ANSI escape codes for styling strings in a terminal. You can see the source code here: https://github.com/chalk/ansi-styles

```
const style = require('ansi-styles');
```

Next, we need to define the colors we want to use for the log, warn, and error, as well as the type of method we would like to use in order to paste messages.

```
var logFunction = console.log,
    logColor = 'green',
    warnColor = 'yellow',
    errorColor = 'red';
```

Notice that we have already set the default values and will be using the good old "console.log" JavaScript function to show the messages.

Now, we'll define each method, log, warn, and error with the color we will be using:

```
log: function(object) {
        logFunction(style[logColor].open + object + style[logColor].close);
        return true;
},
```

We have encapsulated the index.js code so it can be utilized in other files by using the "module.exports" variable once a file is required. You will see how it works once we implement the module:

```
module.exports = {
  // code goes here
}
```

Run Your Module Code

We can now run our library to ensure that we don't encounter any errors. To do so, select the caret from the top right corner in WebStorm and select "Edit Configurations..." See Figure 3-8.

Figure 3-8. *Edit Configurations menu item in WebStorm*

The wizard will open up and we will select the "+" sign to add a new configuration. From the drop-down menu, select "Node.js." See Figure 3-9.

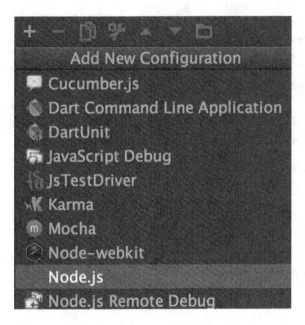

Figure 3-9. *Add new configration in WebStorm*

The program will then allow us to configure the Run/Debug options. We will leave all the default settings as they are, but for the JavaScript file, we'll select the name of the app, "woodenlog," and enter the "index.js" file we created (see Figure 3-10.) Hit "OK" to close this wizard.

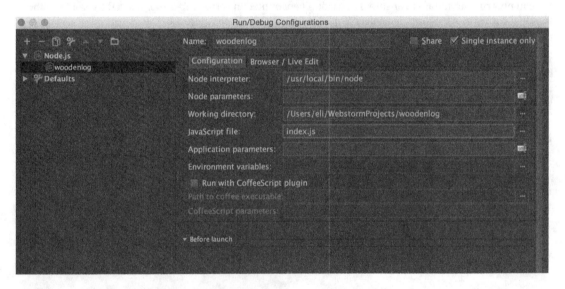

Figure 3-10. *Run/Debug configuration settings for Node.js.*

Now, at the top right corner of WebStorm, we can see "woodenlog" added to the top menu, and also a green "play" icon (see Figure 3-11).

Figure 3-11. *WebStorm top right menu shows "woodenlog" app*

Install Dependencies

We could go ahead and run the application by pressing the play button, but we will encounter errors—see Figure 3-12.

```
Run    woodenlog
    /usr/local/bin/node index.js

    module.js:340
        throw err;
        ^
    Error: Cannot find module 'ansi-styles'
        at Function.Module._resolveFilename (module.js:338:15)
        at Function.Module._load (module.js:280:25)
        at Module.require (module.js:364:17)
        at require (module.js:380:17)
        at Object.<anonymous> (/Users/eli/WebstormProjects/woodenlog/index.js:8:15)
        at Module._compile (module.js:456:26)
        at Object.Module._extensions..js (module.js:474:10)
        at Module.load (module.js:356:32)

 Terminal    4: Run    6: TODO
                                                              6:23  L
```

Figure 3-12. *Woodenlog error message in WebStorm*

From looking at the errors, we can see that we're missing some code, so before we can run the code successfully, we need to install the module we are using called "ansi-styles."

We need our package.json file to store our dependencies before we begin installing the module. Open the Terminal using either WebStorm's built-in Terminal (bottom right corner) or the Mac built-in Terminal and navigate to the project root.

We want to run "npm init" so it will create the "package.json" file for us, the same as we did for the "Tester" application. In the Terminal, run:

```
$ npm init
```

This time, set the package.json file that npm created to read/write permission, so we will be able to manually edit the file, which will be used be as npm when we publish our module. In the command line, type:

```
$ sudo chmod 777 package.json
```

Now, we can install "ansi-styles;" in the command line, type:

```
$ npm install ansi-styles --save
```

Notice that we have used the –save flag to allow the module to be added to the dependencies list in the package.json file.

Now, hit the green "play" button once again and you should see the following output:

```
/usr/local/bin/node index.js

Process finished with exit code 0
```

This means that the code has been run successfully.

Ignore Files

Now that our library is ready and working, we want to prepare to publish to GitHub. We do not want to publish any dependencies, which is what package.json is for. This will allow other users to select "npm install" and thus download npm to all of the libraries, which will decrease any redundancies on the hosting servers.

Also, note that WebStorm has created a hidden ".idea" folder with settings regarding a project that we don't want to upload either. To achieve this, we want to create a "gitignore" file at the root of the project that will instruct Git to ignore these files.

In the WebStorm or Mac Terminal, create the file using vim or your favorite editor:

```
$ vim .gitignore
```

Next, type "i" to insert and paste the following:

```
node_modules
.idea
```

Create Test Stubs

If you recall, earlier we showed you the code that npm generates in package.json for testing; the code looked like this:

```
test": "echo \"Error: no test specified\" && exit 1"
```

We will implement this test now. We won't delve into Test Driven Development (TDD) and Behavior Driven Development (BDD), since it's not necessary to sidetrack from the chapter's main objectives, but feel free to read about it online or in other books. There is a large school of thought that believes writing tests before writing code is superior.

To get started, we need to create a folder in the root of the project and name it "test," and then add a file call "index.js" inside of that folder. See Figure 3-13.

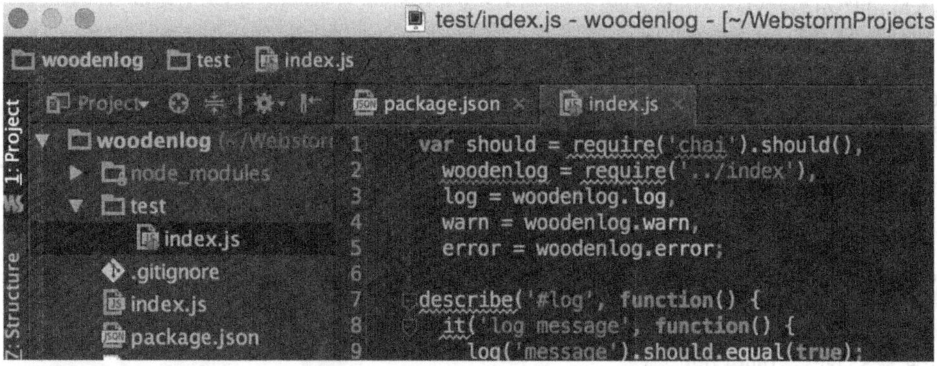

Figure 3-13. *Test folder structure in WebStorm*

For testing, we will be using "chai" (`http://chaijs.com/`). Chai is a BDD / TDD assertion library for Node.js and the browser. It can be easily paired with other JavaScript testing frameworks. We will pair it with a test framework called "mocha" (`https://mochajs.org/`).

Start off by installing "chai" and "mocha." In the Terminal, type:

```
$ npm install chai –save-dev
$ npm install mocha –save-dev
```

Now paste the code from Listing 3-4.

Listing 3-4. Test code for woodenlog module using mocha

```
var should = require('chai').should(),
      woodenlog = require('../index'),
      log = woodenlog.log,
      warn = woodenlog.warn,
      error = woodenlog.error;

describe('#log', function() {
      it('log message', function() {
            log('message').should.equal(true);
      });
});

describe('#warn', function() {
      it('warn message', function() {
            warn('message').should.equal(true);
      });
});

describe('#error', function() {
      it('error message', function() {
            error('message').should.equal(true);
      });
});
```

We define "should" and also our methods:

```
var should = require('chai').should(),
       woodenlog = require('../index'),
       log = woodenlog.log,
       warn = woodenlog.warn,
       error = woodenlog.error;
```

Then, we are able to define each of our test stubs. In our case, the method returns true once the message has been logged successfully:

```
describe('#log', function() {
       it('log message', function() {
               log('message').should.equal(true);
       });
});
```

We have used "log," "warn," and "error" as our test stubs naming conventions, however it is common to see the words "test" or "unit" at the end of each test. For example: "logTest" or "logUnit." It's a matter of preference.

Configure Package.json File

Now we can configure our package.json file with the repo Git URL location, test script, license, version, and other information. See Listing 3-5.

Listing 3-5. Package.json file configure all changes

```
{
  "name": "woodenlog",
  "version": "1.0.1",
  "description": "Minimalist log node messages module",
  "main": "index.js",
  "scripts": {
          "test": "./node_modules/.bin/mocha --reporter spec"
  },
  "repository": {
    "type": "git",
    "url": "git+https://github.com/eladelrom/woodenlog.git"
  },
  "keywords": [
    "log",
    "woodenlog",
    "log",
    "messages"
  ],
  "author": "Elad (Eli) Elrom",
  "license": "MIT",
  "bugs": {
    "url": "https://github.com/eladelrom/woodenlog/issues"
  },
```

```
"homepage": "https://github.com/eladelrom/woodenlog#readme",
"dependencies": {
  "ansi-styles": "^2.2.1"
},
"devDependencies": {
  "chai": "^3.5.0",
  "mocha": "^2.4.5"
}
}
```

Run Test Stubs Using npm

Since we have configured the test field in package.json:

```
"test": "./node_modules/.bin/mocha --reporter spec"
```

We will now be able to run our tests. In the Terminal, type the following command:

```
$ npm test
```

Once you run this command, you should see a pass message for our three methods and a spit-out of our code in the console, already formatted with our colors (Figure 3-14).

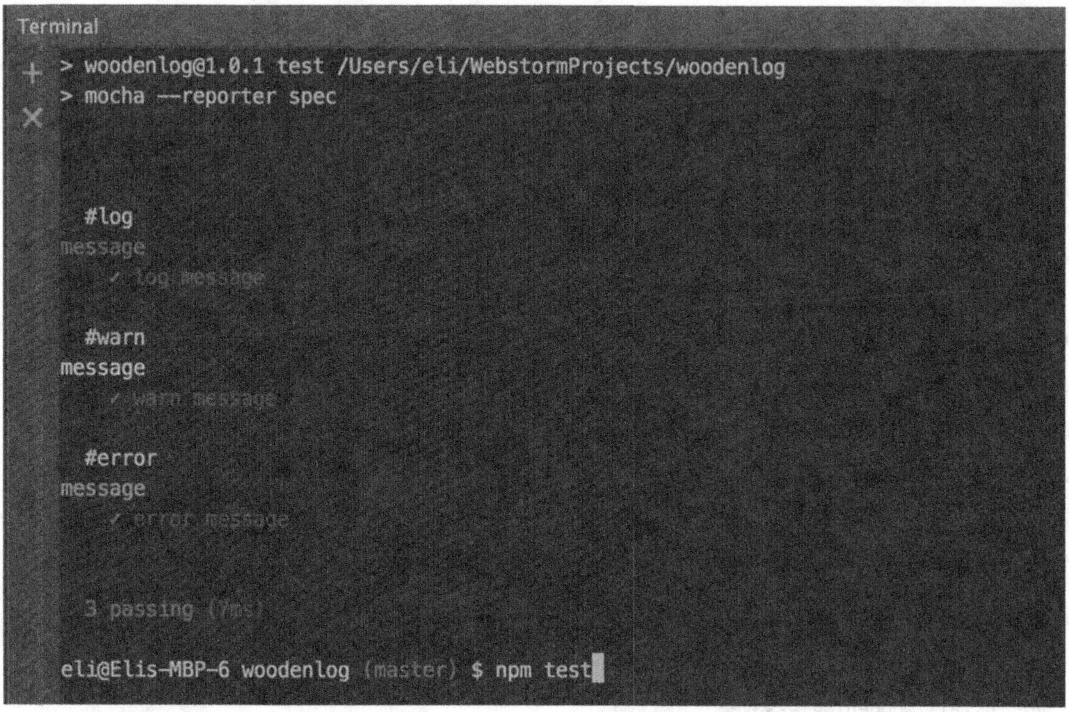

Figure 3-14. npm test results in Terminal

Create Markdown Home Page File

Last but not least, we want to create a README.md file. The ".md" file extension stands for "markdown." Markdown is lightweight syntax for styling your writing on GitHub and other platforms. It uses charcters to instruct styling and it makes styling your document easy.

The README.md file is considered our "home" page; it's configured by default with the package file and GitHub. We will be using this file automatically as your "home" page for the repository.

The markup language is straightforward. For instance, to highlight code, you'll wrap code inside ```js opening tags and ``` closing tags (Listing 3-6).

Listing 3-6. Format code in Markdown syntax

```js
var woodenlog = require('woodenlog');
// woodenlog.configurate(null, 'white', 'green', 'red');

woodenlog.log('just log!');
woodenlog.warn('this is a warning!');
woodenlog.error('this is an error!');

```

This will format your code in a nice, easy-to-see box, complete with colors and spacing. See Figure 3-15.

```
var woodenlog = require('woodenlog');
// woodenlog.configurate(null, 'white', 'green', 'red');

woodenlog.log('just log!');
woodenlog.warn('this is a warning!');
woodenlog.error('this is an error!');
```

Figure 3-15. *Format code in Markdown results*

To see all your available options and different Markdown syntax, feel free to visit this cheat sheet page: https://github.com/adam-p/markdown-here/wiki/Markdown-Cheatsheet

We will be using the following complete code block for our README.md file (Listing 3-7).

Listing 3-7. README.md file content

```
WoodenLog
=========

Minimalist log node messages module to add colors for console.log for specific type of log.

## Installation

```shell
  npm install woodenlog --save
```

Usage
```

```js
var woodenlog = require('woodenlog');
// woodenlog.configurate(null, 'white', 'green', 'red');

woodenlog.log('just log!');
woodenlog.warn('this is a warning!');
woodenlog.error('this is an error!');

```

Tests

```shell
   npm test
```

Release History

* 1.0.0 Initial release

The results can be seen in Figure 3-16.

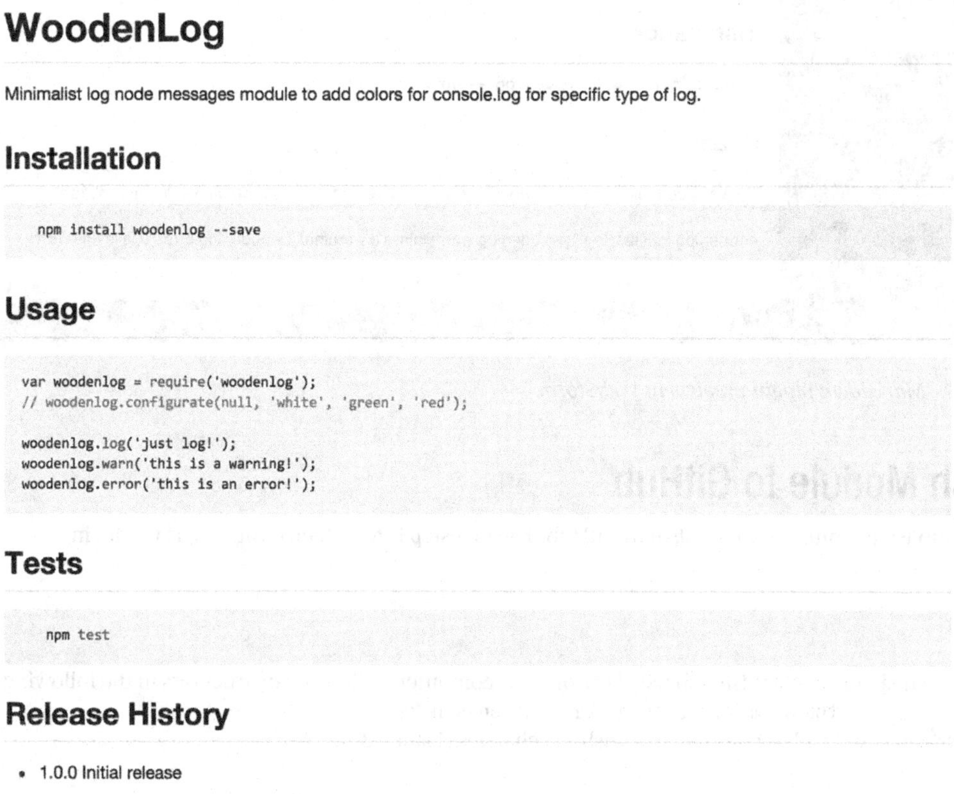

WoodenLog

Minimalist log node messages module to add colors for console.log for specific type of log.

Installation

```
npm install woodenlog --save
```

Usage

```
var woodenlog = require('woodenlog');
// woodenlog.configurate(null, 'white', 'green', 'red');

woodenlog.log('just log!');
woodenlog.warn('this is a warning!');
woodenlog.error('this is an error!');
```

Tests

```
npm test
```

Release History

* 1.0.0 Initial release

Figure 3-16. *README.md formatted*

Markdown Plugin in WebStorm

WebStorm has a Markdown plugin that helps you display and work with Markdown files. To add the Markdown plugin or any other plugins you want, follow the steps below:

1. Open the "Preference" window by selecting "command" + " , " or top menu "WebStorm" ➤ "Preferences..."

2. Select "Plugins."

3. Search for "Markdown" plugin.

4. Click "Install."

Next, toggle between the "Text" and "Preview" tabs to see the code and its results. See Figure 3-17.

Figure 3-17. *Markdown plugin preview in WebStorm*

Publish Module to GitHub

Before we publish to npm, we will publish to GitHub. The first step is to initialize Git, just as we did in Chapter 1.

```
$ git init
```

Next, you need to generate GitHub SSH keys on your computer. Follow the instructions in the following link: https://help.github.com/articles/generating-an-ssh-key/

Now we can add the files, commit, and push the changes (Listing 3-8).

Listing 3-8. Publish module to GitHub

```
$ git add .
$ git commit -m 'init commit'
$ git push --set-upstream origin master
```

Note that if you didn't configure your Git with your GitHub credential, it will ask for your username and password.

```
Username for 'https://github.com': [your user name]
Password for 'https:// [your user name]@github.com':
```

You will see a confirmation in the Terminal, confirming that the repo was published.

```
To https://github.com/eladelrom/woodenlog.git
 * [new branch]      master -> master
Branch master set up to track remote branch master from origin.
```

You may also visit the GitHub page to see your module README.md file and module files. See Figure 3-18:

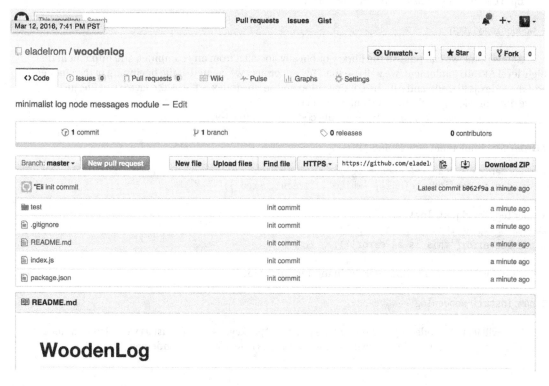

Figure 3-18. *GitHub woodenlog repo home page*

Now, we are ready to publish to npm. In order to publish to npm, run the command:

```
$ sudo npm publish
```

Just like with GitHub, since we haven't configured our user, npm will ask for authentication. See message below:

```
npm ERR! need auth auth required for publishing
npm ERR! need auth You need to authorize this machine using `npm adduser`
```

As you can see, it has given us the command in an error message. Type the command into the Terminal to add a username:

```
$ npm adduser
```

Now that the user has been added, we can publish again:

```
$ npm publish
```

npm confirms that this publishing was correct:

```
+ woodenlog@1.0.0
```

At this point, we can publish the library publically, install it from any computer, and implement the high-level API. To implement, we will use the "Tester" project we created at the beginning of the chapter, add the index.js file, edit and run the configuration and set the index.js file as the JavaScript file, just like we've done previously with the woodenlog project.

Inside the index.js file, paste the following code (see Listing 3-9):

Listing 3-9. Implement woodenlog API

```
var woodenlog = require('woodenlog');
// woodenlog.configurate(null, 'white', 'green', 'red');

woodenlog.log('just log!');
woodenlog.warn('this is a warning!');
woodenlog.error('this is an error!');
```

Next, install the woodenlog module. In the Terminal, type in:

```
$ npm install woodenlog --save-dev
```

This will install woodenlog and update the project's "package.json" file, just as we did in Chapter 1. Open "package.json" and you can see the module added as a developer dependency:

```
  "devDependencies": {
    "woodenlog": "^1.0.1"
  }
```

Run the project and you will see the following results in WebStorm Run Terminal. See Figure 3-19:

Figure 3-19. *WebStorm Run Terminal results*

Summary

In this chapter, we looked at npm popular node modules; learned how to install Node.js; installed dependency modules locally, globally and using different module versions options and flags; and configured an npm package.json file.

We created our own first node modules, learned how to create a GitHub project repository, created our module code and ran the code, learned which files to ignore, and created test stubs using mocha and chai.

We created a Markdown file using the Markdown plugin in WebStorm and published our module to GitHub and npm.

In the next chapter, we will learn how to set up a PhoneGap / Cardova project.

CHAPTER 4

■ ■ ■

Cordova, PhoneGap & Ionic

In this chapter, we will be learning about Cordova, PhoneGap and Ionic. Cordova enables us to write our code only once and deploy our app on just about any platform out there while still using the same code base. We will learn how to create projects, preview them in the platform we selected, and easily deploy our apps. We will also cover how to install plugins and learn about the distribution process.

Apache Cordova

Cordova is an open-source mobile development framework. It allows the use of HTML5, CSS3, and JavaScript for cross-platform development. Because of the technology stack of Cordova, using it will allow us to easily create and integrate MEAN stack apps.

Why Apache? Cordova is licensed under the Apache License, Version 2.0, which allows the royalty-free distribution of your app, making it free of charge worldwide. See the complete license here: `http://www.apache.org/licenses/LICENSE-2.0`

Cordova's applications execute within wrappers, which are targeted to each platform you select and thus rely on plugins to access each device's own specific capabilities. Some examples include camera, push notifications, and device status. In fact, you can view all of the plugin options Cordova offers and filter by device here:

`https://cordova.apache.org/plugins/`

By using the Cordova platform, we can deploy the same code base across the most popular platforms and stores, such as Android, iOS, and Web, without having to re-implement with each platform's specific language and tool set. Additionally, we can create a WebView (special browser window) that is able to access device-level APIs.

■ **Note**   The main advantage of Cordova is that it is budget-friendly and can cross-platform, removing the need to write specific platform native code.

Writing native code for each platform has its own advantages., and many large Fortune 500 companies have specific teams dedicated to each platform. But the ability to re-use your code and deploy it on multiple devices and stores can reduce the development effort and resources for a project. This will allow startups and smaller-sized companies to gain a presence in all popular stores and platforms, just like the "big boys," while utilizing a single development team.

Cordova is supported by all major platforms, including iOS mobile and desktop, Android, Bada, BlackBerry, Windows mobile and desktop, Amazon Fire OS, and much more. Visit Cordova to see the list of supported platforms:

`https://cordova.apache.org/contribute/`

© Elad Elrom 2016
E. Elrom, *Pro MEAN Stack Development*, DOI 10.1007/978-1-4842-2044-3_4

Cordova "Hello World"

You actually already have all of the tools you will need to get started. You will be utilizing Node.js and npm, which we have covered extensively in previous chapters. Let's begin.

The most common way to install Cordova and plugins and maintain a Cordova project is to use the Command Line Interface (CLI) utility, such as Mac OSX's Terminal application. Open Terminal.

To install Cordova, you will need to install the code globally using npm:

```
$ sudo npm install -g cordova
```

■ **Note**   Notice we use the "g" flag to ensure that the code will be available to us locally, for our specific Hello World project, but also globally for future projects. As a rule of thumb, any package that provides command-line tools that you will need to use on multiple projects should be installed globally.

Notice that we have installed Cordova as a "sudo" in order to allow npm to make any changes it needs in our environment. If you encounter any errors, simply try to run the same command again or follow the instructions that the error has given you.

Next, create your first Cordova app:

```
$ cordova create HelloCordova
```

Now we can navigate into the folder and add a platform:

```
$ cd HelloCordova
$ cordova platform add browser
```

Once these commands are run in the Terminal, you should be able to see the same or similar output in your Terminal. See Figure 4-1.

```
            ├── isarray@1.0.0
            ├── process-nextick-args@1.0.6
            └── util-deprecate@1.0.2
        ├── infinity-agent@2.0.3
        ├── is-redirect@1.0.0
        ├── is-stream@1.0.1
        ├── lowercase-keys@1.0.0
        ├── nested-error-stacks@1.0.2
        ├── object-assign@3.0.0
        ├── prepend-http@1.0.3
        ├─┬ read-all-stream@3.1.0
        │ ├─┬ pinkie-promise@2.0.0
        │ │ └── pinkie@2.0.4
        │ └─┬ readable-stream@2.0.6
        │   └── isarray@1.0.0
        └── timed-out@2.0.0
      ├─┬ registry-url@3.0.3
      │ └─┬ rc@1.1.6
      │   ├── deep-extend@0.4.1
      │   └── strip-json-comments@1.0.4
    ├─┬ repeating@1.1.3
    │ └─┬ is-finite@1.0.1
    │   └── number-is-nan@1.0.0
    ├─┬ semver-diff@2.1.0
    │ └── semver@5.1.0
    └── string-length@1.0.1

eli@Elis-MBP-6 ~ $ cordova create HelloCordova
Creating a new cordova project.
eli@Elis-MBP-6 ~ $ cd HelloCordova
eli@Elis-MBP-6 HelloCordova $ cordova platform add browser
Adding browser project...
Running command: /Users/eli/.cordova/lib/npm_cache/cordova-browser/4.0.0/package/bin/create /Users/eli/
HelloCordova/platforms/browser io.cordova.hellocordova HelloCordova
Creating Browser project. Path: platforms/browser
Discovered plugin "cordova-plugin-whitelist" in config.xml. Installing to the project
Fetching plugin "cordova-plugin-whitelist@1" via npm
Installing "cordova-plugin-whitelist" for browser
```

Figure 4-1. *Terminal output installing Apache Cordova*

Running Your App in Cordova

Lastly, run the project in the platform. In the Terminal, run the following command:

```
$ cordova run browser
```

This command will execute and open up the app we just created in your browser. See Figure 4-2.

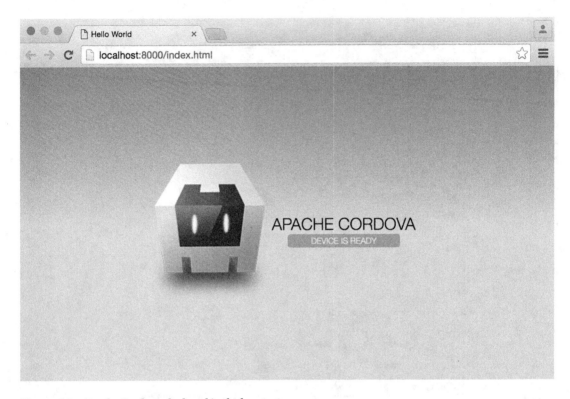

Figure 4-2. *Apache Cordova deployed in the browser*

At any time, you can terminate the app by typing ctrl+c in Terminal. The project's files just created are shown in Figure 4-3 and described in the following list.

```
-rw-r--r--    1 eli   staff   992 Mar 23 07:02 config.xml
drwxr-xr-x    7 eli   staff   238 Mar 23 07:02 .
drwxr-xr-x    6 eli   staff   204 Mar 23 07:03 www
drwxr-xr-x    5 eli   staff   170 Mar 23 07:10 plugins
drwxr-xr-x    4 eli   staff   136 Mar 23 07:11 platforms
drwxr-xr-x    3 eli   staff   102 Mar 23 07:11 hooks
drwx------+ 17 eli   staff   578 Mar 23 07:20 ..
```

Figure 4-3. *HelloCordova project list of files*

- **config.xml**: This file provides information about the app and specifies parameters affecting how it will work, such as whether it responds to orientation shifts or not.

- **www**: This folder holds the actual web app HTML, CSS, and JS files.

- **Plugins**: The plugins folder contains the plugins your app will be using. The plugins are an interface for Cordova and native components to communicate with each other, as well as bindings to standard device APIs. These enable you to invoke native code from JavaScript.

- **Platforms**: This folder contains the platforms you will be using, such as Android, BlackBerry, iOS, and Windows Mobile.

- **Hooks**: The hooks folder holds special scripts, which can be added by applications, plugin developers, or even by your own build system, to customize Cordova commands.

Figure 4-4 (from `https://cordova.apache.org/docs/en/latest/guide/overview/index.html`) provides a high-level architectural overview of the Cordova platform. The "Web App" is your "www" folder and "config.xml" file, and the HTML rendering targets specific platforms and allows added plugins to interact with specific native code from JavaScript.

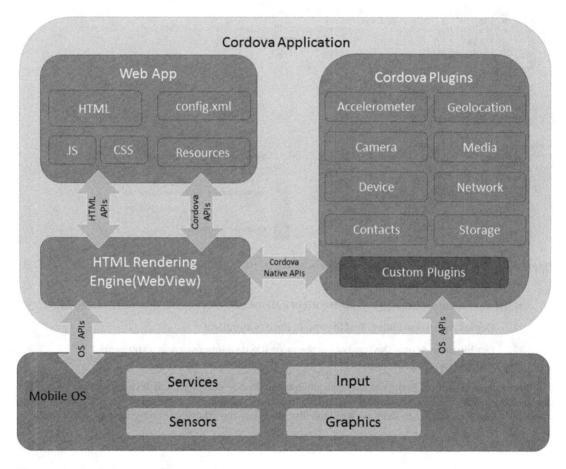

Figure 4-4. *Cordova app architecture*

Cordova Platform Deployment

So far, we have deployed a simple "Hello World" Cordova app on a web browser. Now let's say we want to add a platform, such as iOS. In the Terminal of the project, type ctrl+c to stop the app, and then:

```
$ cordova platform add ios
```

79

Next, navigate to the project files. In the Terminal, type:

```
$ cd platforms/ios/
```

Lastly, we can now open the project in Xcode, which we already installed back in Chapter 1. In the Terminal, type:

```
$ open HelloCordova.xcodeproj
```

The project will open in Xcode if the SDK was properly. See Figure 4-5.

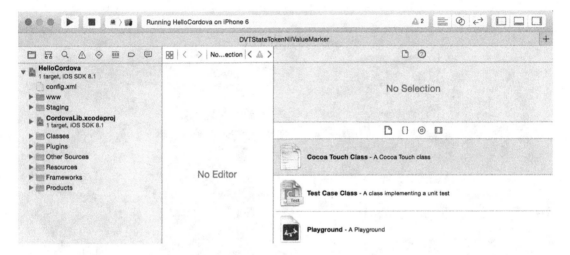

Figure 4-5. *Opening Cordova app iOS platform in Xcode*

The deployment of each platform is different. For iOS, the process consists of the following steps:

1. **Deploy App to Emulator**: Test the app in the iOS Simulator.

2. **Deploy to an Actual Device**: Follow the same iOS developer steps as if you were to deploy a native iOS app.

To see the app running in the emulator, all you have to do is select the type of device you want your app to run under in Xcode. Click the "HelloCordova" icon on the top menu, then select "HelloCordova" and select one of the iOS Simulators from the available list. We chose the iPhone 6 (See Figure 4-6):

Figure 4-6. *Select iOS device in Xcode*

Now that you have selected a device, hit the play icon on the top menu to begin the simulator and the stop icon to close it. See Figure 4-7 to watch our app running in the simulator.

Figure 4-7. *Cordova Hello World app running in iOS Simulator for iPhone 6*

Next, navigate back to the platform folder:

```
$ cd ..
```

To remove the iOS or any other platform, all you have to do is type the following command:

```
$ cordova platform remove ios
```

Of course you would need to replace the platform name, depending on whichever platform you want to remove.

You can also add a specific version of a platform. For example, to add the iOS platform version 4.0.0:

```
$ cordova platform add ios@4.0.0
```

Deployment to the iOS store using the Apple iOS Developer Program will be covered later on in this book (see "Platform Deployment"). You can jump to that section of the book and have the app installed and tested on your actual device if you are anxious to do so.

Notice we used "browser" and now "iOS" as our platform name, but you can use any platform available from the list we previously mentioned. They can be viewed here:

```
https://cordova.apache.org/contribute/
```

A few helpful Cordova commands:

1. "cordova –v": Displays the cordova version

2. "cordova –h": Provides a list of commands and options

3. "cordova platform update ios@4.0.0": Updates a platform to a specific version

4. "cordova platform update ios": Updates a platform to the latest version. At the time of writing, iOS latest version is 4.1.1.

Cordova Plugins

The Apache Cordova project maintains a set of plugins known as the core plugins, which are available on most platforms. These core plugins allow your application to access device capabilities such as battery, camera, and contacts.

In addition to the core plugins Cordova maintains, there are also many third-party plugins, which provide additional features not necessarily available on all platforms.

You can search for Cordova plugins using the command line search or directly on npm. You are also able to develop your own plugins, as described in the Plugin Development Guide on the Cordova website. Some plugins may be necessary, for example, to communicate between Cordova and custom native components.

To find a plugin, visit the plugin page, where you can sort by platform and/or quality: `http://cordova.apache.org/plugins/`

The command line can be used to search for features. For example, let's say we want to find a push notifications feature for our platform. In the command line, type:

```
$ cordova plugin search notifications
```

This opens up your default browser with the following URL:

```
http://cordova.apache.org/plugins/?q=notifications
```

See Figure 4-8 below.

Figure 4-8. *Searching plugins result page*

To install a plugin, type the name of the plugin you would like to add. The following command would not be successful:

```
$ cordova plugin add phonegap-plugin-push
```

If you try to install using the command above, it will spit out an error message in the Terminal because it's expecting a sender ID (see Figure 4-9), and you will see the following error message:

```
Error: Variable(s) missing (use: --variable SENDER_ID=value).
```

Since this is a third-party plugin, it was configured to require a parameter. Clicking on the plugin in the Cordova search results page we opened earlier will result in the Cordova page opening up the npm project URL, located here: `https://www.npmjs.com/package/phonegap-plugin-push`

Follow the Installation link and read the author notes to see what the installation requires. In our case, it will need the store ID for Android. Since we will not be installing this plugin for the Android platform, we can install it with the default ID of "XXXXXXX." Let's try again:

```
$ cordova plugin add phonegap-plugin-push --variable SENDER_ID="XXXXXXX"
```

```
eli@Elis-MBP-6 ios $ cordova plugin add phonegap-plugin-push
Fetching plugin "phonegap-plugin-push" via npm
Error: Variable(s) missing (use: --variable SENDER_ID=value).
eli@Elis-MBP-6 ios $ cordova plugin add phonegap-plugin-push --variable SENDER_ID="XXXXXXX"
Fetching plugin "phonegap-plugin-push" via npm
Installing "phonegap-plugin-push" for browser
Installing "phonegap-plugin-push" for ios
```

Figure 4-9. *Terminal output for installing phonegap-plugin-push*

This time it successfully installed the plugin. Additionally, there are other core plugins that are worth mentioning:

- Basic Device Information (Device API): cordova-plugin-device

- Network Connection Events: cordova-plugin-network-info

- Battery Events: cordova plugin add cordova-plugin-battery-status

- Accelerometer: cordova plugin add cordova-plugin-device-motion

- Compass: cordova plugin add cordova-plugin-device-orientation

- Geolocation: cordova plugin add cordova-plugin-geolocation

- Camera: cordova plugin add cordova-plugin-camera

- Media Capture: cordova plugin add cordova-plugin-media-capture

- Media Playback: cordova plugin add cordova-plugin-media

- Access Files: cordova plugin add cordova-plugin-file

- Network File Access: cordova plugin add cordova-plugin-file-transfer

- Notification via Dialog Box: cordova plugin add cordova-plugin-dialogs

- Notification via Vibration: cordova plugin add cordova-plugin-vibration

- Contacts: cordova plugin add cordova-plugin-contacts

- Globalization: cordova plugin add cordova-plugin-globalization

- Splashscreen: cordova plugin add cordova-plugin-splashscreen

- Open New Browser Windows (InAppBrowser): cordova plugin add cordova-plugin-inappbrowser

- Debug Console: cordova plugin add cordova-plugin-console

To install these plugins, we can use the same syntax that we used to install the "phonegap-plugin-push" plugin:

```
$ cordova plugin add [plugin name]
```

Also notice that some plugins rely on other plugins. For example, "cordova-plugin-media-capture" relies on "cordova-plugin-file." The plugin will be automatically installed on all platforms we add—in our case, iOS and browser.

To see the plugin list, type the following command:

```
$ cordova plugin list
```

In the back stage, you can see that the "config.xml" added configuration for these plugins automatically. For example, for the push notification, there is an entry:

```
<feature name="PushNotification">
    <param name="ios-package" value="PushPlugin" />
</feature>
```

Visit the plugins folder inside the "www" folder and you will see the plugin was added correctly. See Figure 4-10:

```
drwxr-xr-x   3 eli   staff   102 Mar 26 08:04 phonegap-plugin-push
drwxr-xr-x   3 eli   staff   102 Mar 26 08:04 cordova-plugin-network-information
drwxr-xr-x   3 eli   staff   102 Mar 26 08:04 cordova-plugin-device-motion
drwxr-xr-x   3 eli   staff   102 Mar 26 08:04 cordova-plugin-device
drwxr-xr-x   3 eli   staff   102 Mar 26 08:04 cordova-plugin-battery-status
drwxr-xr-x  10 eli   staff   340 Mar 26 08:04 ..
drwxr-xr-x   7 eli   staff   238 Mar 26 08:04 .
eli@Elis-MBP-6 plugins $ pwd
/Users/eli/Desktop/HelloCordova/platforms/ios/www/plugins
```

Figure 4-10. *Plugin folder shows installed plugins*

Cordova Plugman

In addition to installing plugins manually, as we have done, Cordova utilizes a tool called "Plugman" to help you manage plugins.

To install the manager, run this command:

```
$ sudo npm install -g plugman
```

To see a help printout and a version, just as we've done in Cordova, use the "-h" and "-v" flags:

```
$ plugman –h
$ plugman –v
```

The Plugman tool implements the plugin on all device APIs and disables them by default—you decide when to enable the plugin. It also supports two different ways of adding and removing plugins, depending on your choice of workflow, discussed in the Overview:

1. If you use a cross-platform workflow, you will need to use the Cordova CLI utility to add plugins, as described in the Command-Line Interface, which is what we showed you earlier in the chapter. As you have seen, CLI sets the plugin for all of the platforms at once.

2. If you want to use a platform-centered workflow, you will need to use a lower-level Plugman CLI, separately, for each targeted platform.

Here's an example of using Plugman for a specific platform. Type the following commands:

```
$ cd ~/desktop
$ cordova create TestPlugMan
$ cd TestPlugMan/
$ cordova platform add android
$ plugman install --platform android --project platforms/android --plugin cordova-plugin-console
```

In this example, we navigated to our desktop directory, created a new project called "TestPlugMan," added the Android platform and installed a console plugin to that specific platform.

Additionally, Plugman comes handy when you want to create a plugin on your own and it's not published yet.

Cordova Distributions

Apache Cordova is the engine that powers the distribution solutions . Distributions contain additional tools to help the developer deploy and develop apps, which is why they differ in command from Cordova, but technically they do the same thing.

Each tool can provide command line tools, JavaScript frameworks, and cloud services that extend beyond Cordova.

There are many distributions to choose from: Adobe PhoneGap, Ionic, Monaca, Onsen UI, Visual Studio, TACO, Telerik, GapDebug, App Builder, Intel XDK, Cocoon, and Framework7.

You can read more about these here: https://cordova.apache.org/ or visit the sites of each distribution directly.

PhoneGap, the most popular distribution, offers easy cloud deployment, while Ionic is built from CSS with superpowers ("Sass") and optimized for AngularJS, so both are great options for MEAN stack types of apps. Recently, Ionic changed their pricing model, and it's now free for developers up to using limited resources and monthly charges based on resources used. See more information here: https://ionic.io/pricing

PhoneGap Distribution

We have chosen Adobe PhoneGap as our example of a Cordova distribution. The reason we chose PhoneGap is that it's an open source distribution and the original and most popular of Apache Cordova distributions available.

The benefit of using PhoneGap over Cordova directly is that it has a built-in feature that enables developers to deploy their app in the cloud. This means that you may not need to open the app in Xcode or any other native development SDK in order to publish your app, and you can use additional tools and commands offered by the distribution.

In the section below, we will install PhoneGap, start coding, and show you how to preview the PhoneGap App.

Installing PhoneGap

For installing PhoneGap, Adobe offers either a CLI installation or a desktop app.

If you prefer the desktop app, simply download it here:

```
https://github.com/phonegap/phonegap-app-desktop/releases/download/0.2.3/PhoneGapDesktop.dmg
```

To install the CLI, type in the Terminal:

```
$ sudo npm install -g phonegap@latest
```

You can confirm that the installation was successful by typing "phonegap" in the Terminal command line.

In the future, when new versions of PhoneGap are released, you can upgrade your PhoneGap installation by using the following command:

```
$ sudo npm update -g phonegap
```

Install PhoneGap Mobile App

Phonegap offers developers distribution for mobile apps on devices and allows tests and previews of PhoneGap mobile apps across platforms without additional platform SDK setup, which brings tremendous value. It provides access to the PhoneGap core APIs providing access to the native device features without having to install plugins or compile locally first.

1. **iTunes**: https://itunes.apple.com/app/id843536693

2. **Google Play**: https://play.google.com/store/apps/details?id=com.adobe. phonegap.app

3. **Windows Phone Store**: http://www.windowsphone.com/en-us/store/app/ phonegap-developer/5c6a2d1e-4fad-4bf8-aaf7-71380cc84fe3

Additionally, you can find the app directly on a device's store using the "PhoneGap Developer" keyword. See the app installed on an iPhone, Figure 4-11.

Figure 4-11. *PhoneGap Developer app install on an iPhone*

Start Coding

We have already installed PhoneGap and the PhoneGap Developer app, and now we can create our first PhoneGap app. To get started, we will utilize PhoneGap to create the basic scaffolding for our app. In the Terminal, type the following command:

```
$ phonegap create helloPhoneGap
```

This command created a folder for us named "helloPhoneGap," which holds everything we will need to get started.

Navigate into that folder and see what was created.

```
$ cd helloPhoneGap/
```

As you can see, it created a similar structure as Cordova with a "www," platforms, plugins, hooks folders, and a config.xml and package.json file.

Preview Your PhoneGap App

To preview the application that was created, all there is left to do is type one command into the Terminal:

```
$ phonegap serve
```

This command will start up the app server and advise us of the IP address it is listening in on. In our case, it's listening in on 192.168.1.65:3000. See Figure 4-12.

```
[phonegap] starting app server...
[phonegap] listening on 192.168.1.65:3000
[phonegap]
[phonegap] ctrl-c to stop the server
[phonegap]
[phonegap] 200 /__api__/appzip
[phonegap] 200 /__api__/appzip
[phonegap] [console.log] Received Event: deviceready
[phonegap] 200 /socket.io/?EIO=3&transport=polling&t=LFNbaOm&sid=M6iUa9rOpy7l9HxZAAAA
[phonegap] 200 /socket.io/?EIO=3&transport=polling&t=LFNbaOY&sid=M6iUa9rOpy7l9HxZAAAA
```

Figure 4-12. Starting PhoneGap app server and moving files to device

Now, open your device, such as iPhone or Android, and in the PhoneGap Developer app we installed, select the IP address the app server is listening in on (192.168.1.65:3000 in our case, but it will be different for you).

PhoneGap will build and transfer the files via Socket.IO to the device automatically. See Figure 4-13 for a preview of the app. Figure 4-12 shows in the Terminal that the files were moved successfully.

Figure 4-13. *PhoneGap Developer app preview on iPhone*

You can see the value of using PhoneGap over Cordova; we didn't have to install Xcode or follow the tedious process of Apple in order to run the app on our device. In fact, the PhoneGap Developer app gives us access to the device API, so that we can also easily access our device hardware.

PhoneGap Development

Now that we have PhoneGap installed and we know how to install and preview our app on our devices, we can go ahead and make changes in our app and start the actual development process.

We will be using WebStorm to import our project. However, feel free to use any Integrated Development Environment (IDE) you would like.

In WebStorm, select "Open" on the Welcome page (see Figure 4-14). If you have any projects open, close them and the Welcome page will appear.

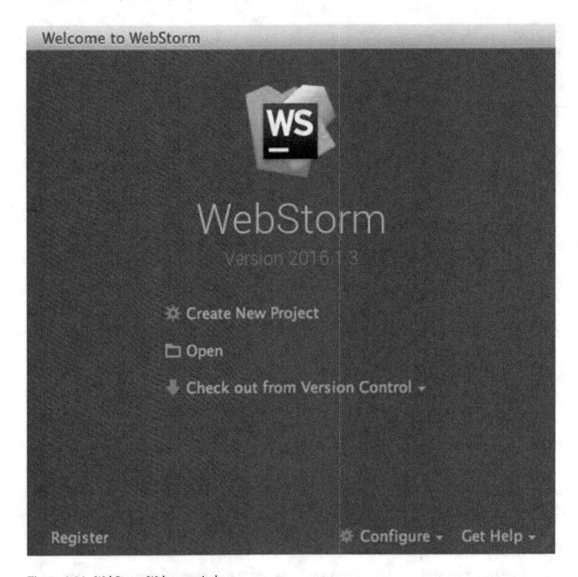

Figure 4-14. *WebStorm Welcome window*

Next, it will open up the "Open File or Project" window. Then, WebStorm asks us to define the project root directory. Navigate to where you placed the "helloPhoneGap" project and click on "Project Root" (see Figure 4-15.)

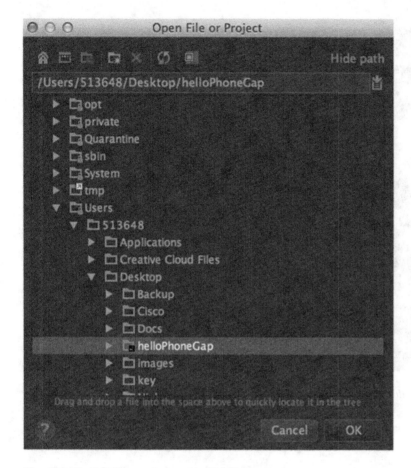

Figure 4-15. *Selecting project root in WebStorm*

Click "Finish" and that's all there is to it. WebStorm will open up with the project configured (see Figure 4-16).

Figure 4-16. *WebStorm with helloPhoneGap project configured*

Navigate into the "www" folder and open the index.html file in WebStorm—see Figure 4-16 and Listing 4-1.

Listing 4-1. Index.js content

```
<body>
    <div class="app">
        <h1>PhoneGap</h1>
        <div id="deviceready" class="blink">
            <p class="event listening">Connecting to Device</p>
            <p class="event received">Device is Ready</p>
        </div>
    </div>
    <script type="text/javascript" src="cordova.js"></script>
    <script type="text/javascript" src="js/index.js"></script>
    <script type="text/javascript">
        app.initialize();
    </script>
</body>
```

The code is straightforward; it shows a title called "PhoneGap" and has a div with text that will change according to the device. Then, it loads the Cordova.js and js/index.js scripts and initializes the app.

Change the heading tag from "Hello":

```
<h1>PhoneGap</h1>
```

To "Hello PhoneGap":

```
<h1>Hello PhoneGap</h1>
```

Now, to see this change on the actual device, all you have to do is run the server command again in the Terminal:

```
$ phonegap serve
```

As you recall, WebStorm has a "Terminal" window, so you don't need to open up the Mac Terminal—simply use the built-in Terminal. To stop the local server created by PhoneGap, click ctrl-c.

You should be able to see the change we have made on your actual device—see Figure 4-17.

Figure 4-17. *"Hello PhoneGap" is showing on device*

Ionic

A second Cordova distribution we would like to point out and cover is Ionic. Ionic distribution is geared toward the AngularJS framework.

Similar to PhoneGap, Ionic has built-in features that enable developers to develop and deploy their app easily. Additionally, it will automatically set your project with structure, libraries, and settings according to AngularJS best practices.

In this section, we will install Ionic, add plugins, preview the app we will be creating, preview the app in an iOS simulator, and review the Ionic resources.

To get started, install Ionic using the following command in the Terminal:

```
$ sudo npm install -g ionic
```

That command will install the Ionic CLI: https://www.npmjs.com/package/ionic. It is a Cordova decorator, meaning all Cordova commands will work plus additional commands added be ionic.

Once Ionic is installed, you can start a new project. We'll call the project "helloionic":

```
$ ionic start helloionic
```

Ionic adds the iOS application by default and uses the "tabs" template project. The command is the same as writing tabs at the end:

```
$ ionic start helloionic tabs
```

See the Terminal output in Figure 4-18:

```
eli@Elis-MBP-6 desktop $ ionic start helloionic
Creating Ionic app in folder /Users/eli/Desktop/helloionic based on tabs project
Downloading: https://github.com/driftyco/ionic-app-base/archive/master.zip
[==============================] 100% 0.0s
Downloading: https://github.com/driftyco/ionic-starter-tabs/archive/master.zip
[==============================] 100% 0.0s
Updated the hooks directory to have execute permissions
Update Config.xml
Initializing cordova project
Adding in iOS application by default
eli@Elis-MBP-6 desktop $
```

Figure 4-18. *Ionic "helloionic" project output*

Ionic offers currently three template starters: tabs (default), sidemenu, and blank.

Next, let's start a new project in WebStorm so we can explore the project easily. Similar to how we imported the "helloPhoneGap" project into WebStorm, we'll do the same with "helloionic"(see Figure 4-19). As you recall:

1. Select "Open."

2. Next, select "Source files are in a local directory, no Web server is yet configured."

3. Now, browse and set the project root, "helloionic," and click "OK"

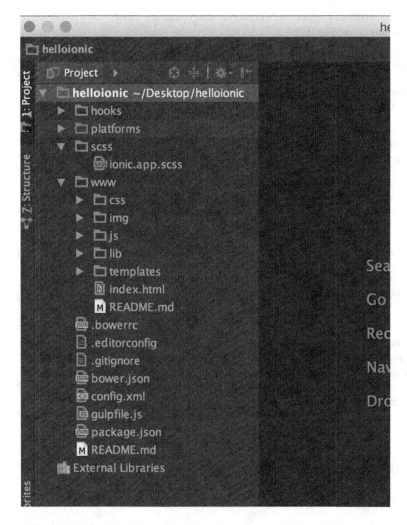

Figure 4-19. *"helloionic" configured in WebStorm*

Ionic automatically created our project and included the same files and folder we have seen before in Cordova and PhoneGap, such as index.html, hooks, platforms, plugins, config.xml, bower.json, and package.json.

Additionally, Ionic includes all the basic AngularJS structures and templates to get you started as soon as possible. For instance:

- www/js/app.js: App file is a global place for creating, registering, and retrieving AngularJS modules.

- www/js/controllers.js: AngularJS controller is the glue that holds the model and view together.

- www/js/services.js: AngularJS services are substitutable objects that are wired together using dependency injection (DI).

- www/templates: The view representation includes the following: chat-detail.html, tab-account.html, tab-chats.html, tab-dash.html, tabs.html.

- www/lib: Includes the following libraries: CSS, SCSS, fonts, and the js folder, which includes Angular libraries and Ionic libraries.

- www/lib/ionic/scss/ionic.scss: SCSS is described on `http://sass-lang.com/` as "CSS with superpowers." Sass is a preprocessor for generating CSS that adds power and elegance to the basic language.

In the next chapter, we will be diving deep into AngularJS, folder structure, and framework, and we don't want to get sidetracked from the chapter objective. Go over the code and you will get an idea, or review this project again after you've completed Chapter 5.

Ionic Front-end

Ionic excels when it comes to front-end, offering pre-made UI components ready to use across different platfroms. To see the available UIs, check the Ionic component page:

`http://ionicframework.com/docs/components/`

Additionally, Ionic follows OS-specific guidelines for following styles, behaviors, and transitions to fit the platform you choose. For example, the menu toggle button is on the left in iOS but on the right in Android.

Ionic also put lots of effort into performance. For instance, for handling lists, Ionic introduced a "collection-repeat" directive to replace ng-repeat and its only showing list that are displaying instead of rendering all the items in a collection.

Add Plugins in Ionic

Adding plugins or re-installing in Ionic is the same as Cordova and PhoneGap:

```
$ ionic plugin add [plugin name]
```

That command will register the plugin inside the "package.json," just as we've seen in Cordova and PhoneGap.

Preview Your App

To run the project, in the Terminal either inside of WebStorm or directly in Terminal, after changing the directory to the Ionic library ("cd helloionic"), type:

```
$ ionic serve
```

The "serve" command deploys the project in the browser. See Figure 4-20:

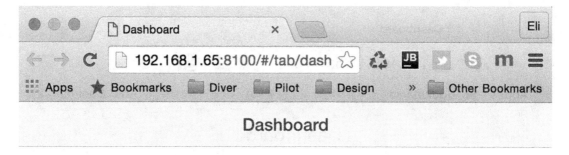

Welcome to Ionic

This is the Ionic starter for tabs-based apps. For other starters and ready-made templates, check out the Ionic Market.

To edit the content of each tab, edit the corresponding template file in `www/templates/`. This template is `www/templates/tab-dash.html`

If you need help with your app, join the Ionic Community on the Ionic Forum. Make sure to follow us on Twitter to get important updates and announcements for Ionic developers.

For help sending push notifications, join the Ionic Platform and check out Ionic Push. We also have other services available.

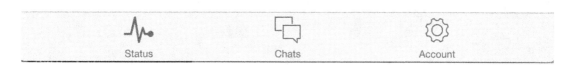

Figure 4-20. *"helloionic" deployed in the browser*

Use the lab flag to see your app in different platforms (see Figure 4-21).

```
$ ionic serve -lab
```

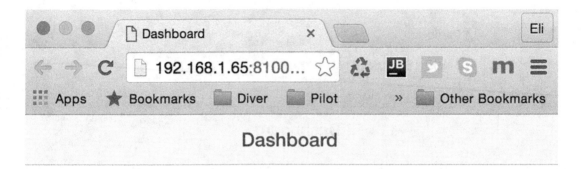

Welcome to Ionic

This is the Ionic starter for tabs-based apps. For other starters and ready-made templates, check out the Ionic Market.

To edit the content of each tab, edit the corresponding template file in `www/templates/`. This template is `www/templates/tab-dash.html`

If you need help with your app, join the Ionic Community on the Ionic Forum. Make sure to follow us on Twitter to get important updates and announcements for Ionic developers.

For help sending push notifications, join the Ionic Platform and check out Ionic Push. We also have other services available.

Figure 4-21. *Ionic serve with lab flag*

Also worth mentioning:

1. livereload flag: Watch for changes and update your app automatically.
2. c flag: Print the console logs to the Terminal.

Let's put it all together:

```
ionic serve --c --lab --livereload
```

iOS Simulator

To deploy the same project on iOS, you need to install the "ios-sim" project using the following command:

```
$ sudo npm install -g ios-sim
```

Then you can run the project in the simulator using the following command (see output in Figure 4-22):

```
$ ionic run ios
```

Figure 4-22. *"helloionic" deployed on iPhone 6*

You can also open the Ionic project in Xcode by typing this command in the Terminal:

```
$ open platforms/ios/HelloCordova.xcodeproj
```

In Xcode, build and run the current scheme, the play icon, just as we did in Chapter 1. Ionic supports the Crosswalk Project (https://crosswalk-project.org/). Crosswalk is an HTML application runtime originally sponsored by Intel and built on open source foundations. It extends the web platform and adds new capabilities, ensuring they are available on your build. Benefits include:

1. Improved performance and visuals using HTML5, CSS3, and JavaScript

2. Access to latest recommended and emerging web standards

3. Ability to try experimental APIs not supported by mainstream web browsers

4. Control over the update cycle of your app by distributing it with its own runtime.

5. Debug easily using Chrome DevTools

To install Crosswalk, run the following commands:

```
$ npm install -g ios-deploy
$ ionic browser add crosswalk
```

After installing Crosswalk, you can provide a rich experience on all Android 4.x devices. Ionic will automatically embed Crosswalk for your Android build, ensuring everything is working correctly.

You can use the browser list command to see the different versions of Crosswalk you can install:

```
$ ionic browser list
```

Ionic Resources

Next, when you are ready to deploy, you'll need icons and a splashscreen for your app on each platform you deploy. This can add a lot of work, since you need to follow each platform's guidelines. Ionic handles that gracefully. All you have to do is follow these templates for icons and splashscreens:

1. Icons: `http://code.ionicframework.com/resources/icon.psd`

2. Splashscreens: `http://code.ionicframework.com/resources/splash.psd`

Place the icon and splash file template in the Ionic resource folder ("helloionic/resources") and run this command:

```
$ ionic resources
```

Alternatively, you can run "ionic resources" first and, once the directory and files are created, add PSD and run the command again.

Running the command will generate all the files and take care of parameters such as image dimension, OS Device, and landscape/portrait. That command will also upload the files to Ionic's servers and create the correct platform folders and edit the "config.xml" file for you automatically.

Summary

In this chapter, we learned about Apache Cordova, created a Cordova "Hello World" sample app, and learned how to run this app. We studied the different platform deployments that Cordova supports and also the different Cordova plugins available and where to locate them. We covered several of the Cordova distributions, such as PhoneGap and Ionic. We installed PhoneGap and the PhoneGap Mobile App and created a PhoneGap Hello World sample project. We began coding and previewed our PhoneGap app on our specific device. Lastly, we configured WebStorm IDE with the PhoneGap project we had created. We then created and configured an Ionic project, previewed some of the features and commands that can help you use Ionic to its fullest potential, and deployed your app in the browser and on iPhone 6.

In the next chapter, we will learn about AngularJS and how to create apps in AngularJS, which can be deployed using Cordova, PhoneGap, and Ionic on most popular devices. This will allow us to leverage and use the same codebase to deploy our app without having to write native code for each specific device.

CHAPTER 5

AngularJS

AngularJS is the "A" in the MEAN stack. AngularJS enables developers to create front-end rich client side applications. The pieces are loosely coupled and structured in a modular fashion, resulting in less code to write, added flexibility, easier-to-read code, and quicker development time.

At the end of the day, AngularJS simply allows the developer to put together a toolset for building a framework, which will fit your exact application's needs. Additionally, AngularJS is well structured and built to be fully accessible, in accordance with Accessible Rich Internet Applications (ARIA) so your app or site can be built correctly for people with disabilities. AngularJS also gets along very well with other JavaScript libraries; its features can be easily modified or replaced to fit your exact needs.

We will be covering AngularJS throughout this chapter, diving deep into one of its most popular skeleton projects, called "Angular Seed." We will be looking at each piece individually, which will allow us to gain a full understanding of the AngularJS framework. Much of the work we have done in past chapters will come in handy here, since we won't need to do much installation and we can hit the ground running right away.

Note   The word "Angular" means having multiple angles or measured by an angle. Visit `https://angularjs.org/` to learn more about AngularJS.

An AngularJS best practice is using a Model View Controller (MVC) style architecture, and in fact, AngularJS supports coding with seperation of concerns. Splitting code into different piles is practiced in most programming languages, and applies to AngularJS as well.

Note   AngularJS MVC includes the model, which is the application's data; the view, which is the HTML and directives (more on these later in this chapter), and the controller, which is the glue holding the model and the view together. The controller takes the data, applies business logic, and sends the results to the view.

The current version of AngularJS is version 1, AKA AngularJS1, however in 2015 a developer preview of AngularJS2 was released, and it's in Release Candidate 5 (RC5) status at the time of this writing. There are differences between the two versions, and it's a good idea to get familiar with AngularJS version 2 now to be able to migrate your code if you ever need to.

AngularJS2's goal is for users to be able to use the same code to develop across all platforms, which aligns very well with this book and will make it easier for us to upgrade to Angular 2.

© Elad Elrom 2016

E. Elrom, *Pro MEAN Stack Development*, DOI 10.1007/978-1-4842-2044-3_5

Angular Seed Project

You can create your project from scratch, download the necessary libraries, test, build scripts, and create your own folder structure, or you can download a skeleton project to quickly bootstrap your project. You can use a pre-set dev environment so that you can begin developing quickly and efficiently, following AngularJS's best practices.

There are pros and cons of using a boilerplate skeleton code. You can decide on your own if you want to use this skeleton for future projects, but it is a good way to start your first AngularJS app and learn the ropes.

A good example of a project boilerplate skeleton project to use is "angular-seed"; visit the page on GitHub to learn more about the project: `https://github.com/angular/angular-seed`.

"Angular-seed" includes the AngularJS framework as well as development and testing tools to help you start coding immediately.

WebStorm already includes a copy of angular-seed, so you can get up and running quickly. Open WebStorm and close any open projects, then wait for the welcome screen to come up.

On the welcome screen, select "Create New Project" ➤ "AngularJS" from the left menu—see Figure 5-1.

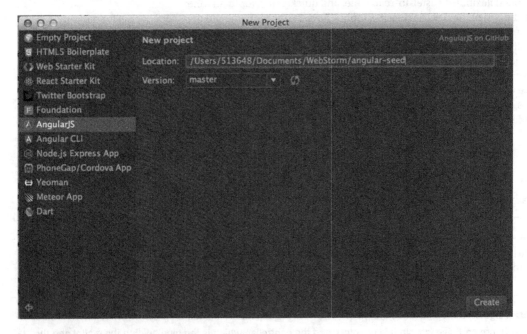

Figure 5-1. *Create New Project: Choose Project Directory window*

Under "New Project" choose the location and name of the app as "angular-seed." Click "Create" and the new project opens up—see Figure 5-2.

Figure 5-2. *"angular-seed" project in WebStorm*

Now that we have the project downloaded, we can fetch all of the libraries we will need. "Angular-seed" is set with a preconfigured npm command to automatically run and install all of these libraries. In the command line, simply type the following in the location of the project:

```
$ sudo npm install
$ sudo bower install --allow-root
```

That's it! These commands install all the libraries we need from npm and Bower. Now we have all we need to start our project. To run the project, all we have to do is run this command:

```
$ sudo npm start
```

Navigate to the following URL, or use the "open" command in the second command line to see the app. See Figure 5-1.

```
$ open http://localhost:8000
```

Now, the project is ready (see Figure 5-3). If you want to shut down the server, click ctrl+c.

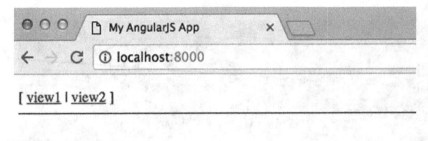

Figure 5-3. angular-seed My AngularJS app showing in a Google Chrome browser

Now that we have the project set up in WebStorm, we can run the project commands from the WebStorm Terminal window. Type "npm start" instead of using the Mac Terminal application—see the WebStorm Terminal window in Figure 5-2.

Let's now dive into the files and libraries that the Angular-seed project includes.

Bower Component

The first folder under the "app" root folder is the "bower_components" folder, located here: "angular-seed/app/bower_components." When we run the command "npm install", it's actually running the "Bower install" command for us.

Open "angular-seed/bower.json" and you will see what has been installed for us in the Bower component folder:

```
"dependencies": {
    "angular": "~1.5.0",
    "angular-route": "~1.5.0",
    "angular-loader": "~1.5.0",
    "angular-mocks": "~1.5.0",
    "html5-boilerplate": "^5.3.0"
}
```

The "bower_components" folder includes the following libraries, and if you open the "README.md" file in each library, you can retrieve all of the information regarding that library. As you may recall, we have already configured WebStorm with a Markdown plugin, so when you open the "README.md" file, it should open in its pre-styled form.

- **Angular**: This is an AngularJS framework code base.

- **Angular-loader**: This is the AngularJS loader library. It will allow your AngularJS scripts to be loaded in any order you want them. To implement this, place it on top of your index file (so that it's executed first) and proceed to load your files in any order you want. There are other libraries that can be used in order to achieve the same goal, such as "RequireJS" or "angular-async-loader," or you can use more modern libraries such as "Browserify" or "webpack," but feel free to search through these libraries online and explore.

- **Angular-mocks**: The library is built to replace functionality for testing purposes. An example is the AngularJS $http service internal API, which is mocked by AngularJS's built-in $httpBackend in ngMocks. Why would you need this? You are able to create a mocked service and use the results in tests. If the backend is tested properly and the interfaces are defined clearly, there will be a clean separation of concerns and the testing strategy will be efficient.

- **Angular-route**: The $route library is used for deep-linking URLs to controllers and views. $route API listens for $location.url() change event and then tries to map a path to route definition; more about that later in this chapter.

- **html5-boilerplate**: HTML5 boilerplate code is aimed at enabling you to build faster and more enterprise-grade web apps or sites. You can check the project and see what it contains here: `https://html5boilerplate.com/`. The HTML5 boilerplate includes analytics, icons, Normalize.css, jQuery, and Modernizr configured Apache setting codes to increase performance.

App Layout File

The "index.html" file is the app entry point layout file (the main HTML template file of the app). It holds the Bower components, styles, routes, controllers, directives, filters, and components. See Listing 5-1.

Listing 5-1. App layout file index.html

```
<div ng-view></div>

<div>Angular seed app: v<span app-version></span></div>

<!-- In production use:
<script src="//ajax.googleapis.com/ajax/libs/angularjs/x.x.x/angular.min.js"></script>
-->
<script src="bower_components/angular/angular.js"></script>
<script src="bower_components/angular-route/angular-route.js"></script>
<script src="app.js"></script>
```

```
<script src="view1/view1.js"></script>
<script src="view2/view2.js"></script>
<script src="components/version/version.js"></script>
<script src="components/version/version-directive.js"></script>
<script src="components/version/interpolate-filter.js"></script>
```

When using the AngularJS script tag, AngularJS will be integrated and initialized automatically.

Notice that the scripts are set at the bottom of the page, which improves the app load time. If the scripts had been at the top, HTML loading would have been blocked by the loading of the JS scripts.

It is recommended that you place the "ng-app" at the root of the app, usually on the "html" tag. This will enable AngularJS to bootstrap your app automatically. Also, it is a good idea to add the "ng-strict-di" directive on the same element as "ng-app" to the HTML tag to ensure the app is annotated correctly. It is recommended that you enable "ng-strict-di" in all of your scripts as soon as possible in order to prevent the app from breaking later on when the annotation is added.

■ **Note** To ensure that your app will be able to be minified once ready for deployment, a good practice is using "strict-di." The app must fail to run when invoking functions that don't use explicit function annotation. This means that the methods used must be declared. Using the "ng-strict-di" will ensure the app is confirming with dependency injection guidelines and will fail to run if not.

You can achieve this by using:

```
<html ng-app="myApp" ng-strict-di>
```

Add the following to each HTML tag:

```
<!DOCTYPE html>
<!--[if lt IE 7]>      <html lang="en" ng-app="myApp" class="no-js lt-ie9 lt-ie8 lt-ie7" ng-
strict-di> <![endif]-->
<!--[if IE 7]>         <html lang="en" ng-app="myApp" class="no-js lt-ie9 lt-ie8" ng-strict-
di> <![endif]-->
<!--[if IE 8]>         <html lang="en" ng-app="myApp" class="no-js lt-ie9" ng-strict-di>
<![endif]-->
<!--[if gt IE 8]><!--> <html lang="en" ng-app="myApp" class="no-js" ng-strict-di>
<!--<![endif]-->
```

The other entry layout file, "index-async.html," holds the same content as "index.html," but it loads the JS files asynchronously instead of synchronously.

These two index files are interchangeable, and either one can be used to build your app. "index-async. html" loads scripts asynchronously, which usually gives you a faster bootstrap time, while "index.html" loads scripts synchronously, which is often a bit slower, but its code is easier to understand for someone new to the AngularJS framework (Listing 5-2).

Listing 5-2. App layout file index-async.html

```
<script>
    // load all of the dependencies asynchronously.
    $script([
      'bower_components/angular/angular.js',
      'bower_components/angular-route/angular-route.js',
```

```
    'app.js',
    'view1/view1.js',
    'view2/view2.js',
    'components/version/version.js',
    'components/version/version-directive.js',
    'components/version/interpolate-filter.js'
  ], function() {
    // when all is done, execute bootstrap angular application
    angular.bootstrap(document, ['myApp']);
  });
</script>
<title>My AngularJS App</title>
<link rel="stylesheet" href="app.css">
</head>
<body ng-cloak>
  <ul class="menu">
    <li><a href="#/view1">view1</a></li>
    <li><a href="#/view2">view2</a></li>
  </ul>

  <div ng-view></div>

  <div>Angular seed app: v<span app-version></span></div>

</body>
</html>
```

AngularJS offers a bootstrap guide, which allows you to learn more about the initialization process—specifically, how you can manually initialize an AngularJS project when necessary:

```
https://docs.angularjs.org/guide/bootstrap
```

In order for "index-async.html" to work, you will need to inject a piece of AngularJS JavaScript code into the HTML page. Luckily for Angular-seek, the project has a predefined script to help you do that. In the command line, just type the following code:

```
$ npm run update-index-async
```

The npm script copies the contents of the "angular-loader.js" file into the "index-async.html" HTML page. Note that you will need to run this script every time you update a version of AngularJS.

There are times that you will need to have even more control over the AngularJS framework and you may want to manually initialize AngularJS. Here is a simple example of manually initializing AngularJS (see Listing 5-3).

Listing 5-3. Manually initialize AngularJS

```
<!DOCTYPE html>
<html>
<body>
<script src="bower_components/angular/angular.js"></script>

  <script>
    angular.module('myApp', [])
```

```
      .controller('MyController', ['$scope', function ($scope) {
        // TODO
      }]);

    angular.element(document).ready(function() {
      angular.bootstrap(document, ['myApp']);
    });
  </script>
</body>
</html>
```

Notice that, only once the AngularJS element received the "ready" event will be dispatch result in bootstrap of AngularJS.

Partial Views

Creating partial views allows you to split the view into separate files. Think of each piece as a stand-alone reusable UI module. "Angular-seed" promotes this type of architecture and comes with two partial templates:

1. angular-seed/app/view1/view1.html

2. angular-seed/app/view2/view2.html

"view1.html" holds a paragraph tag with a copy—see below:

```
<p>This is the partial for view 1.</p>
```

"view2.html" holds a paragraph tag and a binding tag along with the version of the app—see below:

```
<p>This is the partial for view 2.</p>
<p>
  Showing of 'interpolate' filter: {{ 'Current version is v%VERSION%.' | interpolate }}
</p>
```

"Angular-seed" gives us a taste of the data binding's feature available in AngularJS. The code implements two-way data binding and connects the "view" to your "model" seamlessly using a reflection, meaning that once you change the JavaScript object (model), the HTML code (view) will be updated automatically. The result? View is updated without the need for your own DOM manipulation or event handling.

Styles

"app.css" is the default stylesheet for the app. It can be used as the starting point for you to build upon. See the CSS code created for us in Listing 5-4.

Listing 5-4. app.css stylesheet

```
.menu {
  list-style: none;
  border-bottom: 0.1em solid black;
```

```
  margin-bottom: 2em;
  padding: 0 0 0.5em;
}

.menu:before {
  content: "[";
}

.menu:after {
  content: "]";
}

.menu > li {
  display: inline;
}

.menu > li:before {
  content: "|";
  padding-right: 0.3em;
}

.menu > li:nth-child(1):before {
  content: "";
  padding: 0;
}
```

Controllers

The concept of controller is not new; it's the "C" in the "MVC" ("Model-View-Controller") pattern and acts as the glue between the view (HTML) and model (JavaScript object). In AngularJS, the controller is defined by a JavaScript constructor function that used to augment what AngularJS calls a $scope.

■ **Note**   In AngularJS, the $scope is the owner or context of the application's variables and functions. Once the $scope is created, you can then create objects in the controller's $scope, such as variables and functions. The "ng-model" directives can then use the variables and functions in that context.

Behind the scenes, when a controller is attached to the DOM via the "ng-controller" directive, the AngularJS instantiates the controller's constructor function you created, all of which is done automatically for you.

When you create a new controller, a new child $scope is created and can be used as an injectable parameter to the controller's constructor function. See code below as example:

```
.controller('View1Ctrl', ['$scope', function($scope) {
  // Implement
}]);
```

According to AngularJS's guides, controllers should be used to:

1. Set up the initial state of $scope object.

2. Add behavior to the $scope object.

Common implementation mistakes regarding AngularJS Controllers include:

- **Formatting input**: Do not use controllers to format <input> tags. This can be done inside AngularJS form controls.

- **Filtering output**: Do not filter output or results inside of controllers—use filters (more about filters later in this chapter).

- **Sharing state:** Do not share code or state across multiple controllers. You can use services instead (more about service in future chapters).

- **Manipulating the DOM**: Controllers should contain business logic only; it's the "C" in the MVC pattern. Putting view logic into controllers can break the AngularJS MVC framework and reduce testability. As we mentioned, use reflection (data binding) or directives to manipulate the DOM.

These are some common mistakes that developers often make in regards to any MVC. They can be seen in all MVC frameworks where MVC is implemented regardless of the language. It's a good idea to become familiar with MVC patterns— that way, AngularJS will make much more sense.

Take a look at "view1" controller logic. The code is located here: "angular-seed/app/view1/view1.js". See Listing 5-5.

Listing 5-5. Content of view.js

```
'use strict';

angular.module('myApp.view1', ['ngRoute'])

.config(['$routeProvider', function($routeProvider) {
  $routeProvider.when('/view1', {
    templateUrl: 'view1/view1.html',
    controller: 'View1Ctrl'
  });
}])

.controller('View1Ctrl', [function() {

}]);
```

Similarly, "view2," located here "angular-seed/app/view2/view2.js", holds the controller logic for "view2." See Listing 5-6.

Listing 5-6. Content of view2.js

```
'use strict';

angular.module('myApp.view2', ['ngRoute'])

.config(['$routeProvider', function($routeProvider) {
  $routeProvider.when('/view2', {
```

```
      templateUrl: 'view2/view2.html',
      controller: 'View2Ctrl'
  });
}])
```

```
.controller('View2Ctrl', [function() {

}]);
```

AngularJS sets the controls "View1Controller" and "View2Controller" and initiates them. "Angular-seed" leaves the controllers unimplemented but all ready to be coded.

The $scope becomes available to the "view1" and "view2" templates when the controllers are registered. The following example implements "View1Controller," which attaches the greeting property "Hello!" to the $scope.

Change "view1.js" from the following:

```
.controller('View1Ctrl', [function() {
}]);
```

To the implemented code:

```
.controller('View1Ctrl', ['$scope', function($scope) {
  $scope.greeting = 'Hello!';
}]);
```

Now that we have added a variable, we can use the "greeting" property in "view1.html," using binding, to change "view1.html" from:

```
<p>This is the partial for view 1.</p>
```

To the following code:

```
<div ng-controller="View1Ctrl">
    <p>This is the partial for view 1.</p>
    {{ greeting }}
</div>
```

Run the app by typing in the Bash command line the following commands, in two separate Bash terminal windows:

```
$ npm start
$ open http://localhost:8000/app/index.html
```

As mentioned before, it's good practice to open two tabs for the Terminal in WebStorm so that you can type commands without leaving your IDE. The browser opens up to the following URL:

```
http://localhost:8000/app/index.html
```

You can see the binding of the word "Hello!" to the template "view1" (see Figure 5-4).

[view1 | view2]

This is the partial for view 1.

Hello!
Angular seed app: v0.1

Figure 5-4. *angular-seed project implementing controller for "view1"*

We can extend the code and create a custom greeting input box with a button. To submit the change of the greeting, paste the following code into "view1.html." See Listing 5-7.

Listing 5-7. view1.html including custom greeting.

```
<div ng-controller="View1Ctrl">
    <p>This is the partial for view 1.</p>
    <input data-ng-model="customGreeting">
    <button data-ng-click="changeGreeting(customGreeting)">Change Greeting</button>

    <p>{{ greeting }}</p>
</div>
```

Notice that the code is using "data-ng-click" and "data-ng-model," which is the recommended prefix according to the Angulara guide.

■ **Note** "data-ng-model," "ng:model," "ng_model," or even "x-ng-model" are all interchangeable, and the element has matches "ngModel" API for all these examples, the same works for other controller tags. The AngularJS HTML compiler digests all of these the same way, but the AngularJS guide recommends using the data-prefixed "data-ng-model" version. The other forms shown above are accepted for legacy reasons, but AngularJS advises us to avoid using them, so it's better to get into the habit from day one.

As you can see, we added a "customGreeting" function that is marked as an "ng-model" and an "ng-click" to be mapped to the "changeGreeting" function, allowing us to pass the "customGreeting" variable to the controller.

In "view1.js," copy the code in Listing 5-8.

Listing 5-8. view1.js controller including custom greeting code

```
'use strict';

angular.module('myApp.view1', ['ngRoute'])

.config(['$routeProvider', function($routeProvider) {
  $routeProvider.when('/view1', {
    templateUrl: 'view1/view1.html',
    controller: 'View1Ctrl'
  });
}])

.controller('View1Ctrl', ['$scope', function($scope) {
  $scope.greeting = 'Hello!';
  $scope.customGreeting = "Hello Angular";
  $scope.changeGreeting = function(output) {
  $scope.greeting = output;
};
}]);
```

Notice that we added two objects—a "customGreeting" variable and a "changeGreeting" function—to be used to update the greeting variable.

Refresh the page and then you can insert a custom greeting. Once you click "Change Greeting," the text changes accordingly (Figure 5-5).

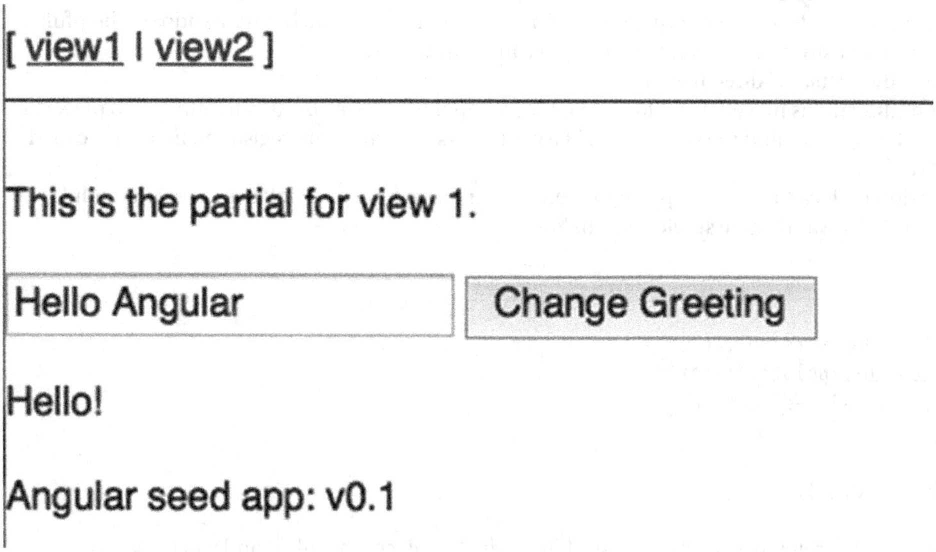

Figure 5-5. *angular-seed project implementing controller component for view1*

AngularJS Directives

Directives are considered by many to be the most complex concept in AngularJS, but understanding and being able to write your own directives very rewarding. You will have the ability to create your own custom HTML tags with just a few lines of code.

At a high level, directives are markers on a DOM element. These markers can point to any DOM component, from an attribute to an element name, or even a comment or CSS class. These markers then tell the AngularJS's HTML compiler to attach a specified behavior or to transform the entire DOM element and its children based on a specific logic.

Angular comes with a set of many of these directives already built-in. In fact, we have already used them—in "view1.html" and "view2.html" we used "ngModel" and "ngClick" directives.

■ **Note** AngularJS directives are usually spelled with lowercase letters and camel case—for example, "ngModel" and "ngClick." You should use the same convention when writing your own custom directives.

See the code below:

```
<input data-ng-model="customGreeting">
```

In these directives, AngularJS extends HTML by providing custom directives that add functionality to the markup and allow us to create powerful, dynamic templates. Adding a reflection via data binding has given us a whole new feature.

In addition to the built-in directives, AngularJS allows us to develop our own, creating reusable components to fill our needs. Abstracting away the DOM manipulation logic creates a great separation of high-level code from implementations and makes JavaScript and HTML more object-oriented languages.

"Angular-seed" aids us in creating directives—in fact, it comes with a directive called "version." The "version" directive includes testing and implementation to get you started, which is tremendously helpful; it comes set with the folder structure and an example you can easily follow.

Let's examine the "version" directive:

The "version" directive is placed in a folder called "components," where you are encouraged to place all directives moving forward. Behind the scenes, just like controllers, directives are registered in what is called "module.directive."

Look at "version.js," located here: "app/components/version/version.js." It holds the version module declaration and basic "version" value service. See below:

```
'use strict';

angular.module('myApp.version', [
  'myApp.version.interpolate-filter',
  'myApp.version.version-directive'
])

.value('version', '0.1');
```

In the code, there is a reference to "interpolate-filter," which replaces the token and will be covered more thoroughly later on in this chapter.

Notice that the "module.directive" API was used to register the directive. The "module.directive" takes the normalized directive name, followed by a factory function, which is the actual directive you are registering.

■ **Note** The AngularJS module is defined as a collection of directives, controllers, services, etc. It's used to register and retrieve modules. All the modules you will be using must be registered before they will work.

Next, look at the "version-directive.js" file. This is the actual custom directive that returns the current app version. See Listing 5-9.

Listing 5-9. Version-directive code

```
'use strict';

angular.module('myApp.version.version-directive', [])

.directive('appVersion', ['version', function(version) {
  return function(scope, elm, attrs) {
    elm.text(version);
  };
}]);
```

As you can see, the directive is defined as "appVersion," and it is used as a factory function. It returns an object with different options to tell the HTML compiler how the directive should behave when it's matched.

■ **Note** AngularJS factory, service, and provider are similar—the difference is in what you get. Service just executes code, factory returns an object and provider executes the code and calls the $get method.

In the background, the "appVersion" factory function gets invoked once the compiler matches the directive for the first time. You can and should perform any initialization work necessary. In the background, the function is invoked on AngularJS using $injector.invoke, which makes it injectable, just like the controllers.

Once the directive is set, you can look at the implementation. Take a look inside of "index.html" or "index-async.html"—they will have the following declaration:

```
<div>Angular seed app: v<span app-version></span></div>
```

The tag "app-version" will be handled by the HTML compiler ($compile) and will attach a specified behavior to that DOM element. Now we see "Angular seed app: v0.1" in each view. Using directive is powerful, since you now have the ability to create your own custom HTML tags.

Template Expanding Directive

Let's create our own custom directives for AngularJS to use.

Let's say you have a chunk of template that represents some information you want to present internally or to the end user. The template must be repeated many times in the code, and when you change the code in one place, you will want to change it in several others places without copying and pasting or doing a refactoring effort.

This is a good opportunity to utilize a directive type called "Template," expanding to simplify your code. Let's create a directive that simply replaces the contents of the HTML code with a static template.

First, create a new directive. We will call our first directive <first>—the name doesn't need to describe the directive functionality since it's just for practice. The folder structure can follow the <version> directive that came out of the box with Angular-seek.

Add the code from Listing 5-10 into the following structure: app/components/first/first-directive.js

Listing 5-10. First directive returns a template

```
'use strict';

angular.module('myApp.first.first-directive', [])

    .directive('myFirstDirective', [function() {
        return {
            template: 'Name: {{info.name}} <br /> version: {{info.version}}'
        };
    }]);
```

As you can see, we are returning a template with the info object that holds the project name and version number. Next, register the directive by pasting Listing 5-11 into app/components/first/first.js:

Listing 5-11.

```
'use strict';

angular.module('myApp.first', [
    'myApp.first.first-directive'
])
```

Now, we can implement the <first> directive, open app/view2/view2.html and place it in Listing 5-12.

Listing 5-12. View2.html with first dircetive

```
<p>This is the partial for view 2.</p>
<p>
  Showing of 'interpolate' filter:
  {{ 'Current version is v%VERSION%.' | interpolate }}
</p>
<div my-first-directive></div>
<br />
```

The div tag with "my-first-directive" will be replaced with the template.
Lastly, don't forget to add the scripts to the index.html and index-async.html files:

```
<script src="components/first/first.js"></script>
<script src="components/first/first-directive.js"></script>
```

See the scripts implemented into "index-async.html" in Listing 5-13.

Listing 5-13. index-async.html with first directive scripts

```
// load all of the dependencies asynchronously.
$script([
  'bower_components/angular/angular.js',
```

```
    'bower_components/angular-route/angular-route.js',
    'app.js',
    'view1/view1.js',
    'view2/view2.js',
    'components/version/version.js',
    'components/version/version-directive.js',
    'components/version/interpolate-filter.js',
    'components/first/first.js',
    'components/first/first-directive.js'
], function() {
    // when all is done, execute bootstrap angular application
    angular.bootstrap(document, ['myApp']);
});
```

The best practices in regards to writing directives:

1. **Naming Convention**: It is important to avoid a naming convention that may conflict with a potential future standard of HTML or AngularJS. It is recommended that you use your own prefix for directive names. For instance, if you create a <calendar> directive, it may collide with a future releases of HTML—the HTML6 <calendar> tag already exists. Instead, use <myCalendar> or <tripCalendar>. The directive <ngCalendar> may also conflict with a future AngularJS directive.

2. **Coding Convention**: It's recommended that you use a definition object instead of returning a function. As you have seen in <first> directive, we used the "info" object defined in the controller and return a template, not a function.

AngularJS Filters

AngularJS offers filters to help sort data. You can select a subset of items from an array and it will be returned as a new filtered array.

Additionally, AngularJS gives us the ability to create our own custom filters. To create a new filter, we need to first create a filter module and then register the custom filter with the newly created module, just as we've done for directives and controllers.

As we've seen in the <version> directive that comes with "angular-seed," it uses a custom filter called "interpolate-filter.js" (Listing 5-14).

Listing 5-14. interpolate-filter.js content

```
angular-seed/app/components/version/interpolate-filter.js

'use strict';

angular.module('myApp.version.interpolate-filter', [])

.filter('interpolate', ['version', function(version) {
  return function(text) {
    return String(text).replace(/\%VERSION\%/mg, version);
  };
}]);
```

117

The filter replaces the value of "version" with a specific version number. As you may recall, "version.js" sets the value of the version:

```
'use strict';

angular.module('myApp.version', [
  'myApp.version.interpolate-filter',
  'myApp.version.version-directive',
])

.value('version', '0.1');
```

Components

In AngularJS, a "component" is defined as a special type of directive that uses a simpler configuration. A component works well when you want to create a reusable component based on application structure. This makes it easier to write an app in a way that's similar to Web Components or Angular 2's style of application architecture, so it's a good idea to start moving in that direction now.

It is important to understand the difference between a directive and a component. Components are triggered by an element, so there's no need to use components for directives that need to be triggered by attribute or a CSS class. Additionally, we shouldn't use components when we want to rely on DOM manipulation or are adding event listeners, because the HTML $compile and link functions will not be available when we need advanced directive definition options.

"Angular-seed" is already set with a component folder, as you may recall, and we have the <version> and <first> directives in that directory.

To create and register a component, use the "component" method with the Angular module, just as we've done with directives, controllers, and filters.

You can find more information here: https://docs.angularjs.org/guide/component. To learn about components in Angular 2, visit this page:

https://angular.io/docs/ts/latest/tutorial/toh-pt3.html

Testing

In Chapter 3, we configured npm with the "mocha" testing library and were able to run a test simply by typing:

```
$ npm test
```

We then terminated the process by hitting ctrl + c—otherwise the test would keep running the process in the background. Mocha tests JavaScripts, but there are times you want to run browser tests.

Karma Testing

"angular-seed" comes with a "Karma" library to run browser tests, and it is already configured, so there's no need to install anything. To see the code in action, just run "npm test" just as we've done with mocha in the Bash command line terminal.

A key feature of Karma is that we can use it to run tests against multiple browsers at the same time. The most common browsers include Chrome, Firefox, Safari, and IE.

When you type "npm test" in the background, it will run the following command: "karma start karma. conf.js".

The code picks up the testing configurations to be used from the "package.json" script tag:

```
"scripts": {
  "pretest": "npm install",
  "test": "karma start karma.conf.js",
  "test-single-run": "karma start karma.conf.js  --single-run",
}
```

To learn more about Karma, check the GitHub open source project located here:

```
https://github.com/karma-runner/karma
```

Karma is a highly visible project, and there are plenty of plugins available on npm that extend the functionality of the base code. You can check out the list of plugins here: `https://www.npmjs.com/browse/keyword/karma-plugin`.

The decision of "angular-seed" to use Karma is not random; the AngularJS team developed Karma, and it is the recommended testing tool for AngularJS projects.

The config file for Karma is called "karma.conf.js." Luckily, it has already been created for us automatically in the root folder. Open the "karma.conf.js" config file. As you can see, it is set to run the unit tests with Karma (Listing 5-15).

Listing 5-15. karma.conf.js config file

```
module.exports = function(config){
  config.set({

    basePath : './',

    files : [
      'app/bower_components/angular/angular.js',
      'app/bower_components/angular-route/angular-route.js',
      'app/bower_components/angular-mocks/angular-mocks.js',
      'app/components/**/*.js',
      'app/view*/**/*.js'
    ],

    autoWatch : true,

    frameworks: ['jasmine'],

    browsers : ['Chrome'],

    plugins : [
            'karma-chrome-launcher',
            'karma-firefox-launcher',
            'karma-jasmine',
            'karma-junit-reporter'
            ],

    junitReporter : {
      outputFile: 'test_out/unit.xml',
      suite: 'unit'
```

```
    }
  });
};
```

Notice that "karma.conf.js" is already configured with each library, including AngularJS, Angular-mocks, and the modules:

```
files : [
  'app/bower_components/angular/angular.js',
  'app/bower_components/angular-route/angular-route.js',
  'app/bower_components/angular-mocks/angular-mocks.js',
  'app/components/**/*.js',
  'app/view*/**/*.js'
],
```

Next, take a look at the actual test—angular-seed/app/view1/view1_test.js—in Listing 5-16.

Listing 5-16. view1_test.js test file

```
'use strict';

describe('myApp.view1 module', function() {

  beforeEach(module('myApp.view1'));

  describe('view1 controller', function(){

    it('should ....', inject(function($controller) {
      //spec body
      var view1Ctrl = $controller('View1Ctrl');
      expect(view1Ctrl).toBeDefined();
    }));

  });
});
```

Notice that the code checks to see that the controller is being defined—the same goes for "view2_test.js" (Listing 5-17).

Listing 5-17. view2_test.js test file

```
'use strict';

describe('myApp.view2 module', function() {

  beforeEach(module('myApp.view2'));

  describe('view2 controller', function(){

    it('should ....', inject(function($controller) {
      //spec body
```

```
    var view2Ctrl = $controller('View2Ctrl');
    expect(view2Ctrl).toBeDefined();
  }));

});
});
```

When we run the test using the command line "npm test" in the terminal, the test fails (Figure 5-6).

Figure 5-6. *Karma tests fails*

The tests fails because there is no $scope service, so the $controller provider cannot instantiate the injected $scope argument, so it creates the following error message:

"Karma Unknown provider: $scopeProvider <- $scope"

To fix this, we need to provide the $scope while instantiating a controller using the $controller provider. Paste the following update in Listing 5-18.

Listing 5-18. view1_test.js file, including creating a new $rootScope instance

```
'use strict';

describe('myApp.view1 module', function() {

  beforeEach(module('myApp.view1'));

  describe('view1 controller', function(){
      var view1Ctrl, scope;

      beforeEach(inject(function ($controller, $rootScope) {
          scope = $rootScope.$new();
          view1Ctrl = $controller("View1Ctrl", {$scope:scope});
```

```
      }));

  it('should ....', inject(function() {
    expect(view1Ctrl).toBeDefined();
  }));

});
});
```

■ **Note**   Notice that we sometimes we use $rootScope and sometimes $scope. The difference between $scope and $rootScope is the context. $rootScope is the parent ("root") of all the scopes we create in our app, inside all the controllers.

We have then injected the $rootScope into the "setUp" stub of the test and the child $scope is then defined as $rootScope.$new(). Now we are able to inject the $scope as an argument into the $controller constructor as a new child scope:

```
view1Ctrl = $controller("View1Ctrl", {$scope:scope});
```

In "view2_test.js", we will do the same thing. See Listing 5-19.

Listing 5-19. view2_test.js includes creating a new $rootScope instance

```
'use strict';

describe('myApp.view2 module', function() {

  beforeEach(module('myApp.view2'));
  describe('view2 controller', function(){
          var view2Ctrl, scope;

          beforeEach(inject(function ($controller, $rootScope) {
                  scope = $rootScope.$new();
                  view2Ctrl = $controller("View2Ctrl", {$scope:scope});
          }));

  it('should ....', inject(function() {
    expect(view2Ctrl).toBeDefined();
  }));

});
});
```

Press ctrl + c and then run the tests again. Now, the tests will pass (Figure 5-7).

Figure 5-7. *Karma tests success*

To test the <version> directive, take a look at this file: angular-seed/app/version-directive_test.js. See Listing 5-20.

Listing 5-20. directive_test.js test file for version directive

```
'use strict';

describe('myApp.version module', function() {
  beforeEach(module('myApp.version'));

  describe('app-version directive', function() {
    it('should print current version', function() {
      module(function($provide) {
        $provide.value('version', 'TEST_VER');
      });
      inject(function($compile, $rootScope) {
        var element = $compile('<span app-version></span>')($rootScope);
        expect(element.text()).toEqual('TEST_VER');
      });
    });
  });
});
```

The test expects that it should print the current version number, and it compares the "TEST_VER" with the element text value to see if they match. We already know that it works, since we have made sure it would pass the tests.

Similarly, there is a code to test the interpolate filter. See the following file: angular-seed/app/interpolate-filter_test.js. Listing 5-21 shows the content of the file:

Listing 5-21. interpolate-filter_test.js test file

```
'use strict';

describe('myApp.version module', function() {
```

123

```
  beforeEach(module('myApp.version'));

  describe('interpolate filter', function() {
    beforeEach(module(function($provide) {
      $provide.value('version', 'TEST_VER');
    }));

    it('should replace VERSION', inject(function(interpolateFilter) {
      expect(interpolateFilter('before %VERSION% after')).toEqual('before TEST_VER after');
    }));
  });
});
```

The code expects to interpolate the filter of "%VERSION%" against "TEST_VER."

Adding New Tests

We have added a new directive <first>, so what we then want to do is to also add a test for our directive template. Add "first-directive_test.js" to the "angular-seed/app/components/first" folder.

This test will ensure that the template has produced the correct text (see Listing 5-22).

Listing 5-22. first-directive_test.js test file

```
'use strict';

describe('myApp.version module', function() {
  beforeEach(module('myApp.first'));

  describe('app-first directive', function() {
    it('should print the template', function() {
      inject(function($compile, $rootScope) {
        var element = $compile('<div my-first-directive></div>')($rootScope);
        expect(element.text()).toEqual('Name: {{info.name}}  version: {{info.version}}');
      });
    });
  });
});
```

Once again, run the tests using "npm test" in the shell command line and you should get "Executed 6 of 6 SUCCESS" results.

Proctractor Testing

Protractor is defined as an "end-to-end" testing framework for the AngularJS applications based on Node.js, and as such it is built to make the process of testing easier. Let's take a look at testing the functionality of an AngularJS app, specifically with Protractor. If you have used Selenium and Selenium WebDriver for creating automated tests, then you will be familiar with how Protractor works. Protractor tests can be run on both regular and headless browsers such as DalekJS or PhantomJS. They are intended to emulate the user's actions on the application.

■ Note End-to-end testing means to test the flow of the application from start to finish. In testing end-to-end, we want to ensure the flow is as expected and that the data is reflected in the view upon change.

This particular testing framework is built with AngularJS apps in mind and can test elements that are specific to the development structure. Protractor testing is also smart enough to automatically wait for a pending task to complete.

Protractor is built on top of WebDriverJS and runs tests against your application in an actual browser, interacting with it as a user would, so if you have ever used behavior-driven development then this should all be familiar to you.

Protractor supports high visibility projects like Jasmine, Mocha, Karma, or Cucumber libraries as well custom frameworks; Jasmine and Mocha are more often used than Cucumber. In fact, Jasmine is set as the default for the Protractor framework.

Take a look at the project in GitHub: https://github.com/angular/protractor

We don't need to install or configure anything, since everything is already pre-set for us by "angular-seed."

Open the "package.json" config file; notice that there is a script for "preprotractor" and "protractor." See below:

```
"scripts": {
  "preprotractor": "npm run update-webdriver",
  "protractor": "protractor e2e-tests/protractor.conf.js",
}
```

As you can see "angular-seed" comes with two configuration files, located in the "e2e-tests" folder:

1. "protractor-conf.js": Protractor config file

2. "scenarios.js": End-to-end scenarios/behavior to be run by Protractor

"Protractor.conf.js" stores each option needed to run such tests, such as timeouts, test directory sources, and suites. See Listing 5-23.

Listing 5-23. protractor.conf.js config file

```
exports.config = {
  allScriptsTimeout: 11000,

  specs: [
    '*.js'
  ],

  capabilities: {
    'browserName': 'chrome'
  },

  baseUrl: 'http://localhost:8000/app/',

  framework: 'jasmine',

  jasmineNodeOpts: {
    defaultTimeoutInterval: 30000
  }
};
```

Scenarios File

The "scenarios.js" file, as, stores the behavior of the app from an end-user standpoint. See Listing 5-24.

Listing 5-24. scenarios.js testing behavior

```
'use strict';

describe('my app', function() {

  it('should automatically redirect to /view1 when location hash/fragment is empty',
function() {
    browser.get('index.html');
    expect(browser.getLocationAbsUrl()).toMatch("/view1");
  });

  describe('view1', function() {

    beforeEach(function() {
      browser.get('index.html#/view1');
    });

    it('should render view1 when user navigates to /view1', function() {
      expect(element.all(by.css('[ng-view] p')).first().getText()).
        toMatch(/partial for view 1/);
    });

  });

  describe('view2', function() {

    beforeEach(function() {
      browser.get('index.html#/view2');
    });

    it('should render view2 when user navigates to /view2', function() {
      expect(element.all(by.css('[ng-view] p')).first().getText()).
        toMatch(/partial for view 2/);
    });

  });
});
```

As you can see, it checks both view1 and view2 to ensure that the user sees these partials as expected.

To begin the Protractor tests, first we must ensure the project is running in a separate command line shell.

```
$ sudo npm start
```

Then, run the following two commands in the command line:

```
$ sudo npm run update-webdriver
$ sudo npm run protractor
```

Running these commands may result in an error messages, while running "npm run protractor" on Mac OS X 10.10. However, this can be resolved easily by making a change in "protractor.conf.js." Simply add the following line:

```
directConnect: true,
```

Here is the complete "protractor.conf.js" file content with the change included:

```
exports.config = {
  allScriptsTimeout: 11000,

  specs: [
    '*.js'
  ],

  capabilities: {
    'browserName': 'chrome'
  },

  directConnect: true,

  baseUrl: 'http://localhost:8000/app/',

  framework: 'jasmine',

  jasmineNodeOpts: {
    defaultTimeoutInterval: 30000
  }
};
```

Now, run "npm run protractor" again and the test results should show success, as you can see in Figure 5-8.

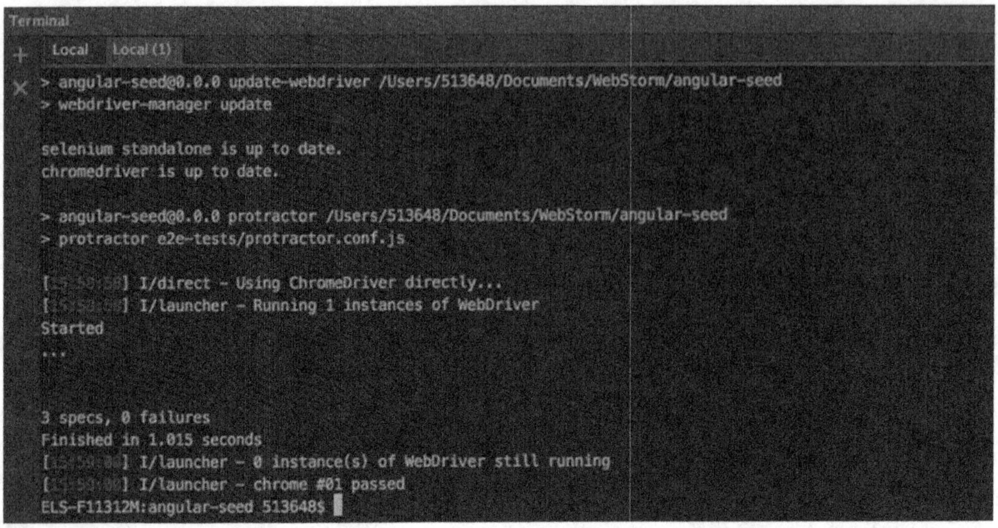

Figure 5-8. *Protractor results*

Routes

$route service in AngularJS is used for deep-linking URLs to controllers and HTML partials (view). AngularJS watches $location.url() and then tries to map the path to an existing route definition, which you set.

The $route service is typically used in conjunction with the "ngView" directive and the $routeParams service. The $routeParams service allows you to retrieve the current set of route parameters that were configured.

Open the "app/app.js" main application module file. See Listing 5-25:

Listing 5-25. app.js with first directive

```
'use strict';

// Declare app level module which depends on views, and components
angular.module('myApp', [
  'ngRoute',
  'myApp.view1',
  'myApp.view2',
  'myApp.version',
  'myApp.first'
]).
config(['$routeProvider', function($routeProvider) {
  $routeProvider.otherwise({redirectTo: '/view1'});
}]);
```

As you can see from Listing 5-25, the $routeProvider is set to the "otherwise" option, to run "view1" as the default view. If, for example, we want to create a routing of "home," we can change that easily; all we have to do is set the route to "home." See Listing 5-26.

Listing 5-26. Adding routeProvider home page

```
config(['$routeProvider', function($routeProvider) {
  $routeProvider.
  when('/home', {redirectTo: '/view2'}).
  otherwise({redirectTo: '/view1'});
}]);
```

To test these changes, ensure "npm start" is running, then open the following URL:

```
localhost:8000/app/index.html#/home
```

The app will change the URL in the browser automatically to:

```
http://localhost:8000/app/index.html#/view2
```

This can come in handy when handling URLs and later on for Search Engine Optimization (SEO), as you will see in future chapters.

Service

Many apps need content to drive the app. As they say, content is king!

AngularJS XMLHttpRequest (XHR) services create a good separation of MVC and can be considered as an "MVCS" for service, you can create high-level code and low-level implementation. Create a service module, register it just like we've done with other modules, then re-use the API calls. This allows you to move your model and business logic out of the front-end code and build back-end agnostic web apps, aligning very well with the MVC pattern. As you've seen with data binding, you can then use reflection to display and filter the data in the view.

In Chapter 7, we will be covering building services and we will use these services in an AngularJS app as an example.

Summary

In this chapter, we covered AngularJS. We installed the "angular-seed" project and took a deep dive into fully understanding how it works under the hood. We looked at the Bower components that are installed, Partial Views, CSS styles, controllers, directives, filters, routes, services, and components. We also created our own first directive and implemented it into the view.

We also looked at testing. Angular-seed comes configured with Karma, we looked at the existing tests' scripts and added new tests, then looked at Protractor testing and executed those tests. Lastly, I also went over best practices, AngularJS 2, and how to prepare and build our app to make it AngularJS2 friendly. Angular guide devoted a section and you can see the difference between AngularJS1 and AngularJS2 here: `https://angular.io/docs/ts/latest/cookbook/a1-a2-quick-reference.html`

Where to go from here: AngularJS provides a good tutorial, which will walk you through AngularJS and can be found here: `https://docs.angularjs.org/tutorial`. After being equipped with what you have learned in this chapter, it should now be a breeze for you to review the examples they provide for you and will allow you to expand your knowledge. In the next chapter, we will expand on CSS and responsive design.

CHAPTER 6

■ ■ ■

CSS, Bootstrap, & Responsive Design

In the previous chapter, we covered AngularJS extensively, but we didn't talk about styling our code. In this chapter, we will cover styling—specifically, Cascading Style Sheets (CSS) classes used by AngularJS. We will also be covering UI Bootstrap, which includes out-of-the-box components such as an accordion or an alert, written in AngularJS by the AngularJS team. These can be used to expedite the development time of your app if it is done according to AngularJS's best practice recommendations. Lastly, we will be covering responsive design, including the two most used techniques: media quieries and creating different views for each device.

CSS Classes Used by AngularJS

AngularJS already has a pre-defined CSS style that it uses right out of the box. In fact, the guide docs offer a page that shows all of the CSS classes used by the AngularJS framework; feel free to visit this page: `https://docs.angularjs.org/guide/css-styling`.

The AngularJS framework offers a list of methods you can tap into, such as:

- "ng-scope"
- "ng-isolate-scope"
- "ng-binding"
- and many more

In this section, you will learn how to utilize different internal AngularJS CSS processes in order to create custom CSS styles.

■ **Note**   Cascading Style Sheets (CSS) is used to properly maintain information such as colors, sizes, and fonts, and provide consistent user experience.

Create a New Project

Let's start by looking at the internal functionality in action. Create a new instance of "angular-seed" or use the one we created in Chapter 5. We encourage you to create a new project to give you a quick reference of how easy it should be to have one up and running by now. To create a new project, in the command line, type:

```
$ git clone https://github.com/angular/angular-seed.git
$ cd angular-seed
```

In WebStorm, import the project and open two terminal windows. In one window, type:

```
$ npm install
$ npm start
```

In the second window, type:

```
$ open http://localhost:8000
```

As you may recall, the "open" command will navigate to the URL in your default browser.

For more details, refer back to Chapter 5. As you can see, in less than two minutes, we were able to start a new project with a mere five commands; not too bad!

We do not need to create a style sheet, since "angular-seed" already comes with a ready-to-use CSS stylesheet. You can see a reference in index.html and index-async.html:

```
<link rel="stylesheet" href="app.css">
```

Similarly, "html5-boilerplate", which is part of the "angular-seed" components, also includes a base CSS file:

```
<link rel="stylesheet" href="bower_components/html5-boilerplate/dist/css/main.css">
```

ng-scope

Open the "angular-seed" app CSS file "/app/app.css" and add the following code:

```
.ng-scope {
    border: 2px solid #000000;
    margin: 5px;
}
```

Refresh the index page in the browser to see the app in action. See Figure 6-1.

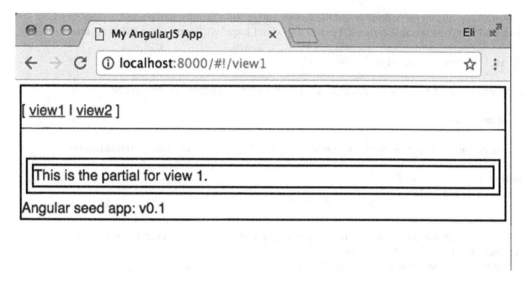

Figure 6-1. *angular-seed app showing in Chrome browser with custom ng-scope*

The style is attached to the "ng-scope" class, and all of the elements with a "new" scope get a border automatically. Since the elements now have a border, it shows us all of the elements that got created.

Applying the style automatically can help with creating a custom style design. Let's say we want to add a 100-pixel padding to each new element. All we have to do is change the code to the following:

```
.ng-scope {
        padding-left: 100px;
}
```

Similarly, AngularJS offers the option to apply CSS style to the following:

- "ng-isolate-scope": for isolating the scope of a directive
- "ng-binding": databinding
- "ng-invalid" and "ng-valid": form validations
- "ng-pristine" and "ng-dirty": user interaction, pristine, not touched by user vs. dirty
- "ng-touched" and "ng-untouched": blur control for form control widget

Let's create another example. If we want to add a red border to any element that uses a data binding, this can be done easily.

Open "view1.js" and implement the controller. Change the code from:

```
.controller('View1Ctrl', [function() {
}]);
```

to the following code:

```
.controller('View1Ctrl', ['$scope', function($scope) {
  $scope.viewCopy = 'This is the partial for view 1.';
}]);
```

As you can see, all that we've done is add the $scope and create a variable in the scope called "viewCopy" and then we attached the text that we want. Next, in the "view1.html," we'll replace the following line:

```
<p>This is the partial for view 1.</p>
```

with a binding tag that uses "viewCopy" variable we've attached to the scope:

```
<p>{{viewCopy}}</p>
```

Now we can add in the style sheet "app.css" the "ng-binding" style definition. See code below:

```
.ng-binding {
  border: 3px solid red;
}
```

Notice that earlier we used #00000, which is a hex color code for black. You can just use a color name if you don't care about the exact color hex code.

Refresh the page and you will see that the binding element has a red style—see Figure 6-2.

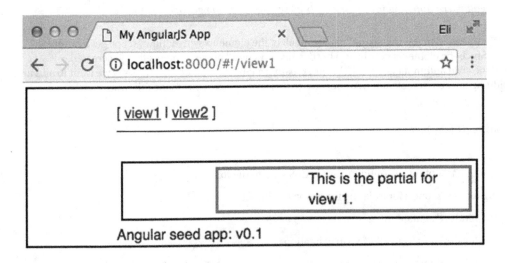

Figure 6-2. *"angular-seed" app showing in a Chrome browser with custom ng-binding style*

■ **Note** Keep in mind that this feature can come handy not just for style—you can use the feature for debugging purposes as well.

---

ng-dirty, ng-invalid, and ng-pristine

Similar to how we used the "ng-binding" style, we can also use the following tags:

- "ng-dirty": for elements that have been interacted with already

- "ng-invalid": for invalid elements

- "ng-pristine": for elements that have not been interacted with yet.

These styles can come in handy for forms.

Add the following styles in the "app.css" file—see Listing 6-1.

Listing 6-1. ng-dirty, invalid, and pristine definitions

```css
.ng-dirty {
  border: 2px solid yellow;
}

.ng-invalid {
  border: 2px solid red;
}

.ng-pristine {
  border: 2px solid green;
}
```

Next, place the following code in the "view1.html" view file—see Listing 6-2.

Listing 6-2. Simple form view using ng style defenitions

```html
<form name="form">
        <input name="input" ng-model="userName" required>
        <span class="error" ng-show="form.input.$error.required">required</span><br/>
        <div>
                form.$valid: {{form.$valid}}<br/>
                form.input.$valid: {{form.input.$valid}}<br/>
                form.input.$error: {{form.input.$error}}<br/>
        </div>
</form>
```

Lastly, in "view1.js," we'll define the user name:

```js
.controller('View1Ctrl', ['$scope', function($scope) {
                $scope.userName = '';
}]);
```

Refresh the page (see Figure 6-3).

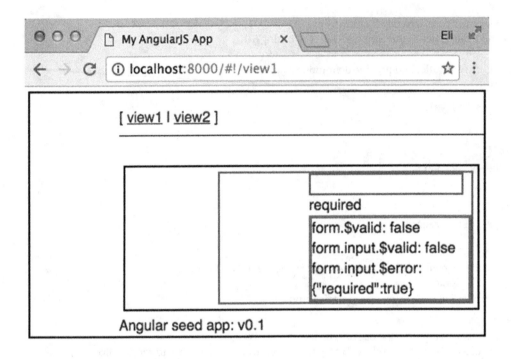

Figure 6-3. *Form validation style*

Next, start typing into the text input box and see the results (Figure 6-4).

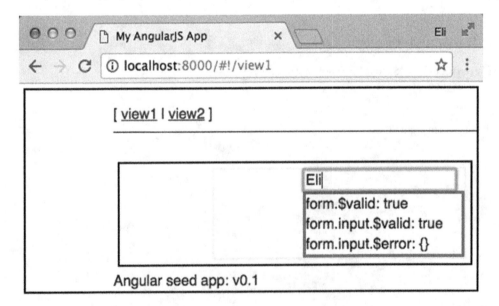

Figure 6-4. *Validate form style*

As you can see, the form was validated and we now see the style we defined. If the form was not validated, we would see the results shown in Figure 6-5.

[<u>view1</u> I <u>view2</u>]

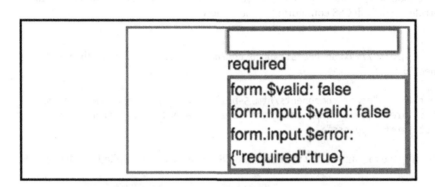

Figure 6-5. *Form not validated*

Install Bootstrap

Bootstrap was released in 2011 as an open source front-end responsive framework for developing mobile first apps as well as web. Bootstrap is considered to be the most popular front-end framework. It is often associated with AngularJS because they are often used together. Bootstrap is the second most popular library on GitHub at the time of writing. Visit the GitHub page here:

```
https://github.com/twbs/bootstrap
```

Bootstrap requires HTML5. In order to use HTML5, we need to declare the document as HTML5. Open "index.html" in the "angular-seed" project.

Bootstrap utilizes HTML5 and the HTML doctype uses "<!DOCTYPE>" and must be declared. Luckily, unlike HTML 4.01 where there are three different "<!DOCTYPE>" declarations, in HTML5 there is only one declaration: "<!DOCTYPE html>".

At the time of this writing, the current production version of Bootstrap is 3.3.6 and Bootstrap 4 is at Alpha version 4. Although Bootstrap 4 is not out yet, having knowledge as to where the platform is heading can benefit you greatly. While writing the code, take into account future releases of Bootstrap; we encourage you to read more about version 4 here:

```
http://blog.getbootstrap.com/2015/08/19/bootstrap-4-alpha/
```

```
Bootstrap is composed of two libraries:
```

- **Bootstrap JavaScript**: a set of reusable and common components

- **Bootstrap CSS**: commonly used styles

```
They do not need to be used together within a project.
```

To install Bootstrap, simply run the following Bower command:

```
$ bower install bootstrap
```

Next, add the Bootstrap CSS file to the "index.html" page inside of the "<head>" tag:

```
<!-- Bootstrap CSS -->
<link rel="stylesheet" href="//maxcdn.bootstrapcdn.com/bootswatch/3.3.6/paper/
bootstrap.min.css " rel="stylesheet">
```

Make sure you add the "bootstrap.min.css" prior the other CSS stylesheets, since we want our specific CSS delcalartions to override the default CSS configurations. See below:

```
<!-- Bootstrap CSS -->
<link rel="stylesheet" href="//maxcdn.bootstrapcdn.com/bootswatch/3.3.6/paper/bootstrap.
min.css" rel="stylesheet">

<link rel="stylesheet" href="bower_components/html5-boilerplate/dist/css/normalize.css">
<link rel="stylesheet" href="bower_components/html5-boilerplate/dist/css/main.css">
<link rel="stylesheet" href="app.css">
```

Refresh the "index.html" page to confirm that the Bootstrap CSS style sheet was applied. See Figure 6-6.

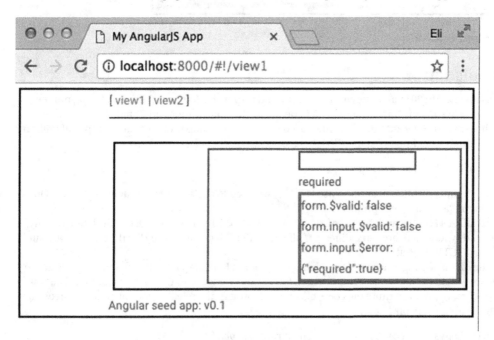

Figure 6-6. *Bootstrap CSS style sheet in "angular-seed" project*

UI Bootstrap

We've added the Bootstrap CSS to our project, but what about the Bootstrap JavaScript file? The Bootstrap JavaScript relies on jQuery for its component set, but AngularJS best practices dictate that it's not recommended for use with the full version of jQuery.

AngularJS has already shipped with a version of jQuery, the lite version (jqLite), and it is already available for your use. When you call "angular.element," it's actually an alias for the "jQuery lite" library. With that being said, if you want, you can install the full jQuery and reference "angular.element" to jQuery.

■ **Note**   jqLite is a compatible API to jQuery. It implements only the most-used functionality and enables AngularJS cross-browser manipulation.

Bootstrap v3.x is based on the full jQuery library, and thus it is not ideal to use with AngularJS. However, AngularJS offers UI Bootstrap, which provides common components as the Bootstrap UI. See: http://angular-ui.github.io/bootstrap/.

Why is the full version of jQuery being integrated and used in AngularJS considered bad practice? jQuery is based on manipulating the DOM, using events, and injecting elements, while AngularJS is based on data binding, having Angular bind variables and JQuery injecting elements at the same time, which can make our project messy and buggy.

The AngularJS version of UI Bootstrap is a rewrite of Bootstrap's component developed by the AngularUI team, built specifically for the AngularJS framework. UI Bootstrap is based on Bootstrap's markup and CSS, and the components are coded in native AngularJS using directives. These integrate well with the AngularJS mindset without depending on jQuery or Bootstrap JavaScript files.

In the previous chapter, we learned how to create a directive, which is the recommended way to code in AngularJS when we want to manipulate the DOM. We are basically telling our app how to watch data changes for specific elements. UI Bootstrap requires the Bootstrap CSS file, which we have already added.

Next, replace the content of "view1.html" with the following code, which was taken directly from the https://angular-ui.github.io/bootstrap/ tutorial page—see Listing 6-3.

Listing 6-3. Buttons utilizing UI Bootstrap and Bootstrap CSS

```
<div class="btn-group">
    <label class="btn btn-primary" ng-model="checkModel.left" uib-btn-checkbox>Left</label>
    <label class="btn btn-primary" ng-model="checkModel.middle" uib-btn-checkbox>Middle</
label>
    <label class="btn btn-primary" ng-model="checkModel.right" uib-btn-checkbox>Right</
label>
</div>
```

Lastly, add the declaration of "ui-bootstrap" in "index.html" at the bottom of the page, where we declare all of our components:

```
<script src="//angular-ui.github.io/bootstrap/ui-bootstrap-tpls-2.1.4.js"></script>
```

Refresh "index.html" and you should be able to see the button group (see Figure 6-7).

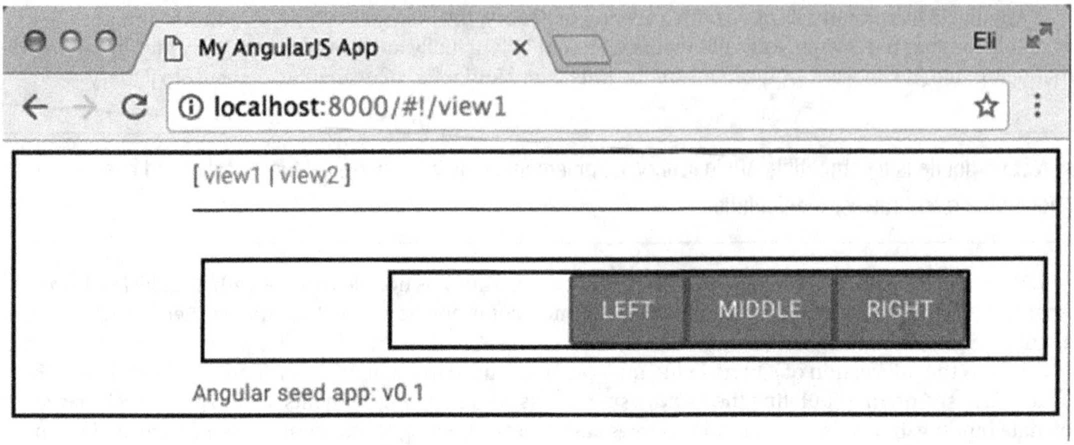

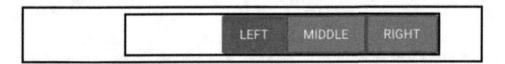

Figure 6-7. *"angular-seed" with UI Bootstrap and Bootstrap CSS utilizing the group button*

Try clicking the buttons—nothing will happen. Visually they seem fine, but they are not working. Once you click, they do not stay selected as you would expect from a button group. To fix this, we will need to include "ui.bootstrap" in the module declaration.

To do so, open "view1.js" and change the following code from:

```
angular.module('myApp.view1', ['ngRoute'])
```

to:

```
angular.module('myApp.view1', ['ngRoute', 'ui.bootstrap'])
```

Now that we've declared the UI Bootstrap in our module, buttons will stay in an active state once clicked (see Figure 6-8):

Figure 6-8. *UI Bootstrap button group implementation*

Next, let's say we want to know the buttons' state as we click them, so we can trigger a user gesture. To do so, take a look at Listing 6-4. We declare the logic in "view1.js" to handle the data of the group button.

Listing 6-4. View1.js group button logic

```
'use strict';

angular.module('myApp.view1', ['ngRoute', 'ui.bootstrap'])

.config(['$routeProvider', function($routeProvider) {
  $routeProvider.when('/view1', {
    templateUrl: 'view1/view1.html',
```

```
        controller: 'View1Ctrl'
    });
}])

.controller('View1Ctrl', ['$scope', function($scope) {
        $scope.data = {
          left: true,
          middle: false,
          right: false
        };
}]);
```

Then, in Listing 6-5, we'll set "view1.html" with the actual buttons we will be using and bind the properties we've set in the controller.

Listing 6-5. View1.html group button view

```
<div ng-controller="View1Ctrl">
    <pre>{{data}}</pre>
    <div class="btn-group">
        <label class="btn btn-primary" ng-model="data.left" uib-btn-checkbox>Left</label>
        <label class="btn btn-primary" ng-model="data.middle" uib-btn-checkbox>Middle</label>
        <label class="btn btn-primary" ng-model="data.right" uib-btn-checkbox>Right</label>
    </div>
</div>
```

Lastly, remove "padding-left: 100px;" and line in app.css ".ng-scope" class, since it's distracting.

That's it! Simply refresh the page and you will be able to see the text changes as you click the buttons—see Figure 6-9. As we click a button, the AngularJS data binding sets the label element with the correct data.

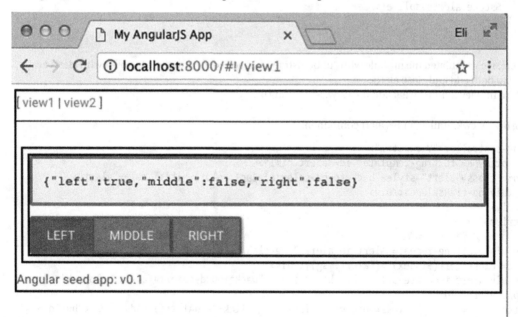

Figure 6-9. *Adding logic to group buttons to know the state of the buttons*

Similarly, let's say we want to implement the alert code in the https://angular-ui.github.io/ bootstrap/ tutorial page. We can easily implement the alert messages in "view2."

Open "view2.js" and replace the code with Listing 6-6.

Listing 6-6. view2.js logic to handle adding, closing, and showing alert messages

```
'use strict';

angular.module('myApp.view2', ['ngRoute', 'ui.bootstrap'])

.config(['$routeProvider', function($routeProvider) {
  $routeProvider.when('/view2', {
    templateUrl: 'view2/view2.html',
    controller: 'View2Ctrl'
  });
}])

.controller('View2Ctrl', ['$scope', function($scope) {
    $scope.alerts = [
        { type: 'danger', msg: 'Oh snap! Change a few things up and try submitting again.' },
        { type: 'success', msg: 'Well done! You successfully read this important alert
        message.' }
    ];

    $scope.addAlert = function() {
      $scope.alerts.push({ msg: 'Another alert!' });
    };

    $scope.closeAlert = function(index) {
      $scope.alerts.splice(index, 1);
    };
}]);
```

Here, we've initiated the module with "ui.bootstrap" and added logic to the controller with alerts and a method to both add and close alerts.

Next, in "view2.html," we'll add the view. See Listing 6-7.

Listing 6-7. view2.html includes alert components

```
<div ng-controller="View2Ctrl">
  <script type="text/ng-template" id="alert.html">
    <div class="alert" style="background-color:#fa39c3;color:white;" role="alert">
      <div ng-transclude></div>
    </div>
  </script>

  <div uib-alert ng-repeat="alert in alerts" ng-class="'alert-' + (alert.type || 'warning')"
  close="closeAlert($index)">{{alert.msg}}</div>
  <div uib-alert template-url="alert.html" style="background-color:#fa39c3;color:white">A
  happy alert!</div>
  <button type="button" class='btn btn-default' ng-click="addAlert()">Add Alert</button>

</div>
```

142

We specifically used the code straight from the https://angular-ui.github.io/bootstrap/ tutorial page so you can see how to implement a component. Now you can do the same with every single component on the page on your own, whenever you need them.

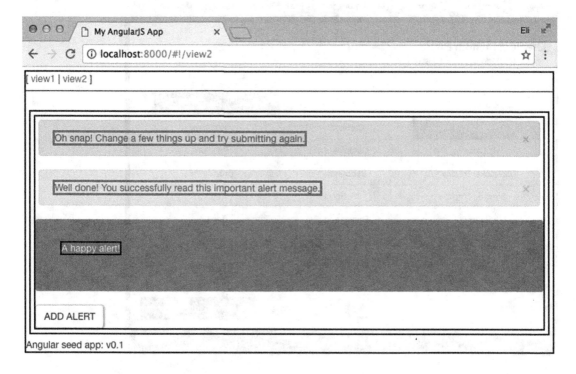

Figure 6-10. *"angular-seed" with UI Bootstrap alerts*

Creating a Custom UI Bootstrap Build

So far we have used two of the UI Bootstrap components: an alert and a group button. However, the entire UI Bootstrap min library is loaded to 121kb, which is a large-sized file for a mere two components. To solve this, UI Bootsrap allows for the creation of custom builds based on the components you are using, instead of loading the entire library. This is a good practice for optimizing your app.

1. To create your own custom build, go to: https://angular-ui.github.io/ bootstrap/ and click "Create a Build."

2. Select the modules you will be using. In this case, we'll be selecting Alert and Buttons (see Figure 6-11). Select "Download 2 Modules."

3. Place the "ui-bootstrap-custom-tpls-1.3.3.min.js" in the "components" folder and change the index.html reference: <script src="components/ui-bootstrap-custom-tpls-1.3.3.min.js"></script>.

See Figure 6-11.

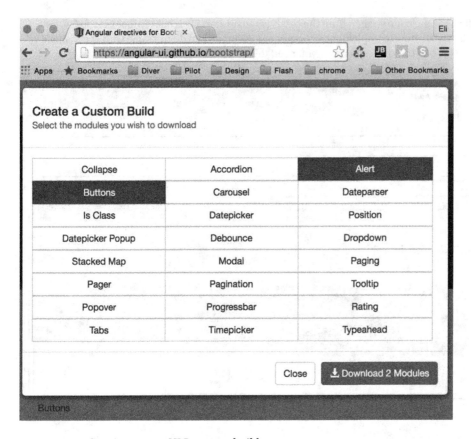

Figure 6-11. *Creating custom UI Bootstrap build*

The potential gain is significant: we are able to reduce the library size from 121Kb to 3Kb. If you want to add additional components, all you will have to do is replace the current build with a new one.

CSS Bootstrap

We have added CSS Bootstrap and we are now able to see the style in our app change automatically. Since Bootstrap comes with definitions for common elements, we are also able to see Angular UI Bootstrap styled with CSS Bootstrap automatically, but there is still more to learn regarding CSS Bootstrap.

One of the most useful features that CSS Bootstrap has to offer is its grid system, which consists of containers and media queries. These features are very useful for page layouts; forget about tables or HTML divs.

■ **Note** Media queries are an advanced CSS3 technique that uses "@media" rule to add a block of CSS code, only under certain conditions—think "if" statements in CSS.

There are different grid options, which can be used based on the device's screen size:

- Extra small devices <768px (such as phones): ".col-xs-"

- Small devices ≥768px (such as tablets): ".col-sm-"

- Medium devices ≥992px (such as desktops): ".col-md-"

- Large devices ≥1200px (such as desktops): ".col-lg-"

Let's create an example: place the following code inside of "view1.html." See Listing 6-8.

Listing 6-8. Bootstrap grid system

```
<div ng-controller="View1Ctrl">
        <div class="row grid">
                <div class="row">
                        <div class="col-md-8">.col-md-8</div>
                        <div class="col-md-4">.col-md-4</div>
                </div>
        </div>
</div>
```

The code is straightforward—we'll create two medium rows and set the div class "grid," then we will need to add the "grid" class to the "app.css" style sheet. See Listing 6-9.

Listing 6-9. Setting grid style in "app.css"

```
.grid [class^=col-] {
        padding-top: 10px;
        padding-bottom: 10px;
        background-color: #ffff00;
        border: 1px solid #ddd;
}
```

Also delete all the CSS "ng" classes from "app.css" we added earlier, so we can see the changes better:

```
.ng-scope {
  border: 2px solid #000000;
  margin: 5px;
}

.ng-binding {
  border: 3px solid red;
}

.ng-dirty {
  border: 2px solid yellow;
}

.ng-invalid {
  border: 2px solid red;
}

.ng-pristine {
  border: 2px solid green;
}
```

The style sheet code will apply to any style that has a class name "col-*". Now refresh the page (see Figure 6-12).

Figure 6-12. *Bootstrap grid system*

As you can see in Figure 6-12, we were able to apply a style to our grid. However, we now have an issue—the text can be cut off in the current screen size selected. To solve this, Bootstrap includes a container called "container-fluid." It can be used for full-width containers, utilizing the complete width of the screen. Change "view1.html" and the class from "row" to "container-fluid" (see Listing 6-10).

Listing 6-10. view1.html container fluid grid

```
<div ng-controller="View1Ctrl">
        <div class="container-fluid grid">
                <div class="row">
                        <div class="col-md-8">.col-md-8</div>
                        <div class="col-md-4">.col-md-4</div>
                </div>
        </div>
</div>
```

In the "app.css" style sheet, we are also able to define the width of the container, which will be adjusted for use in whatever size we decide and will center the container for us automatically. Add the following class in the "app.css" style sheet:

```
.container-fluid {
   width: 940px;
   .center-block();
}
```

Refresh the screen. Now we can see the complete text copy. Once we adjust the screen to a size larger than 940px, the page will center the container for us automatically (see Figure 6-13).

Figure 6-13. *Bootstrap grid utilizing container-fluid*

Bootstrap CSS best practices for grid dictate:

- ".row" class should be used to create horizontal groups of columns.

- ".container" should be used for "fixed-width" containers.

- ".container-fluid" should be used to utilize the full width of the screen.

For more information, visit: `http://getbootstrap.com/css/`

Responsive CSS Media Queries

As we have previously discussed, CSS3 offers @media rules in order to help us define style rules for different screens. These media queries can be used for the following tasks:

- Resolution

- Width and height of view and device screen

- Landscape / portrait orientation

- Print view

In fact, this is such a common practice that the "angular-seed" "main.css" file already comes with pre-defined settings for @media queries. For example, "angular-seed" off default media query for "view" port and for "print" settings.

Add "main.css" in "index.html" <head> tag:

```
<link href="bower_components/html5-boilerplate/dist/css/main.css" rel="stylesheet">
```

Next, search for the following comment inside of "angular-seed/app/bower_components/html5-boilerplate/dist/css/main.css":

```
/* ========================================================================
   EXAMPLE Media Queries for Responsive Design.
   These examples override the primary ('mobile first') styles.
   Modify as content requires.
   ======================================================================== */
```

As you can see, "angular-seed" is already a defined media query for a screen size of 35em, which equals 560px.

```
@media only screen and (min-width: 35em) {
    /* Style adjustments for viewports that meet the condition */
}
```

Next, change the @media tag to the following code (see Listing 6-11):

Listing 6-11. Set background color to yellow on screen size

```
body {
    background-color: red;
}

@media only screen and (min-width: 35em) {
```

```
    /* Style adjustments for viewports that meet the condition */
    body {
        background-color: yellow;
    }
}
```

Now, refresh the browser and change the size of your screen. Once the size is smaller than 560px, the color will be red, while over 560px, the color will be yellow. See Figures 6-14 and 6-15.

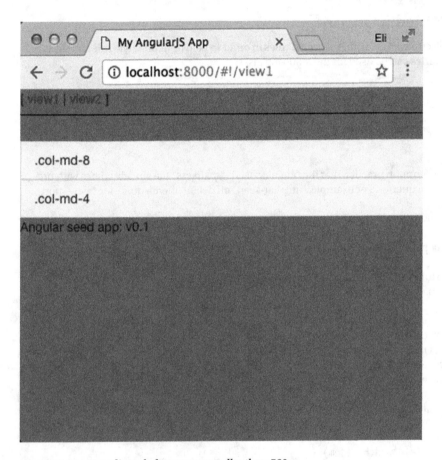

Figure 6-14. *@media style for screens smaller than 560px*

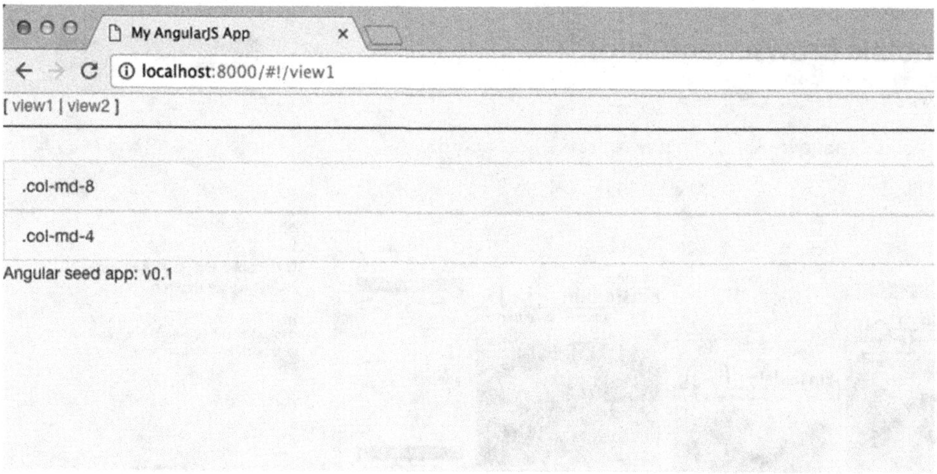

Figure 6-15. *Background color for desktop-sized screens*

Take another look at Listing 6-11. Inside the "@media only screen and (min-width: 35em)," you can set all of the CSS classes you want to change once the screen size is over 560px.

Here, we've created a responsive design that adjusts our style based on screen size with a minimal amount of code.

Portrait and Landscape Orientation

We can also set custom style settings for both portrait and landscape orientations. See Listing 6-12.

Listing 6-12. Using custom style settings

```
@media only screen and (orientation: landscape) {
    body {
        background-color: green;
    }
}
```

Once you turn the device orientation to landscape, the background color will be green. Obviously we don't need to set the portrait orientation, since it is the default.

Emulating Mobile Browsers

Chrome and Firefox offer different plugins that you can use to easily emulate mobile devices; one example is "Mobile Browser Emulator." You can download it free from the Google Chrome webstore (see Figure 6-16.)

```
https://chrome.google.com/webstore/detail/mobile-browser-emulator/lbofcampnkjmiomohpbaihdcb
jhbfepf?hl=en
```

Figure 6-16. *Mobile browser emulator*

Once you install the plugin, you will see an "m" icon close to your Chrome's address bar. Clicking the icon will give you drop-down options to emulate a mobile device. See Figure 6-17.

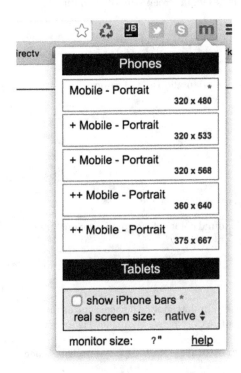

Figure 6-17. *Mobile browser emulator drop-down menu*

CSS Responsive Design Utilizing a Break Point

When working with responsive design, best practices dictate that mobile should be taken into account first, and then other devices. The reasoning behind this is, if the user displays our content on a smaller device, which is less capable than a desktop, we want the content to be optimized and come up as soon as possible. With that in mind, let's create a page that takes screen size into account. We want to change the style once the device screen size is at least 800px.

Ideally, we want our design to be optimized for device size, which will result in a better user experience. Media queries are built for this. We add breakpoints so that a portion of the content will behave differently on each size of the breakpoint we create.

Take a look at Listing 6-13. Place the code inside of "main.css" right after the "EXAMPLE Media Queries for Responsive Design" comment, as we have done previously.

Listing 6-13. Adding breakpoints

```css
body {
    background-color: black;
}

.left-menu ul {
    list-style-type: none;
    padding: 15px;
}

.left-menu li {
    padding: 10px;
    margin-bottom: 10px;
    background-color : darkgrey;
}
.left-menu li:hover {
    background-color: slategray;
}
.copy {
    padding: 25px;
}

/* mobile */
[class*="col-"] {
    float: left;
    width: 100%;
}

/* desktop */
@media only screen and (min-width: 800px) {
    .col-1 {width: 8.33%;}
    .col-2 {width: 16.66%;}
    .col-3 {width: 25%;}
```

```
    .col-4 {width: 33.33%;}
    .col-5 {width: 41.66%;}
    .col-6 {width: 50%;}
    .col-7 {width: 58.33%;}
    .col-8 {width: 66.66%;}
    .col-9 {width: 75%;}
    .col-10 {width: 83.33%;}
    .col-11 {width: 91.66%;}
    .col-12 {width: 100%;}
}
```

As you can see, we have defined a custom list to be used as our left menu and set the style to be used as a mobile style, unless the screen size is bigger than 800px. We have set the width size for each column. In our example, we will only be using "col-3," but it's good practice to set everything up front so that we can then adjust our style as needed (Listing 6-14).

Listing 6-14. Adjusting the style

```
<div class="row">
    <div class="col-3 left-menu">
        <ul>
            <li>Left item 1</li>
            <li>Left item 2</li>
            <li>Left item 3</li>
        </ul>
    </div>
    <div class="col-6 copy">
        <h1>Lorem Ipsum</h1>
        <p> Lorem ipsum dolor sit amet, consectetur adipiscing elit. Vestibulum vestibulum
metus vitae magna viverra, id venenatis dui egestas. Suspendisse tincidunt rhoncus nisi.
Suspendisse tristique commodo sapien, eu dictum erat. Vivamus accumsan quis orci et
pulvinar. Ut efficitur placerat arcu, ut dapibus mauris egestas sit amet. Proin convallis
massa justo, eu molestie nunc sodales in. Proin facilisis non arcu id venenatis. Interdum et
malesuada fames ac ante ipsum primis in faucibus. Integer lacus ipsum, interdum eu maximus
id, gravida a metus. Mauris sed pharetra tellus. Donec in pretium augue.</p>
    </div>
</div>
```

We have created a left menu, a title, and a copy in the middle. When the user views this content using a small device (less than 800px), the menu will extend to 100%, and when viewed on a desktop, the menu list will decrease in size so that the copy can fit. See Figures 6-18 and 6-19.

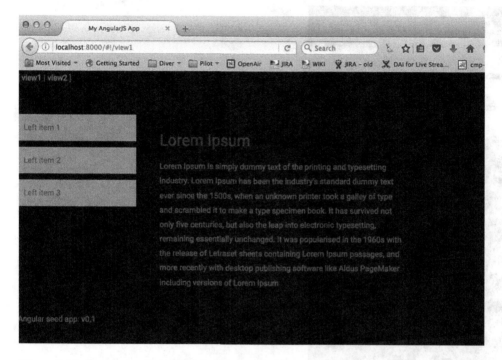

Figure 6-18. *Responsive design with breakpoint desktop view*

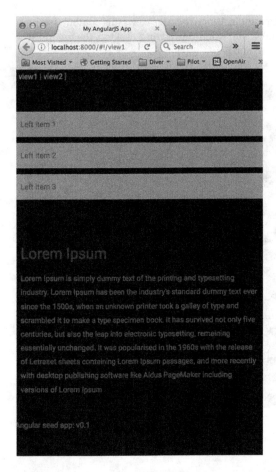

Figure 6-19. *Responsive design with breakpoint mobile view*

Responsive Design Breakpoint Bootstrap

In the previous example, we used lists to create our containers using list HTML components and CSS, but it's not necessary. Bootstrap CSS already has a container and rows, which we can style easily and then adjust for the container automatically. To do so in "bower_components/html5-boilerplate/dist/css/main.css," add the following code (see Listing 6-15):

Listing 6-15. Breakpoint Bootstrap "main.css"

```
.content {
  background: lightgray;
  padding: 15px;
  margin-bottom: 15px;
```

```
  min-height: 300px;
}
.content.slategrey {
  background: slategrey;
}
```

In "view1.html," replace the existing code with following code (see Listing 6-16):

Listing 6-16.

```
<div class="container">
    <div class="row">
        <!-- 1 Columns at a time on mobile and 2 columns on desktop -->
        <div class="col-xs-12 col-sm-6">
            <div class="content">.col-xs-12 .col-sm-6</div>
        </div>
        <div class="col-xs-12 col-sm-6">
            <div class="content slategrey">.col-xs-12 .col-sm-6</div>
        </div>
    </div>
    <hr>
    <!-- 2 /8 desktop or 1 column at a time for desktop -->
    <div class="row">
        <div class="col-sm-2">
            <div class="content">.col-sm-4</div>
        </div>
        <div class="col-sm-10">
            <div class="content slategrey">.col-sm-8</div>
        </div>
    </div>
</div>
```

This code automatically takes mobile into account and adjusts the first set of columns to display one column at a time, and will adjust to two columns for desktop. For the second set of columns, the code displays 20% and 80% widths for desktop and full size for mobile. See Figure 6-20.

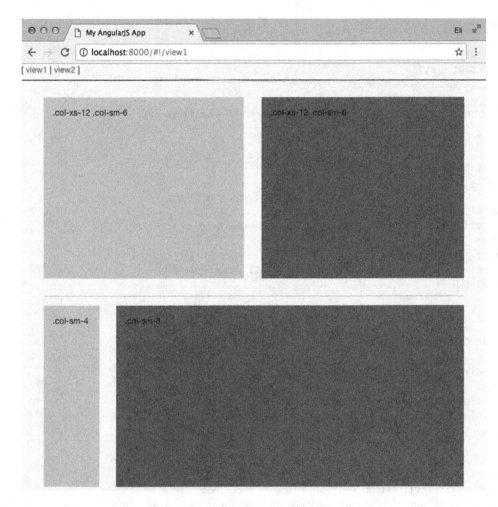

Figure 6-20. *Responsive design breakpoint Bootstrap CSS desktop view*

Now, just as we've done before, change the container from:

```
<div class="container">
```

to:

```
<div class=".container-fluid">
```

As I have mentioned, the ".container-fluid" style changes a fixed-width grid layout into a full-width layout. See Figure 6-21.

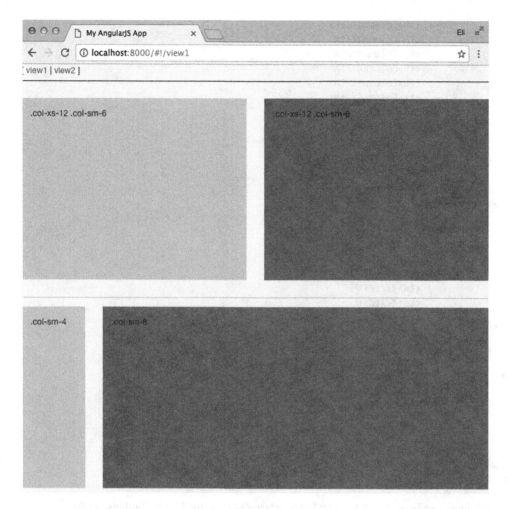

Figure 6-21. *Responsive design breakpoint Bootstrap CSS desktop view using ".container-fluid"*

Bootstrap Responsive Tables

There are cases when you will want to design a responsive table, which hides columns that are less important, based on screen size. For instance, let's say your table has twelve columns but only five are important. We can use Bootstrap CSS to set the table as "unseen" and then set which columns we want to hide based on the user's screen size.

To implement this type of design, in "view1.html," place the following code (see Listing 6-17):

Listing 6-17. Bootstrap responsive tables "view1.html"

```
<section id="unseen">
        <table class="table-striped table-condensed table-bordered">
                <thead>
                <tr>
```

```
                <th>Column1</th>
                <th>Column2</th>
                <th>Column3</th>
                <th>Column4</th>
                <th>Column5</th>
                <th>Column6</th>
                <th>Column7</th>
                <th>Column8</th>
                <th>Column9</th>
                <th>Column10</th>
                <th>Column11</th>
                <th>Column12</th>
        </tr>
        </thead>
        <tbody>
        <tr>
                <td>1</td>
                <td>2</td>
                <td>3</td>
                <td>4</td>
                <td>5</td>
                <td>6</td>
                <td>7</td>
                <td>8</td>
                <td>9</td>
                <td>10</td>
                <td>11</td>
                <td>12</td>
        </tr>
        </tbody>
    </table>
</section>
```

Notice the following code on the table class: "<table class="table-striped table-condensed table-bordered">". The different Bootstrap CSS files indicate the following:

1. **"table-striped"**: sets zebra striping style for the rows

2. **"table-condensed"**: makes tables more compact by cutting cell padding in half

3. **"table-bordered"**: sets borders on all sides of the table and cells

If we wanted to add a hover state for the table, we would just add "table-hover".

Next, set the "bower_components/html5-boilerplate/dist/css/main.css" with the columns you want to hide based on the media screen size (see Listing 6-18).

Listing 6-18. "main.css" style with hidden columns

```
@media only screen and (max-width: 800px) {
        #unseen table td:nth-child(2),
        #unseen table th:nth-child(2) {display: none;}
        #unseen table td:nth-child(10),
        #unseen table th:nth-child(10){display: none;}
        #unseen table td:nth-child(11),
```

```
        #unseen table th:nth-child(11){display: none;}
}

@media only screen and (max-width: 640px) {
        #unseen table td:nth-child(4),
        #unseen table th:nth-child(4),
        #unseen table td:nth-child(7),
        #unseen table th:nth-child(7),
        #unseen table td:nth-child(8),
        #unseen table th:nth-child(8){display: none;}
        #unseen table td:nth-child(9),
        #unseen table th:nth-child(9){display: none;}
        #unseen table td:nth-child(10),
        #unseen table th:nth-child(10){display: none;}
        #unseen table td:nth-child(11),
        #unseen table th:nth-child(11){display: none;}
}
```

Also, to remove the previous yellow and red background body colors, we added in "bower_components/html5-boilerplate/dist/css/main.css",

```
body {
    background-color: red;
}

@media only screen and (min-width: 35em) {
    /* Style adjustments for viewports that meet the condition */
    body {
        background-color: yellow;
    }
}
```

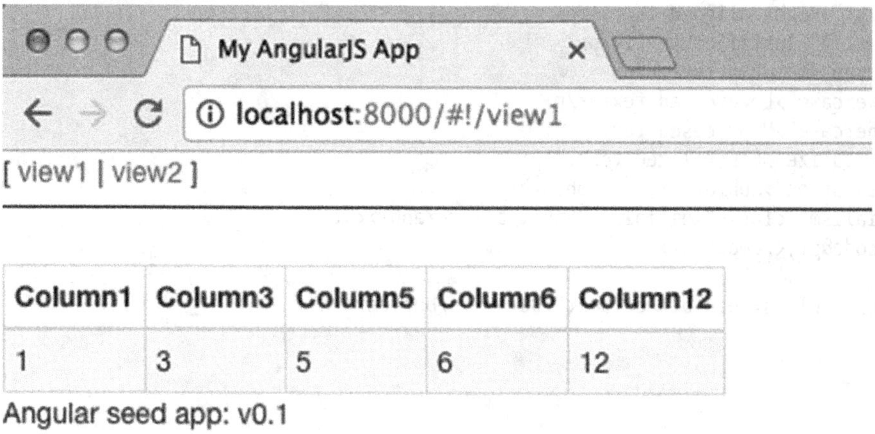

Column1	Column3	Column5	Column6	Column12
1	3	5	6	12

Angular seed app: v0.1

Figure 6-22. *Bootstrap responsive tables style with hidden columns, mobile view*

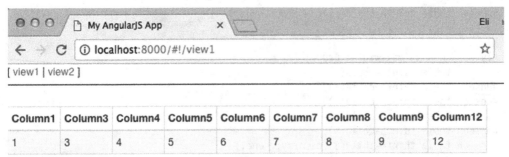

Column1	Column3	Column4	Column5	Column6	Column7	Column8	Column9	Column12
1	3	4	5	6	7	8	9	12

Angular seed app: v0.1

Figure 6-23. *Bootstrap responsive tables style with hidden columns, desktop view*

Bootstrap CSS Common Styles

Take a look at Listing 6-19. These are some commonly used CSS styles. Bootstrap CSS already offers default settings for these common elements—they are self explanatory. Copy them into "view1.html" to replace the existing code (see Listing 6-19).

Listing 6-19. Bootstrap CSS common styles code example

```
<h1>h1. Bootstrap heading <small> with a secondary text</small></h1><br>
<p class="lead">Stand out with lead style</p><br>
<mark>Highlight with the mark tag</mark><br>
<del>Cross off a line</del><br>
<s>No longer accurate</s><br>
<u>Underlined</u><br>
<p class="text-left">Left aligned text.</p>
<p class="text-center">Center aligned text.</p>
<p class="text-right">Right aligned text.</p>
<p class="text-justify">Justified text.</p>
<p class="text-nowrap">No wrap text.</p>
<p class="text-lowercase">Lowercased text.</p>
<p class="text-uppercase">Uppercased text.</p>
<p class="text-capitalize">Capitalized text.</p>
<abbr title="abbreviation">abbreviation</abbr><br>
<abbr title="initialism" class="initialism">initialism</abbr><br>
<code>&lt;inline code&gt;</code><br>
<kbd>ctrl</kbd>
<button type="button" class="btn btn-default">Default</button>
```

```
<button type="button" class="btn btn-primary">Primary</button>
<button type="button" class="btn btn-success">Success</button>
<button type="button" class="btn btn-info">Info</button>
<button type="button" class="btn btn-warning">Warning</button>
<button type="button" class="btn btn-danger">Danger</button>
<button type="button" class="btn btn-link">Link</button>
<button type="button" class="btn btn-primary btn-xs">Extra small button</button>
<button type="button" class="btn btn-primary btn-sm">Small button</button>
<button type="button" class="btn btn-primary btn-lg">Large button</button>
<address>
        <strong>Name</strong><br>
        123 Rainbow Street<br>
        Los Angeles, CA 90210<br>
        <abbr title="Phone">P:</abbr> (310) 111-1111
</address>
```

Responsive Images with Bootstrap CSS

There are times you will need to implement an image on different screen sizes. Creating a responsive image with Bootstrap CSS is easy—all you have to do is use the "img-responsive" class in the image tag (see below):

```
<img src="[url]" class="img-small" alt="Responsive image">
```

When you use "img-responsive," the images will respond automatically, which means that the width will adjust on its own based on the screen size.

You can then customize the image height with the "@media" tag.

In "bower_components/html5-boilerplate/dist/css/main.css," set the following small class:

```
@media screen and (max-width: 480px) {
        img.small {
                max-height: 250px;
                min-height: 50px;
        }
}
```

Then, in "view1.html," set the image class to "responsive" and "small," and replace the existing "view1.html" with the following:

```
<img src="http://goo.gl/fcpsyI" class="img-responsive small">
```

See Figure 6-24.

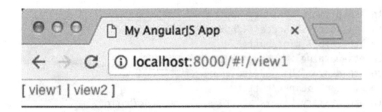

Angular seed app: v0.1

Figure 6-24. *Responsive image using Bootstrap CSS. Photo credit "National geographic."*

Angular-Responsive Library

In the previous sub-chapters, we've shown you how to create media queries using pure CSS and Bootstrap CSS to build elegant views. However, using media queries is often less than ideal, and although we can set "unseen" content and optimize the content, the DOM is still going to process the content using valuable device resources.

Instead of using media queries, the other most common option is to create a completely different view for each screen size. It's easy enough to create it on your own, check screen size, and apply the view, but you don't need to. There are already libraries that include directives to do just that—here's one example: https://github.com/lavinjj/angular-responsive.

The "angular-responsive" directive is set to not add content unless it's displayed on the targeted device. This reduces the expensive use of network traffic and DOM processing, but still requires you to create different views for each device, so it's a bit of a trade-off. To install the libraries, type the following command:

```
$ bower install angular-responsive
```

You can confirm that the library was added here: "angular-seed/app/bower_components/angular-responsive."

Alternatively, you can check out the library directly from GitHub and add it manually to the component folder using the following commands:

- Git clone https://github.com/lavinjj/angular-responsive

- Create a "components/angular-responsive" folder and copy "responsive-directive.js" to the target folder.

Why are we showing you both options? The "angular-responsive" library on Bower may not include the latest code, so it's good to have both options handy.

Next, add the directive to the "view1.js" module:

```
angular.module('myApp.view1', ['ngRoute', 'ui.bootstrap', 'angular-responsive'])
```

Don't forget to load the directive in "index.html" add at the end of the page, the responsive directive:

```
<script src="bower_components/angular-responsive/src/responsive-directive.js"></script>
```

Now, we can use different images (content) for each device, without taxing the device. Swap the images in brackets with an image of your choice with the image size listed. For example: [image50x50] should be replaced with an image with 50-by-50-pixel dimentions.

Listing 6-20. "angular-responsive" used to display different images on different devices

```
<div class="container-fluid" ng-controller="View2Ctrl">
        <div class="row-fluid">
                <div data-ar-mobile>
                        mobile devices<br>
                        <img ng-src="[image50x50]" alt="mobile"
                                        height="50"/>
                </div>
                <div data-ar-tablet>
                        Tablet devices<br>
                        <img ng-src="[image100x100]" alt="tablets"
                                        height="100"/>
                </div>
                <div data-ar-desktop>
                        desktop devices<br>
                        <img ng-src="[image500x500]" alt="desktop"
                                        height="500"/>
                </div>
                <div data-ar-responsive="{ 'Mobile': true, 'Tablet': true, 'Desktop': false }">
                        mobile or tablet devices<br>
                        <img ng-src="[image150x150] " alt="tablets and mobile"
                                        height="150"/>
                </div>
        </div>
</div>
```

As you can see in Figure 6-25, we can emulate the different devices and see the results. The code will be using different images, and we can ensure that, for mobile, we're using smaller-sized images that require fewer resources.

Figure 6-25. *"angular-responsive" using different images on different devices. Photo credit "National Geographic."*

Summary

In this chapter, we put a bucket of paint on our app and learned how to use the built-in CSS classes used by AngularJS. We creaed a new project and used "ng-scope," "ng-dirty," "ng-invalid," and "ng-pristine." We installed Bootstrap CSS and UI Bootstrap and learned how to create a custom UI Bootstrap build.

We covered CSS Bootstrap and how to create and use responsive CSS media queries to adjust to device screen sizes, as well as portrait and landscape orientation. We installed a plugin to emulate mobile browsers and used CSS and Bootstrap CSS to create responsive design to utilize breakpoints.

We also created Bootstrap CSS responsive tables and showed you some of the common styles that Bootstrap CSS has to offer. We created content utilizing responsive images with Bootstrap CSS and, finally, implemented the "Angular-responsive" library to reduce processing time on different devices.

In the next chapter, we will be covering the process of creating services that our app can use utilizing Node.js and ExpressJS.

Write Services Once

As you may recall, in Chapter 1, we installed Node.js on our local machine using the installer from http:// nodejs.org. In Chapter 2, we rolled out servers and installed Node.js on Ubuntu servers. In Chapter 3, we installed modules and created our very own first Node.js module and published it to both npm and GitHub.

In this chapter, we will put it all together and utilize Node.js to create a service layer that can be used on any machine.

Note   A service layer, middle layer, or middle tier is the processing taking place between the front end and the database. It include business logic and processing data. The service layer allows for creating different presentations of the same data.

Express App

Our first step is to set up our server so that we can have an address that the client side can call and be able to receive a result from a service call.

Node.js and Express are built without a strict folder structure, but there are better practices out there. WebStorm includes a folder structure based on these best practices, but of course, what fits one project may not fit another. Regardless, it is recommended that we start by creating a new Node.js Express project.

We'll create a Node.js Express server, examine best practices, and create services.

Note   Express is a flexible Node web application framework based on Node.js with a small footprint that provides a set of features for application development. Remember, the "E" in the MEAN Stack stands for Express, and using Express can help simplify and accelerate development over creating a separate server for front end. The same Node.js server can be used for the middle layer and presentation layer. Visit the Express website here: http://expressjs.com.

Installing Express

To start an Express skeleton project, open WebStorm, select "Create New Project," then select "Node.js Express App," and lastly, "Create" (Figure 7-1).

E. Elrom, *Pro MEAN Stack Development*, DOI 10.1007/978-1-4842-2044-3_7

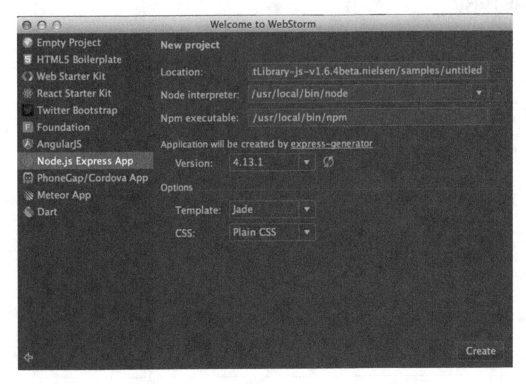

Figure 7-1. *Creating a new Express project in WebStorm*

Look at the directory list and you will see that we have a project with the following directories and files:

1. **node_modules folder**: the Node.js module dependencies being used by the project

2. **public folder**: where we will place our static files, such as images, JavaScript files, and stylesheet CSS files

3. **routes folder**: currently includes index.js and users.js JavaScript files (the services we will be using for our app)

4. **views folder**: holds Jade (now called Pug) templates rendered and served by the routes. Jade/Pug uses a concise, readable syntax to make authoring HTML pages easier.

5. **app.js file**: initializes and glues the app components together.

6. **package.json file**: stores references to the modules (installed in node_modules) and their versions that the app depends on

7. **bin/www file**: Node.js entry point that creates servers and loads required dependencies

If you look at the "package.json" file, notice that "express" "~4.13.4" is the current stable version is 4 and Express 5 is in alpha state. Feel free to visit Express to see the list of changes in Version 5: http://expressjs.com/en/guide/migrating-5.html

Hello World Express

Now that we have a project set up in WebStorm, we'll create a server locally and get a "Hello World." In the upper right corner of WebStorm, click the green caret to run the "www" file. See Figure 7-2.

Figure 7-2. *Run "www" Node.js Express app*

You will see in the left button in the corner, the run window shows that the app is running successfully on port 3000. See Figure 7-3.

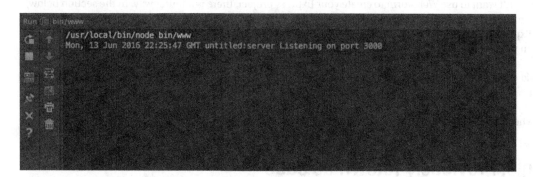

Figure 7-3. *App running successfully on port 3000*

Open http://localhost:3000/ and you will be able to see the app running (Figure 7-4).

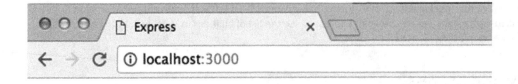

Welcome to Express

Figure 7-4. *Express app running on port 3000*

Express Generator Tool

If you don't want to use WebStorm to create your Express project, there is another way. In the section below, we'll create the same project with a generator.

Express has a generator tool called "express-generator." You can create the same seed project as the one built in to WebStorm with just two commands:

```
$ sudo npm install express-generator -g
$ express untitled
```

The app the Express tool creates is the same as the one in WebStorm.

Pugjs, Previously Known as Jade

Jade's name was changed to Pugjs, and it is one of the most popular template engines. You can take a look at the project here: `https://github.com/pugjs/pug`. It allows us to quickly write intuitive, easy-to-read code that will convert to HTML, saving development time and making the code readable. We have seen Pugjs in action in the previos example. In this section, we will cover Pugjs more, showing you how to integrate it into your app and utilize it.

Add the pug library to our project:

```
$ npm install pug --save-dev
```

Next, create the following file inside of the views folder `views/index.pug`, as shown in Listing 7-1.

Listing 7-1. Index.pug

```
doctype html
html(lang="en")
  head
```

```
    title= pageTitle
    script(type='text/javascript').
      if (foo) bar(1 + 5)
  body
    h1 Pug - node template engine
    #container.col
      if youAreUsingPug
        p You are amazing
      else
        p Get on it!
      p.
        Pug is a simple templating language with a
        strong focus on performance and powerful features.
```

Listing 7-1 was taken straight from a Pug project; it illustrates how to write an easy-to-read HTML code in Pugjs. It creates an HTML document, sets the page title, performs some simple JavaScript calculation, and adds "h1" and "p" tags to the document.

Similarly, the code creates another file ("views/hello.pug"). The file will create an HTML document, add an "h1" tag and set "body" as the value (Listing 7-2).

Listing 7-2. hello.pug

```
html
  head
  body
    h1=body
```

Now that we have two template documents, all we have to do is wire our app and set the view folder. Inside of "app.js," after setting the app "app.set('view engine', 'jade')", add the following code (see Listing 7-3):

Listing 7-3. Set app.js to map to the view folder

```
// set pug
app.set('view engine', 'pug');
// pass variables to pug
app.get('/hello', function (req, res) {
    res.render('hello', { body: 'hello world pug'});
});
```

Notice that we're passing the value of "body" to the hello.pug template page.

To view the template (Figure 7-5), open the documents:

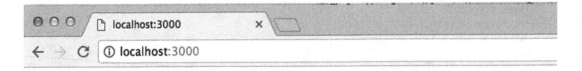

Pug - node template engine

Get on it!

Pug is a simple templating language with a strong focus on performance and powerful features.

Figure 7-5. Index.pug template page

```
$ Open http://localhost:3000
```

Now, open the hello.pug page (Figure 7-6):

```
$ Open http://[computer name]:[port]/hello
```

hello world pug

Figure 7-6. Hello.pug template page

As you can see, creating a template is a powerful tool to put in your bag of tricks when creating Express apps. It can be used for many different things, such as static pages, content, and HTML emails, as we will see later in this chapter.

Setting Up a Service Layer

Next, to set up a service layer, we can utilizie Express's built-in functionality. Express handles service requests using "routing."

■ **Note** Routing in Express is the application end point (URI, or path) and an HTTP request method (GET, POST, HEAD, PUT, DELETE, etc) and how the end point responds to a client's request.

Open the "routes" folder in your app and you will see that there are two files:

- index.js
- users.js

index.js is the default "home" page file, and app.js routes the "routes/index.js" file with the "views/index.jade" template file. When the client calls http://localhost:3000/, it sets the index as the route. In app.js (Listing 7-4), it also creates the app as Express, sets the views as a Jade template, and uses routes we define.

Listing 7-4. app.js sets routes

```
var routes = require('./routes/index');
var users = require('./routes/users');

var app = express();

// view engine setup
app.set('views', path.join(__dirname, 'views'));
app.set('view engine', 'jade');

app.use('/', routes);
app.use('/users', users);
```

Now, in index.js and users.js, we define how to handle the request. For "views/index.js," the script sets the title as "Express," which the Jade template will be using (Listing 7-5).

Listing 7-5. Content of index.js file

```
var express = require('express');
var router = express.Router();

/* GET home page. */
router.get('/', function(req, res, next) {
  res.render('index', { title: 'Express' });
});

module.exports = router;
```

In the "views/index.jade" template file, the code defines the front-end representation (Listing 7-6).

Listing 7-6. Content of "index.jade" file

```
extends layout

block content
  h1= title
  p Welcome to #{title}
```

The Jade template code is similar to HTML, but without the tags. h1 is the same as the HTML heading <h1> tag, and p is the same as the HTML <p> paragraph tag. More on Jade (Pugjs) later in this chapter.

For "routes/users.js," the service responds with the message, "respond with a resource" (Listing 7-7). You can also open the URL to see the message: http://localhost:3000/users.

Listing 7-7. Content of users.js file

```
var express = require('express');
var router = express.Router();

/* GET users listing. */
router.get('/', function(req, res, next) {
  res.send('respond with a resource');
});

module.exports = router;
```

The service is using the route "get" HTTP method router.get(). Additionally, Express supports all of the following methods: get, post, put, head, delete, options, trace, copy, lock, mkcol, move, purge, unlock, report, mkactivity, checkout, merge, m-search, notify, subscribe, unsubscribe, patch, search, and connect.

Express also supports "all()", which will accept any type of HTTP method.

Setting Up a POST Service

In this section, we will be setting up a POST Service Layer and testing it. Change the code inside of "routes/users.js" to the following (Listing 7-8):

Listing 7-8. users.js POST HTTP method

```
var express = require('express');
var router = express.Router();

/* GET users listing. */
router.get('/', function(req, res, next) {
  res.send('GET');
});

/* POST users listing. */
router.post('/', function(req, res, next) {
  res.send('POST: ' + req.body.query);
});

module.exports = router;
```

We have added a "router.post" HTTP method, and when the client sends a POST request, it expects a query param in the body of the request. To see this service at work, create a new HTML file and name it "test.html" (Listing 7-9).

Listing 7-9. test.html form

```html
<form action="http://localhost:3000/users" method="post">
    <input type="text" name="query" id="query"/>
    <button id="btn">submit</button>
</form>

<script>
    var button = document.getElementById('btn');
    button.addEventListener(function() {
        document.getElementById('btn').submit();
    });
</script>
```

Now open test.html in a browser. The content of the file is simple—use "vim test.html" or your personal favorite editor to create the code. In the Terminal, type "$ open test.html", or just double click the file. See Figure 7-7.

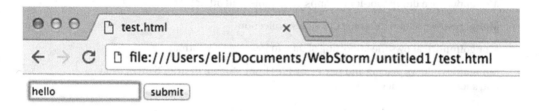

Figure 7-7. Test.html form test page

Reload the server (or click the Rerun button in WebStorm) for the Express changed files to apply. Next, type anything into the text input box and hit submit (Figure 7-8).

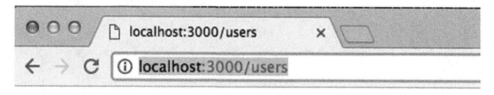

POST: hello

Figure 7-8. Users POST HTTP method return form data

As you can see, the service displays the results of the text input box. This data can be used to retrieve a user from a database or any other data source.

MongoDB Database Integration

In this section, we will be installing the MongoDB database, integrating the database using Express, and creating a service.

MongoDB consists of the following tools:

- **mongod**: the actual database process

- **mongos**: MongoDB Shard—like a controller routing service for MongoDB. It processes queries from the application layer and determines location of the data in the sharded cluster.

- **Mongo**: the database shell (which uses interactive JavaScript)

and the following utilities:

- **Mongodump**: a dump tool-for backups, snapshots, and other tasks

- **Mongorestore**: allows dumping of a single collection

- **Mongoimport**: allows the importing of data in JSON or CSV format

- **Mongofiles**: allows placing and retrieving files from MongoDB GridFS mongostat and shows performance statistics

Install MongoDB

To install MongoDB

```
http://www.mongodb.org/downloads
```

Select "Community Server" tab, select "Current Stable Release," and lastly, "Download (tgz)," as shown in Figure 7-9.

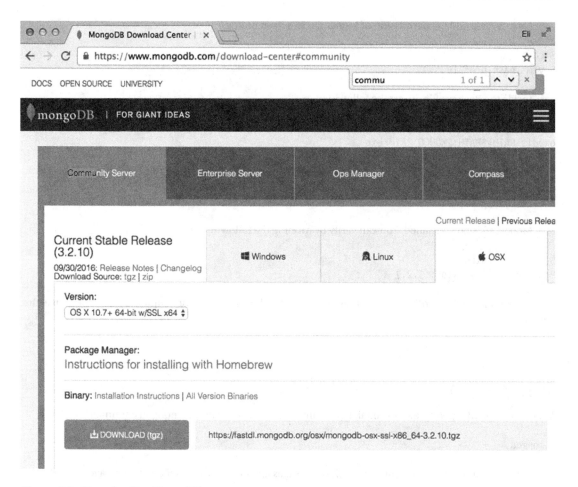

Figure 7-9. *Downloading MongoDB*

Next, navigate to the download folder and extract the gzip compressed tar file:

```
$ cd ~/Downloads
$ tar xzf mongodb-osx-ssl-x86_64-3.2.10.tgz
```

Note that the version at the time of writing is 3.2.10, but the version may have changed by the time you install. Next, move the file to a user local folder under MongoDB.

```
$ sudo mv mongodb-osx-x86_64-3.2.10 /usr/local/mongodb
```

Now we can set a data folder for our MongoDB database:

```
$ sudo mkdir -p /data/db
$ whoami
$ [user name]
$ sudo chown [user name] /data/db
```

Next, we will add the permission of MongoDB to a Bash profile.

```
$ cd ~
$ vim .bash_profile
```

Inside the Bash profile, insert the following:

```
export MONGO_PATH=/usr/local/mongodb
export PATH=$PATH:$MONGO_PATH/bin
```

To save and quit, click "ESCAPE" + ":wq" + "Enter." Run the Bash profile for these changes to take effect:

```
$ . ~/.bash_profile
```

MongoDB is now installed. You can verify by running the following command:

```
$ mongo -version
MongoDB shell version: 3.2.7
```

As you can see, MongoDB replies with the version number. Similarly, for command line options, use the help flag:

```
$ mongod --help
```

Start MongoDB

To start MongoDB, open a new Terminal, type "command" + "t", and run the mongod command.

```
$ mongod
```

MongoDB shows all the output connection messages and ends with the following message:

```
[initandlisten] waiting for connections on port 27017
>
```

A few troubleshooting tips:

1. To stop MongoDB on a mac in Terminal, open "$ top," identify the process, and type "$ kill [pid]", where pid should be the MongoDB process ID.

2. If you get a message such as "Failed to obtain address information for hostname [COMPUTER NAME]: nodename nor servname provided, or not known," you need to add the host of your computer: "$ vim /etc/ hosts". Then, add the host: "127.0.0.1 [COMPUTER NAME]".

3. If you receive the message "Do you want the application mongod to accept incoming network connection," select "Allow."

Visit MongoDB docs regarding FAQ diagnostics: https://docs.mongodb.com/manual/faq/ diagnostics/

Next, open another Terminal tab instance while "waiting for connections on port 27017" mongod is still running.

```
$ mongo
MongoDB shell version: [version]
```

If you go back to the mongod Terminal tab, it will confirm that mongod is connected: "[initandlisten] connection accepted from 127.0.0.1:49360 #1 (1 connection now open)."

As you can see, it replies with a connection and we see ">," and MongoDB is ready for a command.

```
> show dbs
local  0.000GB
```

We don't have a database yet, so it returns with no data size.

Create a Database

Now that we have mongod running and we can interact and type commands, we can create our first MongoDB database. In the MongoDB command line, switch to the username (as you recall, we discover ouruser name by using "whoami"):

```
> use [username]
```

The server will reply in the Terminal output:

```
switched to db [username]
```

Next, we'll create a user collection under our username and insert information about our user:

```
> db.usercollection.insert({ "username" : "someuser", "email" : "someuser@gmail.com" })
```

The server replies in the Terminal output:

```
WriteResult({ "nInserted" : 1 })
```

Now we can confirm that the information was inserted correctly:

```
> db.usercollection.find().pretty()
```

The server replies in the Terminal output:

```
{
        "_id" : ObjectId("5771bc5a4c127a7131da18e2"),
        "username" : "someuser",
        "email" : "someuser@gmail.com"
}
```

Also, running "show dbs" will show us that the user has a collection; the size is still insignificant.

```
> show dbs
```

The server replies in the Terminal output:

```
[username] 0.000GB
local 0.000GB
```

We have created our first MongoDB database, inserted a user collection under our username, and confirmed that the information was inserted correctly.

Read Results from MongoDB into our Express App

Next, we want to be able to interact with the MongoDB database we created and set our Node.js service layer to be able to execute CRUD (create, read, update, and delete) operations and interact with the express front layer.

MongoDB API

In this section, we'll install an API that can create the connection between Node.js and MongoDB. Navigate back to the Express project we created in the previous section. We want to add the following two libraries:

1. MongoDB: the official Node.js driver for MongoDB. See: `https://www.npmjs.com/package/mongodb`

2. Monk: substantial usability improvements for MongoDB usage within Node.JS. See `https://www.npmjs.com/package/monk`

Install these two libraries locally and save them in the package.json file by typing:

```
$ npm install mongodb monk --save-dev
```

app.js

Now that we have an API that can do the talking, we can go back to our "app.js" file and make our MongoDB database accessible to all of our routers. Place Listing 7-10's code after "var app = express();".

Listing 7-10. "app.js" connected to MongoDB

```
var mongo = require('mongodb');
var monk = require('monk');
var db = monk('localhost:27017/[USER NAME]');

// Make our db accessible to our router
app.use(function(req,res,next){
  req.db = db;
  next();
});
```

Notice that we set our database as our username. We got it by running "$ whoami" in the Terminal. Ensure you change the bracketed username ("[USERNAME]") to your username.

users.js

Now in users.js, we can query the database and return the users (Listing 7- 11).

Listing 7-11. users.js get service

```
/* GET users listing. */
router.get('/', function(req, res, next) {
  console.log('start get');
  var db = req.db;
  var collection = db.get('usercollection');
  collection.find({},{},function(e,docs){
    res.send(docs);
  });

});
```

Similarly, a post request will look like Listing 7-12.

Listing 7-12. users.js post service

```
/* POST users listing. */
router.post('/', function(req, res, next) {
  var db = req.db;
  var collection = db.get('usercollection');
  collection.find({'username': req.body.query},{},function(e,docs){
    res.send(docs);
  });
});
```

You can just copy the complete code into routes/users.js as shown in Listing 7-13.

Listing 7-13. users.js complete code

```
var express = require('express');
var router = express.Router();

/* GET users listing. */
router.get('/', function(req, res, next) {
  console.log('start get');
  var db = req.db;
  var collection = db.get('usercollection');
  collection.find({},{},function(e,docs){
    res.send(docs);
  });

});
```

```
/* POST users listing. */
router.post('/', function(req, res, next) {
  var db = req.db;
  var collection = db.get('usercollection');
  collection.find({'username': req.body.query},{},function(e,docs){
    res.send(docs);
  });
});
```

```
module.exports = router;
```

Remember to ensure "mongod" is running by typing "mongod" in a Terminal instance.

Be sure to "run" the Node.js app by clicking the green return icon in WebStorm or by typing command + R while on the run window for the changes to take effect.

To test these changes, go to the user URL and you should be able to see the results of users:

```
http://localhost:3000/users
```

You will see the results in the browser:

```
[{"_id":"57f303a9ed4425e3f6a7724e","username":"someuser","email":"someuser@gmail.com"}]
```

Now open "test.html" again, and this time give "someuser" as the user name and hit submit. You'll get the same results:

```
[{"_id":"57f303a9ed4425e3f6a7724e","username":"someuser","email":"someuser@gmail.com"}]
```

Hit the back button in the browser and try a false username—you will get an empty result: "[]".

We were able to create a MongoDB database connect to the MongoDB database through Node.js and create a Service Layer in Express to perform CRUD operations. In the following sections, we'll add more interactions using Socket.IO.

Express and Socket.IO

In the section below, we will be covering creating a Service Layer that utilizes Web Socket to transfer data. Web Socket is often used to transfer real-time messages such as chats or streaming videos. Web Socket is a valuable feature that can be added that realism features to your application.

Install Socket.IO

Socket.IO allows us to easily create real-time event communications. This is a core feature and a good technology to keep in your bag of tricks for any type of app you will be building. Let's start off by installing Socket.IO. Run the following command in the project root location:

```
$ npm install socket.io --save-dev
```

Add Socket.IO to the App

To add Socket.IO, open app.js and create a server variable, then initialize Socket.IO. We also want to add Socket.IO to our response so it will be available (Listing 7-14). Place code after "var app = express();".

Listing 7-14. Update app.js to set a Socket.IO server

```
// NOTE: add socket.io
var server = require('http').Server(app);
var io = require('socket.io')(server);

app.use(function(req, res, next){
  res.io = io;
  next();
});
```

Lastly, we want to change our Express app signature to pass the app and server. bin/www need both app and server instead of just app. Be sure to add the following line at the bottom of the app.js file:

```
// NOTE: change from: module.exports = app;
module.exports = {app: app, server: server};
```

Next, open the "bin/www" file and make changes so that the app variable will point to the app and server. This accomodates the changes we've made in app.js(Listing 7-15).

Listing 7-15. "bin/www" changes to changes of Express app

```
// NOTE: changed from: var app = require('../app');
var app = require('../app').app;

// NOTE: changed from: var server = http.createServer(app);
var server = require('../app').server;
```

Update Users Service to Include Socket.IO

Now we can update our "routes/users.js" service file and send Socket.IO event notifications. Open "routes/users.js" and replace the service router.get with Listing 7-16.

Listing 7-16. users.js calling "helloSocketIO" and passing data

```
/* GET users listing. */
router.get('/', function(req, res, next) {
  var db = req.db;
  var collection = db.get('usercollection');
  collection.find({},{},function(e,docs){
    // NOTE: EE: added socket IO call
    res.io.emit("helloSocketIO", docs);
    res.send(docs);
  });
});
```

Note that once we have the results from the database, we are able to send these results as event notifications using Socket.IO, so that any subscriber to "helloSocketIO" can retrieve data.

You can return "bin/www" and refresh "http://localhost:3000/users," which will produce the same results, since we are sending the data back "res.send(docs);".

Retrieve a Socket.IO Event Using MongoDB Results

On the front end, our index can subscribe to the event notification and display an alert showing the data. In "views/index.jade," change the code to that in Listing 7-17.

Listing 7-17. Update "index.jade" to include socket.io connection and results from database

```
extends layout

block content
  h1= title
  p Welcome to #{title}
  script(src="/socket.io/socket.io.js")
  script.
    var socket = io('//localhost:3000');
    socket.on('helloSocketIO', function (data) {
      alert('Hello ' + data[0].username);
    });
```

Test Socket.IO App

To test our app, restart the app using the run command in WebStorm and open an instance of the app in your browser:

```
$ open http://localhost:3000
```

Now, when we call the users service using a browser, it will display our user in an alert:

```
$ open http://localhost:3000/users
```

You can also do it without user interaction using cURL:

```
$ curl http://localhost:3000/users
```

▪ **Note** cURL is a Linux tool that can be used without user interaction and is built to transfer data to or from a server using protocols such as FTP, HTTP, HTTPS, POP3, RTMP, and others. It's available for Mac OS X out of the box in Terminal.

---

rooms.js

An easy way to integrate Engine.IO and Socket.IO, or any other transporters, with your app is to use an implementation layer that sits on top of these engines. There are many implementations out there, and we will review one as an example.

rooms.js is a JavaScript Node.js module for creating rooms and streaming data between the front end and back end. It uses Engine.IO or Socket.IO for sending messages and provides a way to send and receive messages and switch different transporters for creating rooms and streaming data between users, streaming data from a database and even streaming from a third-party CDN.

Take a look at Figure 7-10 to better understand the flow. rooms.db connects to a database or a CDN, and through rooms.js, it uses Socket.IO to send messages through a controller to an app.

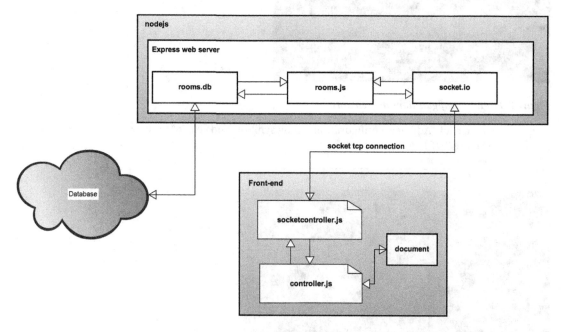

Figure 7-10. *rooms.js high-level architecture*

rooms.js, rooms.db and rooms.js-client together combine a light-weight back-end/front-end libraries built to stream live data and solve problems related to real-time communications.

To start a new project, open WebStorm and select "Create New Project," then select "Node.js Express App." Name the project "rooms". Lastly, click the "Create" button.

Next, open the Terminal in WebStorm and run the following commands:

```
$ npm install roomsjs rooms.db http  --save-dev
```

We will be using Mongoose as the database connector:

```
$ npm install mongoose --save-dev
```

If you didn't install Bower in Chapter 1, you can run the following command prior to installing the rooms.js-client to install Bower:

```
$ npm install -g bower
```

Next, install the front-end client:

```
$ bower install roomsjs-client
```

Next, we want to add app.js as an entry point, since we will be configuring the server and connection there instead of using "bin/www":

1. Click "Run/Debug configurations" ➤ "Edit configurations..." (Figure 7-11).

Figure 7-11. *Edit configurations in WebStorm*

2. Next, click "Add new configuration" (plug symbol) and select "Node.js" (Figure 7-12).

Figure 7-12. *Add new configuration in run/debug wizard*

3. Name the configuration "app"

4. Set the working directory as [location of WebStorm Projects]/rooms

5. Set the "JavaScript file" field to "app.js" (Figure 7-13).

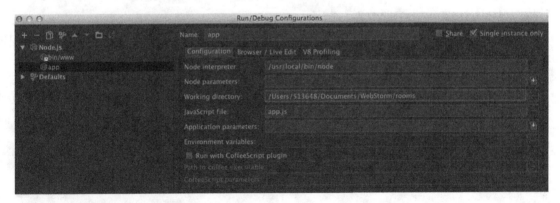

Figure 7-13. *Run/Debug configrations window in WebStorm*

184

Now copy the following into the "rooms/app.js" file (Listing 7-18):

Listing 7-18. app.js application entry point

```
'use strict';

var os = require('os'),
    rooms = require('roomsjs'),
    roomdb = require('rooms.db'),
    port = (process.env.PORT || 8081);

// create express server if needed
var express = require('express'),
    app = express().use(express.static(__dirname + '/client'));

// engine.io, socket.io
var server = require('http').createServer(app).listen(port, function () {
    console.log('Listening on http://' + os.hostname() + ':' + port);
});

// services
roomdb.setServices('services_sample/', app); // pass the app to get rest services or null

// set rooms
rooms = new rooms({
    isdebug : true,
    transporter : {
        type: 'engine.io', /* options: engine.io|socket.io|sockjs */
        server : server
    },
    roomdb : roomdb /* or null if db not needed */
});
```

We've created an Express server and set the services we will be using as well as passed reference of the server we will be using, decided on the Web Socket type and database.

If you try to run the application at this point, you will received an error message, since we didn't set any services yet but defined them here:

```
roomdb.setServices('services_sample/', app);
```

Creating Static Service

In this section, we will create a service that can interact with the database and create a Web Socket connection for us to use. What we've done so far is create a server and pass the app, then have the app scan the services folder for any services.

For services, we'll create a static data service that just returns names. First, create a folder in the project root and name it "services_sample." Next, create a "services_sample/getnames.js" file in the "services_sample" directory.

Copy Listing 7-19.

Listing 7-19. getnames.js service with static data

```
'use strict';
function getnames(data, dbconnectorCallBackToRooms) {
  var vo = ['Liam', 'Samuel', 'Noah'];
  dbconnectorCallBackToRooms(data, vo);
}
module.exports.getnames = getnames;
```

The code creates an array with names and passes it back to the database connector. The "dbconnectorCallBackToRooms" command returns the value object with the names "Liam," "Samuel," and "Noah."

To test the code, run "app" in WebStorm. You should see the Terminal output:

```
/usr/local/bin/node app.js
adding service method: getnames
created rest API: /getnames
Listening on http://[computer name]:[port]
```

Navigate to a browser and give it a try:

```
http://localhost:8081/getnames
```

See Figure 7-14.

```
["Liam","Samuel","Noah"]
```

Figure 7-14. *rooms.js getnames service*

This example is simple in nature, but it shows you how to create a service and how the app can return the data from any data provider you want.

Creating MongoDB Service

In the next section, we can connect to an actual mongo database and insert and read data. To do so, all we need to do is define the data source we will be connecting to. In app.js, add the following line after we set the services:

```
roomdb.connectToDatabase('mongodb', 'mongodb://localhost/usercollection', {});
```

Listing 7-20 provides the updated code for app.js.

Listing 7-20. app.js include connection to Mongo database

```
'use strict';

var os = require('os'),
    rooms = require('roomsjs'),
    roomdb = require('rooms.db'),
    port = (process.env.PORT || 8081);

// create express server if needed
var express = require('express'),
    app = express().use(express.static(__dirname + '/client'));

// engine.io, socket.io
var server = require('http').createServer(app).listen(port, function () {
    console.log('Listening on http://' + os.hostname() + ':' + port);
});

// services
roomdb.setServices('services_sample/', app); // pass the app to get rest services or null
roomdb.connectToDatabase('mongodb', 'mongodb://localhost/usercollection', {});

// set rooms
rooms = new rooms({
    isdebug : true,
    transporter : {
        type: 'engine.io', /* options: engine.io|socket.io|sockjs */
        server : server
    },
    roomdb : roomdb /* or null if db not needed */
});
```

In services, create a service to insert data and name the file "services_sample/insertchatmessage.js". (Listing 7-21). The service will be creating a connector to connect to the database and create the schema (if it does not exist already) then enter chat message and lastly, display the existing message.

Listing 7-21. insertchatmessage service

```
'use strict';

function insertchatmessage(data, dbconnectorCallBackToRooms) {
  var connector = this.getConnector(),
    Chat;

  if (connector.isModelExists('Chat')) {
    Chat = connector.getModel('Chat');
  } else {
    var schema = connector.setSchema({
      chatMessage: 'string',
      roomId: 'Number',
      gravatar: 'string',
      email: 'string',
```

```
      userName: 'string'
    });
    Chat = connector.setModel('Chat', schema);
  }

  var chatMessage = new Chat({
    chatMessage: data.params.chatMessage,
    roomId: data.params.roomId,
    gravatar: data.params.gravatar,
    email: data.params.email,
    userName: data.params.userName
  });

  chatMessage.save(function (err) {
    if (err) {
      console.log('error' + err.message);
    } else {
      Chat.find(function (err, messages) {
        if (err) {
          console.log('error getting messages: ' + err.message);
        }
        dbconnectorCallBackToRooms(data, messages);
      });
    }
  });
}
module.exports.insertchatmessage = insertchatmessage;
```

To test the service, rerun the app.

When you rerun the app, you should see the new service we have added in the run output:

```
/usr/local/bin/node app.js
adding service method: getnames
created rest API: /getnames
adding service method: insertchatmessage
created rest API: /insertchatmessage
Listening on http://[computer name]:[port]
```

To see the code in action, call the service in the browser:

```
http://localhost:8081/insertchatmessage?chatMessage=test&roomId=1&email=test@example.
com&userName=eli
```

Ensure MongoDB is still open. As you may recall, we ran mongod by typing "mongod" in the command line in Terminal.

```
$ mongod
```

Creating a MongoDB GUI Client

In order to mange MongoDB more easily, it's recommended to download a GUI tool such as mongoclient in order to view the data entered.

```
https://github.com/rsercano/mongoclient
```

The link to download the OSx software is at the bottom of the page:

```
https://github.com/rsercano/mongoclient/releases/download/1.2.2/osx-portable.zip
```

Move the software to the "Applications" folder or your favorite software location. To create a connection to the local database, click "connect" from the right top corner, select "Create New," and fill in the following information:

Connections:

1. Connection Name: local

2. Hostname: localhost

3. Port: 27017 (default)

4. DB Name: usercollection

Select "Save changes," as shown in Figure 7-15.

Figure 7-15. MongoClient connect wizard

Select "Connect Now." Under the "Collections" item in the left-hand sidebar, you should be seeing "chats," which is the data collection we just created using the "insertchatmessage" service. Click the "chats" collection and click the "execute" button, leaving all the default form settings in place.

Connect Front-End Application to Service

Now that we know how to create services, we can create front-end code to consume the data into our app. room.js comes with predefined examples for creating a front-end app for Angular, Engine.IO, Socket.IO, or SockJS. To get started:

1. Copy "bower_components/roomsjs-client/client" to the "rooms" root directory:

```
$ cp -rf bower_components/roomsjs-client/client ~/WebstormProjects/rooms
```

2. Rerun "app.js."

3. Open a few instances of the examples:

```
$ Open http://[computer name]:[port]/examples/engineio/
```

Look at the console and click "get results." You will be able to see the data from the service being retrieved (Figure 7-16).

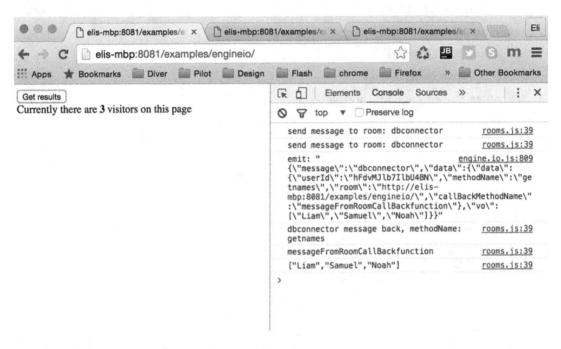

Figure 7-16. *Engine.IO example connecting to service getnames*

As we open more instances of our app, we can see how we are able to consume the data from Engine.IO to determine how many users are connected to our room. Once we click "get results," we can connect to our room to retrieve the data from the service we created.

Open "client/examples/engineio/index.html" and take a look at the code (Listing 7-22).

Listing 7-22. Retrieved data

```html
<html>
<head>
  <script src="http://code.jquery.com/jquery-1.10.1.min.js"></script>
  <script type="text/javascript" src="libs/engine.io.js"></script>
  <script type="text/javascript" src="../../dist/libs/rooms.js"></script>
  <script type="text/javascript" src="libs/autostartcontroller.js"></script>
<body>
<button id="getResultsButton">Get results</button>
<div id="visitors"/>
</body>
</html>
```

This example is adding the libraries we're using—jQuery, Engine.IO.js, rooms.js, and autostartcontroller.js—and including a button and a div for displaying the visitor count.

Take a look at "client/examples/engineio/libs/autostartcontroller.js" (Listing 7-23). The code includes methods to "connectUser" and "listenToUserActions". The code connects to a room, and once there are changes in the room, we listen to the change and update the front end.

Listing 7-23. autostartcontroller.js control rooms.js

```
'use strict';

var isAutoConnect = false,
  rooms,
  userId,
  roomName;

function listenToUserActions() {
  $("#getResultsButton").bind('click', function () {
    rooms.callDbConnector(userId, 'getitems', 'messageFromRoomCallBackfunction');
    rooms.callDbConnector(userId, 'getnames', 'messageFromRoomCallBackfunction');
  });
}

function connectToSocket() {
  var hostName = window.location.hostname,
    port,
    roomSetup,
    transporter,
    connectURL;

  userId = Rooms.makeid(16);
  roomName = window.location.href;
  port = (hostName !== '0.0.0.0' && hostName !== 'localhost') ? '80' : '8081';
  connectURL = 'http://' + hostName + ':' + port;

  roomSetup = {
    roomName : roomName,
    subscriptions : {
      RoomInfoVO : true
    }
  };

  rooms = new Rooms({
    roomSetup : roomSetup,
    userConnectedCallBackFunction : userConnectedCallBackFunction,
    userRegisteredCallBackFunction : userRegisteredCallBackFunction,
    numOfUsersInARoomCallBackFunction : numOfUsersInARoomCallBackFunction,
    stateChangeCallBackFunction : stateChangeCallBackFunction,
    debugMode : true
  });

  transporter = new eio.Socket('ws://localhost/');
  rooms.start({
```

```
    transporter : transporter,
    type : 'engine.io'
  });
}

function stateChangeCallBackFunction(data) {
  // impl
}

function userConnectedCallBackFunction() {
  if (isAutoConnect) {
    rooms.registerUser(userId);
  }
}

function userRegisteredCallBackFunction() {
  rooms.getNumberOfRegisteredUsersInRoom(userId);
}

function numOfUsersInARoomCallBackFunction(data) {
  var numofppl = data.size;
  document.getElementById('visitors').innerHTML = '<div style="font-size: 15px; top:
5px">Currently there are <b>'+numofppl+'</b> visitors on this page</div>';

  if (data.hasOwnProperty('register')) {
    sendMessageToLog('register userId: ' + data.register);
  } else if (data.hasOwnProperty('disconnect')) {
    sendMessageToLog('disconnect userId: ' + data.disconnect);
  }
}

function messageFromRoomCallBackfunction(data) {
  sendMessageToLog('messageFromRoomCallBackfunction');
  sendMessageToLog(JSON.stringify(data.vo));
}

function messageFromRoomCallBackfunction2(data) {
  sendMessageToLog('messageFromRoomCallBackfunction2');
  sendMessageToLog(JSON.stringify(data.vo));
}

function connectUser() {
  isAutoConnect = true;
  connectToSocket();
}

if (typeof jQuery !== 'undefined') {
  $(document).ready(function () {
    'use strict';
    connectUser();
```

```
    listenToUserActions();
  });
} else {
  sendMessageToLog('jQuery not loaded');
}
```

rooms.js with Angular

Similarly, we can create an Angular app that connects with rooms.js. Run this command a few times in order to open a few instances of the app:

```
$ open http://localhost:8081/examples/angular/
```

Take a look at the console in the browser. You can see the interaction of users entering and leaving the room:

> numberOfUsersInRoom message: 1

> disconnect userId: 0r1sO64uyQGIl42m

The app entry point index.html is located here: "client/examples/angular/index.html" (Listing 7-24). This loads all the libraries we will be using: Engine.IO, Angular, rooms and angular-rooms.

Listing 7-24. rooms.js utilizing Angular index.html page

```html
<!doctype html>
<html ng-app="myModule">
<head>
</head>

<body>
<script type="text/javascript" src="../engineio/libs/engine.io.js"></script>
<script src="http://code.angularjs.org/1.0.6/angular.min.js"></script>
<script type="text/javascript" src="../../dist/libs/rooms.js"></script>
<script src="angular-rooms.js"></script>
<script src="scripts/app.js"></script>
</body>
</html>
```

In the angular app, we define the module we will be using and create a connection; see "client/examples/angular/scripts/app.js" (Listing 7-25).

Listing 7-25. Defining module and creating a connection

```javascript
angular.module('myModule', ['rooms'])
  .run(['roomsGateway', function (roomsGateway) {
    'use strict';
    roomsGateway.connectToGateway('ws://localhost:8081/', true);
  }]);
```

angular-rooms (see "client/examples/angular/angular-rooms.js"), is where the heavy lifting is happening. It's similar to what we've done in autostartcontroller.js; we create a room, connect to it, and receive messages.

node-email-templates Library

Sending emails is a crucial and common task that is needed when creating a service, and there are many template libraries out there. One of the more popular ones is "node-email-templates." Visit the project here:

https://github.com/niftylettuce/node-email-templates

It allows us to integrate a template with popular template engines and services. To get started, install the following libraries into the project:

```
$ npm install email-templates async ejs node-sass -save-dev
```

To create an example, we will be creating a service that loads an email template we can use to send emails. Create a new service here: "services_sample/newsletter.js" (Listing 7-26).

Listing 7-26. Newsletter service

```
'use strict';
function newsletter(data, dbconnectorCallBackToRooms) {

    var EmailTemplate = require('email-templates').EmailTemplate
    var path = require('path')

    var templateDir = path.join(__dirname, '../templates', 'newsletter')

    var newsletter = new EmailTemplate(templateDir)
    var user = {name: 'Joe', pasta: 'spaghetti'}
    newsletter.render(user, function (err, result) {
        // result.html
        // result.text
    })

    var async = require('async')
    var users = [
        {name: 'John', email: 'john@aol.com'},
        {name: 'Jane', email: 'jane@aol.com'}
    ]

    async.each(users, function (user, next) {
        newsletter.render(user, function (err, result) {
            if (err) return next(err)

            result.subject = user.name + ' newsletter email';
            console.log(result);
            // send an email via a service
        })
    }, function (err) {
        console.log('error');
        console.log(err);
    })

    dbconnectorCallBackToRooms(data, 'sending emails to users');
}

module.exports.newsletter = newsletter;
```

This service is based on the example "node-email-templates" provided on their GitHub landing page. It cycles through an array of users and creates a template HTML email using the data. Then, we can set the email. In a real life example, we can easily wire our MongoDB into this service, so we pull the data from the database instead of a static variable.

Next, add these three pages to the "templates/newsletter" folder: html.ejs, style.scss, and text.ejs:

1. "templates/newsletter/html.ejs" is the HTML template. Notice that it expects "name" to be passed.

```
<h1>Hi there <%= name %></h1>
```

2. "templates/newsletter/style.scss" utilizes SASS (Syntactically Awesome Style Sheets). It uses "common.scss" and sets some properties:

```
@import '../common';

body {
  background-color: #ddd;
  color: white;
}

h1 {
  text-align: center;
}
```

3. "templates/newsletter/text.ejs" is a text version of "html.ejs" stripted out of any HTML tags.

```
Hi there <%= name %>.
```

Lastly, we want to create a global "common" SASS-style "templates/_common.scss" that we can utilize with any template we will be using:

```
h1 {
  font-family: 'Avenir Next', sans-serif;
}
```

That's it! Rerun the app, and once we navigate to the new service we've created, we can see in the Node.js console that the email template is being generated.

```
$ open http://localhost:8081/newsletter
```

Here's the Node.js console output for our example:

```
{ html: '<h1 style="font-family: \'Avenir Next\', sans-serif; text-align: center;">Hi there
John</h1>',
  text: 'Hi there John.',
  subject: 'john@aol.com newsletter email' }
{ html: '<h1 style="font-family: \'Avenir Next\', sans-serif; text-align: center;">Hi there
Jane</h1>',
  text: 'Hi there Jane.',
  subject: 'jane@aol.com newsletter email' }
```

From here, we can wire it up to a mail service, such as "nodemailer" (`https://github.com/nodemailer/nodemailer`).

Summary

In this chapter, we covered the process of creating services utilizing Node.js and ExpressJS. We created a new project in WebStorm, installed Express, and created a Hello World Express application. We covered the Express Generator Tool and set up a simple Express GET / POST service, then we added MangoDB database integration to the mix, installed MongoDB, started the MongoDB server, and created a database. After that, we integrated and read the results from MongoDB into our Express app and viewed the database using the command line and a mongoclient GUI.

In this chapter, we also covered Socket.IO, Engine.IO, and the integration of Express and these transporters. We updated the users service to include Socket.IO and retrieved a Socket.IO event using MongoDB results. We also used rooms.js to easily create services that can consume data from any CDN. Lastly, we took a look at creating templates utilizing both PugJS and node-email templates. In the next chapter, we will be covering AngularJS SEO.

CHAPTER 8

■ ■ ■

AngularJS SEO

In previous chapters, we covered the process of building an AngularJS application from front-end to back-end services. It's easy to see why AngularJS is popular, with its millions of available libraries, ease of use, and ability to build code that can be deployed on any device. However, many developers and companies still refuse to use AngularJS due to a lack of understanding, SEO and thought that AngularJS can not be crawled by search engines the same as other HTML static pages. In this chapter, we will walk you through the steps of how to set your site to be SEO friendly, so that the robots can crawl and display the pages as if you built a purely HTML site. Sure, Google has updated their crawler and can now execute JavaScript, but other search crawlers, as well as social media web sites, still crawl pages after being rendered by JavaScript, so you will still need to create a static HTML page for the best SEO results.

Config AngularJS Redirect Settings

The redirect happens in your AngularJS apps when using the hashbang "#!" tag in your route. This is a common practice; you can see large sites such as Twitter doing the same.

Using Twitter as an example, pick a user and add the "hashbang" tag:

```
http://twitter.com/#!/EliScripts
```

This will redirect you to http://twitter.com/EliScripts.

Start a New AngularJS Seed Project

To get started, open WebStorm and create a new "angular-seed" project.
As you may recall:

1. "Create New Project" ➤ "AngularJS"

2. Call the project "SEOTester" and click "Create."

3. Open the WebStorm Terminal window (bottom left corner) and run these two commands: "npm install" and "npm start".

4. Open a separate terminal by clicking the plus sign ("New Session") and type the following command: "open http://localhost:8000".

That's it. You should see the same page with the tabs we created in Chapter 5 (Figure 8-1).

© Elad Elrom 2016
E. Elrom, *Pro MEAN Stack Development*, DOI 10.1007/978-1-4842-2044-3_8

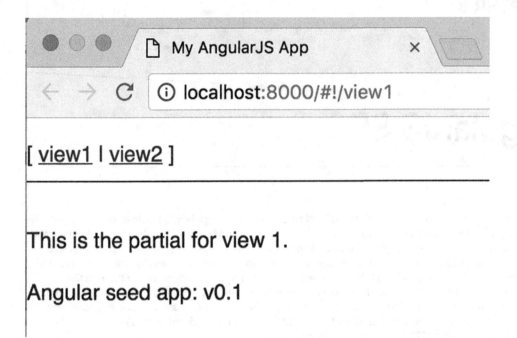

Figure 8-1. *"angular-seed" landing page: index.html*

Now that we have a seed project, we will be following this process:

1. Change the AngularJS project to use HTML5 routing mode.

2. Create a snapshot of your pages.

3. Redirect the pages to the static snapshot.

4. Submit the pages to search engines.

AngularJS HTML Mode and Hashbang

AngularJS offers Hashbang and HTML5 routing modes.

Out of the box, AngularJS seed projects use Hashbang mode. You can try it yourself by redirecting to the following URL: http://localhost:8000/#!/view1

The first step is to update how AngularJS routes pages so that it redirects a page without the hashbang. The URL will look like this: localhost:8000/view1.

To do so:

Open SEOTester/app/app.js and you will see the $locationProvider with the hashPrefix('!') attached:

```
config(['$locationProvider', '$routeProvider', function($locationProvider, $routeProvider) {
  $locationProvider.hashPrefix('!');

  $routeProvider.otherwise({redirectTo: '/view1'});
}]);
```

The $location service is the API used by AngularJS to redirect our app based on the URL. $location API can be used to watch URL changes, history links, and back and forward buttons. It is similar to the "window. location" in JavaScript, but with some extra capabilities for HTML5. You can learn more about the $location API in AngularJS docs: `https://docs.angularjs.org/guide/$location`

Looking at the app.js, the code looks for a Hashbang tag and redirects accordingly—otherwise it would use the default view: "view1." You can confirm this by typing the root URL, `http://localhost:8000/`, which redirects to view1: `http://localhost:8000/#!/view1`.

We want to update the URL and remove the Hashbang for a more standard URL (HTML5 mode). The first step is to set your app.js for HTML5 mode. It's better to use a URL that includes a description of the product or article than just an item ID. Google search engine Page Rank (PR) formula published that they give priority to sites with a URL that hits the keywords you will want to promote on your page.

In fact, according to Google, "Some users might link to your page using the URL of that page as the anchor text. If your URL contains relevant words, this provides users and search engines with more information about the page than an ID or oddly named parameter would (2)." See: `http://static.googleusercontent.com/media/www.google.com/en/us/webmasters/docs/search-engine-optimization-starter-guide.pdf`

The link above is the Engine Optimization Starter guide. I encourage you to read it if you plan on taking SEO seriously.

The first step is setting the AngularJS $location API with "html5Mode" to "true" in "app/app.js":

```
$locationProvider.html5Mode(true).hashPrefix('!');
```

Change the complete "app/app.js" location configuration tag from:

```
config(['$locationProvider', '$routeProvider', function($locationProvider, $routeProvider) {
    $locationProvider.hashPrefix('!');

    $routeProvider.otherwise({redirectTo: '/view1'});
}]);
```

To the following:

```
config(['$locationProvider', '$routeProvider', function($locationProvider, $routeProvider) {
    $locationProvider.html5Mode(true).hashPrefix('!');
    $routeProvider.otherwise({redirectTo: '/view1'});
}]);
```

By default, "html5Mode" requires the use of <base href="/" /> in the header, so add that to your code inside of the "index.html" file. We also want to give the search engines instruction to look for the Hashbang in the URL.

Consequently, the "SEOTester/app/index.html" file should include these two lines inside of the header tag:

```
<head>
        <base href="/" />
                <meta name="fragment" content="!">
</head>
```

Next, we want to add a forward slash ("/") to all of the links in our app—otherwise, it will add the link URL at the end of the address bar. On the index.html page, change from:

```
<body>
...
    <li><a href="#!/view1">view1</a></li>
    <li><a href="#!/view2">view2</a></li>
...
</body>
```

To:

```
<body>
...
    <li><a href="/#!/view1">view1</a></li>
    <li><a href="/#!/view2">view2</a></li>
...
</body>
```

Now you are able to test the HTML5 mode by opening the index page again. In the WebStorm Terminal, type:

```
$ open http://localhost:8000
```

As you can see, it has redirected the page to "localhost:8000/#!/view1," then the page was redirected to "localhost:8000/view1" (Figure 8-2).

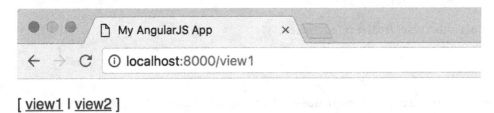

Figure 8-2. *Address bar without hashbang*

Now that we are using the HTML5 mode, we can set routing with SEO-friendly URLs. Open "SEOTester/app/view1/view1.js" and add the following route provider command:

```
$routeProvider.when('/view1/:id/:date/:title', {
  templateUrl: 'view1/view1.html',
  controller: 'View1Ctrl'
});
```

It's common practice to send end users to a specific URL, passing information such as product ID and date. Our app will be able to query the database and render results. The title we are adding is not necessary, since we already passed a product ID, but it will make things more search-engine friendly. Your complete view1/view1.js should look like Listing 8-1.

Listing 8-1. view.js adding a redirect for a URL with information

```
'use strict';

angular.module('myApp.view1', ['ngRoute'])

.config(['$routeProvider', function($routeProvider) {
  $routeProvider.when('/view1', {
    templateUrl: 'view1/view1.html',
    controller: 'View1Ctrl'
  });
  $routeProvider.when('/view1/:id/:date/:title', {
    templateUrl: 'view1/view1.html',
    controller: 'View1Ctrl'
  });
}])

.controller('View1Ctrl', [function() {

}]);
```

Now you can open the following URL:

```
http://localhost:8000/#!/view1/1/08-05-2016/some_title
```

In our code, we redirected to the same view1.html URL, and we can now extract the URL params inside of the controller. Inside of "view1/view1.js," update the controller to the following code:

```
.controller('View1Ctrl', ['$scope','$routeParams', function($scope, $routeParams) {
    $scope.id =   $routeParams.id;
    $scope.date = $routeParams.date;
    $scope.title = $routeParams.title;
}]);
```

Listing 8-2 shows the complete view1/view1.js content:

Listing 8-2. view1.js complete code extracting params

```
'use strict';

angular.module('myApp.view1', ['ngRoute'])

.config(['$routeProvider', function($routeProvider) {
  $routeProvider.when('/view1', {
    templateUrl: 'view1/view1.html',
    controller: 'View1Ctrl'
  });
  $routeProvider.when('/view1/:id/:date/:title', {
```

```
    templateUrl: 'view1/view1.html',
    controller: 'View1Ctrl'
  });
}])

.controller('View1Ctrl', ['$scope','$routeParams', function($scope, $routeParams) {
  $scope.id = $routeParams.id;
  $scope.date = $routeParams.date;
  $scope.title = $routeParams.title;
}]);
```

Now that we've set these params in the controller, we can update the view "app/view1/view1.html" and display these params:

```
<p>This is the partial for view 1. </p>
<p>Id: {{id}}</p>
<p>Date: {{date}}</p>
<p>Title: {{title}}</p>
```

Redirect to the URL once again:

```
http://localhost:8000/#!/view1/1/08-05-2016/some_title
```

We can now see that the param has passed to the view (Figure 8-3).

[view1 | view2]

_____

This is the partial for view 1.

Id: 1

Date: 08-05-2016

Title: some_title

Angular seed app: v0.1

Figure 8-3. *params passed to view*

As you can see, we have passed params in the URL. In the controller, we can call a service that will call a database to retrieve results.

Snapshot

Our next step is to create snapshots of the app pages and give these to the search engine. The snapshot will have a pure static HTML code that the search engines will understand and crawl. If we leave the code as is with the hashbangs and AngularJS code, the search engine won't be able to interpet the binding and variables we are passing, and the content will be missing on the page when the search engines crawl.

There are a few ways to do this, including using a hosted service that will cache your pages and serve them back to Google quickly.

Paid services will take care of a "PhantomJS" or a similar server as well as look after maintenance for a fee, or you can choose to do it on your own.

If you prefer to use a paid service, there are services such as "Prerender.io" (https://prerender.io/), available. Their service is free when you use up to 250 pages and reasonably priced after that.

Often, you will want to serve thousands of pages and customize the process, so it's good to know how to deploy the snapshots yourself.

This process can be broken down into the following steps:

- Install and configure a PhantomJS server
- Apply "angular-seo" script.
- Create a deployment script.
- Update the ".htaccess" file.
- Submit the URL to Google.

Install and Config PhantomJS

Our first step is to install the PhantomJS server.

■ **Note** PhantomJS is a headless WebKit (web browser) that is scriptable with a JavaScript API. It allows running a page without displaying the actual visual page on a browser.

A PhantomJS project can be seen here: https://github.com/amir20/phantomjs-node. To get started, install and run the following command:

```
$ sudo npm install -g phantom --save
```

The command will install PhantomJS globally. During installation, it will show the location of PhantomJS in the Terminal console:

```
Done. Phantomjs binary available at /usr/local/lib/node_modules/phantom/node_modules/
phantomjs-prebuilt/lib/phantom/bin/phantomjs
```

Copy the location, since we will configure the server to be accessible from any folder location on your machine. Call PhantomJS and be sure to point to the location of the libraries we have just copied:

```
$ /usr/local/lib/node_modules/phantom/node_modules/phantomjs-prebuilt/lib/phantom/bin/phantomjs
```

Once you run the command, the Terminal then replies with:

```
phantomjs>
```

This is a sign that PhantomJS is working correctly. Hit "control + c" to exit. It's a good idea to copy PhantomJS to be accessible without typing in the entire location of PhantomJS; you can do so by copying PhantomJS to your local bin folder:

```
$ sudo cp /usr/local/lib/node_modules/phantom/node_modules/phantomjs-prebuilt/lib/phantom/bin/
phantomjs /usr/local/bin/
```

Now, you can simply type "phantomjs" into the command line:

```
$ phantomjs
```

Hit "control + c" to exit.

Apply Angular-SEO Script

For our next step, we'll install an open source code called an "angular-seo" library, which will utilize PhantomJS to render our app in HTML code. You can learn more about "angular-seo" projects here: https://github.com/steeve/angular-seo
To install "angular-seo," we'll use Bower. In the "SEOTester" project in WebStorm, type the following command into the Terminal to install "angular-seo":

```
$ sudo bower install angular-seo --allow-root
```

Depending on the version you're using, you may receive the following message:

```
Unable to find a suitable version for angular, please choose one by typing one of the
numbers below:
    1) angular#1.3.13 which resolved to 1.3.13 and is required by angular-seo#d6b50c5b48
    2) angular#~1.5.0 which resolved to 1.5.8 and is required by angular-seed
    3) angular#1.5.8 which resolved to 1.5.8 and is required by angular-route#1.5.
```

At the time of writing, "Angular-seed" in WebStorm is utilizing version "0.0.0" and AngularJS version "1.5.8." Select option 2.
Now that installation is complete, you can test that the "Phantomjs" server is working properly with "angular-seo"; run the PhantomJS server on your machine and point to the "angular-seo" script and the local server:

```
$ phantomjs --disk-cache=no app/bower_components/angular-seo/angular-seo-server.js 8888
http://localhost:8000
```

If you're asked to allow incoming connections from PhantomJS, select "allow."
Hosts are pointing to localhost:8000. Now we need to test that the PhantomJS server is creating static pages and that we can point to a URL and serve pure HTML pages.
If everything is set correctly, once you go to your pages and replace the hashbang with _escaped_ fragment_, you should see an HTML version of your page, clear of any AngularJS or Ajax codes.
For instance, take the page we previously created:

```
http://localhost:8000/#!/view1/1/08-05-2016/some_title
```

Open up a browser and type the following URL in a second tab in the browser:

```
http://localhost:8888/?_escaped_fragment_=/view1/1/08-05-2016/some_title
```

This may take a minute to open up, since it's generating a static page. Now look at the page source of this page—in some browsers, you can add "view-source:" in front of the URL:

```
view-source:http://localhost:8888/?_escaped_fragment_=/view1/1/08-05-2016/some_title
```

As you can see, the entire code is static HTML, which the search engine is able to crawl.

For the data, you should see the static HTML code:

```
<p class="ng-binding ng-scope">Id: 1</p>
<p class="ng-binding ng-scope">Date: 08-05-2016</p>
<p class="ng-binding ng-scope">Title: some_title</p>
</div>
```

Deployment Script

Now that we can generate static pages, it's good practice to tie the snapshots deployment process with the deployment script, so on each deployment a new set of snapshots will be updated.

There are many ways to create the deployment script, but we will be using Grunt to create our snapshots and upload these files to the server. The Grunt is broken down to create files, change the base, and upload to the server.

If you did not install GruntJS during our earlier chapters, you can do so by typing the following command:

```
$ sudo npm install -g grunt grunt-cli
```

To get Hello World, we'll create a task to uglify and minify our app.js JavaScript file.

Create a Grunt build file, "SEOTester/Gruntfile.js," and copy the code in Listing 8-3.

Listing 8-3. Gruntfile.js complete Hello World code

```
module.exports = function(grunt) {
    // Project configuration.
    grunt.initConfig({
        pkg: grunt.file.readJSON('package.json'),
        uglify: {
            options: {
                banner: '/*! <%= pkg.name %> <%= grunt.template.today("yyyy-mm-dd") %> */\n'
            },
            build: {
                src: 'app/app.js',
                dest: 'build/<%= pkg.name %>.min.js'
            }
        }
    });
```

```
// Load the plugin that provides the "uglify" task.
grunt.loadNpmTasks('grunt-contrib-uglify');

// Default task(s).
grunt.registerTask('default', ['uglify']);
```

```
};
```

The Gruntfile.js file includes the following:

1. Loading the plugins we'll be using
2. Project configurations
3. Creating tasks

We will be using the uglify plugin, so first we want to install the plugin. In the WebStorm Terminal, type the following command:

```
$ sudo npm install grunt grunt-contrib-uglify --save-dev
```

Now we can run the default task:

```
$ grunt
```

After you run the command, you should get:

```
Running "uglify:build" (uglify) task
>> 1 file created.
```

Grunt has created a new file inside of "SEOTester/build/angular-seed.min.js." The app.js file was uglified and minified, and a comment was added. See part of the file below:

```
/*! angular-seed 2016-08-21 */
"use strict";angular.module("myApp",["ngRoute","myApp.view1","myApp.view2",
```

Now, let's continue by creating a task to handle the snapshots. These tasks will consist of the following:

1. Clean folder directory
2. Create a snapshot static page
3. Upload files to server

First, we want to install the plugins we will be using: a cURL command and a shell command. Lucky for us, there are modules for that functionality. Install the modules using the following commands in the WebStorm Terminal:

```
$ npm install grunt-curl grunt-shell --save-dev
```

Copy the complete code shown in Listing 8-4 to the "Gruntfile.js" file on the root of the project:

Listing 8-4. Gruntfile.js generate snapshots files, complete code

```
module.exports = function(grunt) {
    // Project configuration.
    grunt.initConfig({
```

```
        pkg: grunt.file.readJSON('package.json'),
        uglify: {
            options: {
                banner: '/*! <%= pkg.name %> <%= grunt.template.today("yyyy-mm-dd") %> */\n'
            },
            build: {
                src: 'app/app.js',
                dest: 'build/<%= pkg.name %>.min.js'
            }
        },
        shell: {
            clean_snapshots: {
                command: 'rm -rf /[PATH to project]/SEOTester/snapshots'
            },
            server_upload: {
                command: 'scp -r -i /[location to amazon key]/amazon-key.pem /[location to
project]/SEOTester/snapshots/* ec2-user@[server ip]:/var/www/html/[location of snap folder]'
            }
        },
        curl: {
            'snapshots/view1': 'http://localhost:8888/?_escaped_fragment_=/view1/1/08-05-
2016/some_title',
        }
    });

    // Load the plugin that provides the "uglify" task.
    grunt.loadNpmTasks('grunt-contrib-uglify');
    grunt.loadNpmTasks('grunt-curl');
    grunt.loadNpmTasks('grunt-shell');

    // Default task(s).
    grunt.registerTask('default', ['uglify']);
    grunt.registerTask('snap', ['shell:clean_snapshots', 'curl' /*, 'shell:snap_upload'*/
]);

};
```

Let's examine the code. First, we load the Grunt plugins. Add the following commands inside of the Grunt file:

```
grunt.loadNpmTasks('grunt-curl');
grunt.loadNpmTasks('grunt-shell');
```

Now we can register the task. We will call the task "snap":

```
grunt.registerTask('snap', ['shell:clean_snapshots', 'curl' /*, 'shell:snap_upload'*/ ]);
```

Notice that we have commented out the server upload for now, since we are going over the basics and will not actually upload the files to the server.

We'll create the actual tasks of cleaning the snapshot folder and use a cURL command to generate a snapshot.

```
    shell: {
        clean_snapshots: {
            command: 'rm -rf /[path to project]/SEOTester/snapshots'
        },
        server_upload: {
            command: 'scp -r -i /[path to amazon key]/amazon-key.pem /[path to project]/
            SEOTester/snapshots/* ec2-user@[server ip]:/var/www/html/[path to snap folder]'
        }
    },
    curl: {
        'snapshots/view1': 'http://localhost:8888/?_escaped_fragment_=/view1/1/08-05-
        2016/some_title',
    }
```

Be sure to replace the path to project, path to snap folder, and server IP address or public DNS address. We are deploying the snap files to the Linux server we created in Chapter 2.

You can ensure the connection to the Linux server is still working by using the SSH connection shortcut we set in ~/.ssh/config "$ ssh app." If you don't get a connection, make sure the server is still running in AWS and the SSH connection is open for your IP address. Refer to Chapter 2 for more details.

Keep in mind that for the script to work, you will need to still have two terminal windows open with the following commands:

```
$ npm start
$ phantomjs --disk-cache=no app/bower_components/angular-seo/angular-seo-server.js 8888
http://localhost:8000
```

We are downloading the files using cURL; Grunt has utilized the grunt-curl plugin for that. The task goes in and calls any page that we want to be crawled.

Lastly, take note that we want to upload these files to the server. We will be using a grunt-shell for this:

```
server_upload: {
    command: 'scp -r -i /[path to amazon key]/amazon-key.pem /[path to project]/SEOTester/
snapshots/* ec2-user@[server ip]:/var/www/html/[path of snap folder]'
        }
```

Run the Grunt command:

```
$ grunt snap
```

The console will show you the following responses:

```
$ grunt snap
Running "shell:clean_snapshots" (shell) task

Running "curl:snapshots/view1" (curl) task
File "snapshots/view1" created.

Done.
```

Also, notice that a new folder has been created with the name "snapshots," and it includes a snapshot of the view file, which includes the params we had passed through the URL (Figure 8-4).

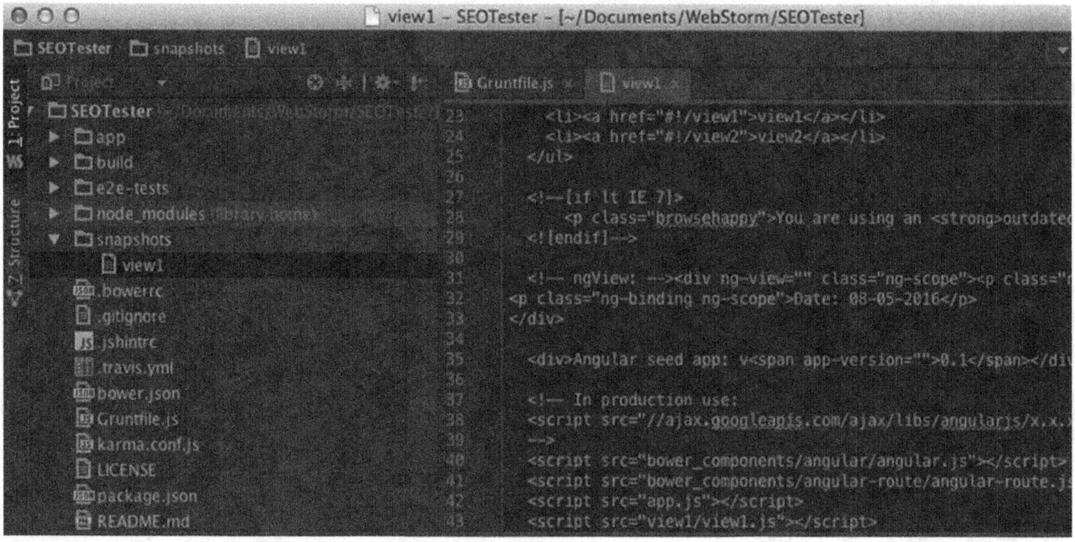

Figure 8-4. *Snapshots folder created with a static file*

When our app is created, we can use the server's upload tasks to automatically upload all of these snapshots to the production server.

Update .htaccess

Apache web server, which we installed on the AWS Linux server, is a one of the most common web servers used to deploy web app pages, and we have already created a task to upload our static snapshots to that server.

All we have to do now is modify the .htaccess file and redirect any files that include _escaped_fragment_ to the corresponding snapshot. We want our deployment server to redirect from:

```
http://[some domain name]/view1/1/08-05-2016/some_title
```

to:

```
http://[some domain name]/?_escaped_fragment_=/view1/1/08-05-2016/some_title
```

This will use the file "view1" we've created, instead of the complete URL structure. Here is the .htaccess code snippet:

```
RewriteEngine On
RewriteCond %{REQUEST_URI}   ^/$
RewriteCond %{QUERY_STRING} ^_escaped_fragment_=/?([^/]+(?:/[^/]+|))
RewriteRule ^(.*)$ /snapshots/%1? [P,L]
```

Lastly, we want any hashbang URL to be redirected to the HTML none hashbang URL:

```
<IfModule mod_rewrite.c>
    Options +FollowSymlinks
    RewriteEngine On
    RewriteBase /
    RewriteCond %{REQUEST_FILENAME} !-f
    RewriteCond %{REQUEST_URI} !^/$
    RewriteRule (.*) /#!/$1 [NE,L,R=301]
</IfModule>
```

Set .htaccess Redirect

Listing 8-5 is an example of a complete ".htaccess" code that handles the redirect.

Listing 8-5. .htaccess complete redirect script

```
<IfModule mod_rewrite.c>
  <IfModule mod_negotiation.c>
    Options -MultiViews
  </IfModule>

  RewriteEngine On

  RewriteCond %{QUERY_STRING} ^_escaped_fragment_=/?([^/]+(?:/[^/]+|))
  RewriteRule ^(.*)$ /snapshots/%1? [NC,PT]

  # Redirect Trailing Slashes...
  RewriteCond %{REQUEST_FILENAME} !-d
  RewriteRule ^(.*)/$ /$1 [L,R=301]
</IfModule>

<IfModule mod_rewrite.c>
    Options +FollowSymlinks
    RewriteEngine On
    RewriteBase /
    RewriteCond %{REQUEST_FILENAME} !-f
    RewriteCond %{REQUEST_URI} !^/$
    RewriteRule (.*) /#!/$1 [NE,L,R=301]
</IfModule>
```

That's it! The site should be set. You can confirm that it was successful by trying out links and seeing whether they have been redirected automatically, like this:

```
http://[some domain name]/?_escaped_fragment_=/view1/1/08-05-2016/some_title
```

AngularJS Metadata Tags

An important portion of an organic SEO is setting up the page's HTML metadata tags—but what is the page metadata tag?

■ **Note**　Organic SEO is achieving high search engine placement/ranking in the unpaid section. You can achieve this by better understanding the search engine algorithm and applying principles that have proven to work.

The metadata tags are set as part of the <head> tag and are not visible to the end user, but they can provide search engines with information about your page. There are different types of metadata that you can include in each page, but the most well-known are title, description, and keywords. There are a few good practices to take into consideration regarding these metadata in order to achieve the best results possible.

The <meta> tag provides metadata with the HTML document. Metadata will not be displayed on the page, but will parse the machine. Meta elements are typically used to specify a page's description, keywords, the author of the document, when it was last modified, and other metadata.

You are able to either roll your own solution or use open source solutions.

We are not done here yet. You probably want to customize each page to have its own unique metadata for the best exposure. There are many ways to do this, but we will show you two possible approaches—creating your own solution using the service module and using a solution library.

Update Metadata Using a Service Module

We can create a service factory method to help us handle the page's metadata. Using a service module is great because it can provide us with a centralized script that will handle the data.

To get started, create a new service file and place it here: "SEOTester/app/components/services.js" (Listing 8-6).

Listing 8-6. Service factory to handle pages metadata

```
'use strict';

/* Services */

angular.module('myApp.services', [])
    .value('version', '0.1')
    .factory('Page', ['$rootScope', function ($rootScope) {

        var defaultTitle = 'defaultTitle',
            defaultDescription = 'defaultDescription',
            defaultKeywords = 'defaultKeywords';

        return {
            getDefaultTitle: function() {
                return defaultTitle;
            },
            getDefaultDescription: function() {
                return defaultDescription;
            },
            getDefaultKeywords: function() {
                return defaultKeywords;
            },
            setMeta: function(title, description, keywords) {
                $rootScope.meta = {
                    title: title,
                    description: description,
                    keywords: keywords
                }
            },
            setDefaultMeta: function() {
                $rootScope.meta = {
                    title: defaultTitle,
                    description: defaultDescription,
                    keywords: defaultKeywords
```

```
            }
        }
    };
}]);
```

As you can see, we can set default values for title, description, keywords, and any other metadata you may want. We can get these values and also set our own custom values via setMeta and setDefaultMeta functions, as well as retrieve each metadata value.

Now, include a reference to the service file we created in the app index.html page.

```
<script src="components/services.js"></script>
```

Also, bind the metadata values to the title, description, and keywords in the index.html "<head>" tag:

```
<title>{{meta.title}}</title>
<meta name="description" content="{{meta.description}}">
<meta name="keywords" content="{{meta.keywords}}" />
```

Next, add a reference to the service module in the "app.js" file:

```
angular.module('myApp', [
  'ngRoute',
  'myApp.view1',
  'myApp.view2',
  'myApp.version',
  'myApp.services'
]).
```

Now we can use the service in any of the view scripts. See the "view1/view1.js" controller script we're adding:

```
.controller('View1Ctrl', ['$scope', '$rootScope', '$routeParams', 'Page', function($scope,
$rootScope, $routeParams, Page) {


  Page.setDefaultMeta();
  console.log($rootScope.meta);

  $scope.id = $routeParams.id;
  $scope.date = $routeParams.date;
  $scope.title = $routeParams.title;
}]);
```

Test the results by opening the app again and inspecting the object we've placed at the console when we set the "console.log", console.log($rootScope.meta) in the view1 controller (Figure 8-5).

```
Object { title: "defaultTitle", description:          view1.js:18:3
"defaultDescription", keywords: "defaultKeywords" }
```

Figure 8-5. *Console log values showing at the inspector*

```
$ open http://localhost:8000
```

We can even build a custom solution where we pick the values out of our database. All we have to do is set the metadata in the controller to each page, or use the default values, in the "view1/view1.js" controller tag instead of what we have now: "Page.setDefaultMeta();" we can set the following:

```
Page.setMeta(title, description, Page.getDefaultKeywords() + hashtags);
```

And the hashtag variables can be fetched from an AngularJS service module. Don't copy that code—it's just for illustration purposes.

To actually see the values being parsed, we can create a snapshot and then look at the source file:

```
$ open http://localhost:8888/
```

You will see the default values we have assigned if you view the source file:

```
<title class="ng-binding">defaultTitle</title>
<meta name="description" content="defaultDescription">
<meta name="keywords" content="defaultKeywords">
```

Update Metadata with ngMeta

The service solution works fine, but there are a few other good solutions on GitHub, such as "ngMeta" (https://github.com/vinaygopinath/ngMeta) and "ui-router-metatags" (https://github.com/tinusn/ui-router-metatags) that can also be utilized for updating metadata.

We will install and utilize ngMeta. To set the module, follow these steps:

Start by installing the module using npm:

```
$ bower install ngMeta --save
```

Next, in the index.html file, add ngMeta script:

```
<script src="bower_components/ngMeta/dist/ngMeta.min.js"></script>
```

Your complete code should appear as follows:

```
<script src="bower_components/angular/angular.js"></script>
<script src="bower_components/angular-route/angular-route.js"></script>
<script src="app.js"></script>
<script src="view1/view1.js"></script>
<script src="view2/view2.js"></script>
<script src="components/version/version.js"></script>
<script src="components/version/version-directive.js"></script>
<script src="components/version/interpolate-filter.js"></script>
<script src="components/services.js"></script>
<script src="bower_components/ngMeta/dist/ngMeta.min.js"></script>
```

Now, for the <head> metadata, replace the title, description, and keywords with the following:

```
<title>{{ngMeta.title}}</title>
<meta property="og:type" content="{{ngMeta['og:type']}}" />
```

```
<meta property="og:locale" content="{{ngMeta['og:locale']}}" />
<meta name="author" content="{{ngMeta.author}}" />
<meta name="description" content="{{ngMeta.description}}" />
```

Then, add "ngMeta" to the modules in app.js and set the default values:

```
'use strict';

// Declare app level module which depends on views, and components
angular.module('myApp', [
  'ngRoute',
  'myApp.view1',
  'myApp.view2',
  'myApp.version',
  'ngMeta'
]).
config(['$locationProvider', '$routeProvider', 'ngMetaProvider', function($locationProvider,
$routeProvider, ngMetaProvider) {
  $locationProvider.html5Mode(true).hashPrefix('!');
  $routeProvider.otherwise({redirectTo: '/view1'});

    ngMetaProvider.useTitleSuffix(true);
    ngMetaProvider.setDefaultTitle('Fallback Title');
    ngMetaProvider.setDefaultTitleSuffix(' - the best site');
    ngMetaProvider.setDefaultTag('author', 'Eli Elrom');
}])
.run(['ngMeta', function(ngMeta) {
  ngMeta.init();
}]);
```

Now we are able to use "ngMetaProvider" to set the default values and initialize the "ngMeta" module. We can do so by setting the metadata to each page, as shown below for "view1/view1.js":

```
'use strict';

angular.module('myApp.view1', ['ngRoute', 'ngMeta'])

.config(['$routeProvider', 'ngMetaProvider', function($routeProvider) {
  $routeProvider.when('/view1', {
    templateUrl: 'view1/view1.html',
    meta: {
      'title': 'title1',
      'description': 'description1'
    },
    controller: 'View1Ctrl'
  });
  $routeProvider.when('/view1/:id/:date/:title', {
    templateUrl: 'view1/view1.html',
    meta: {
      'title': 'title2',
      'description': 'description2'
```

```
    },
    controller: 'View1Ctrl'
  });
}])
.controller('View1Ctrl', ['$scope','$routeParams', function($scope, $routeParams) {
  $scope.id = $routeParams.id;
  $scope.date = $routeParams.date;
  $scope.title = $routeParams.title;
}]);
```

Lastly, install the "ng-inspector" Chrome extension to see the values:

```
http://ng-inspector.org/
```

Now we can see the changing metadata (Figure 8-6).

```
http://localhost:8000/#!/view1/1/08-05-2016/some_title
```

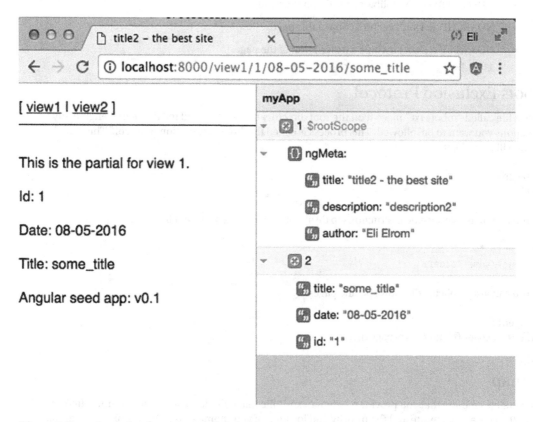

Figure 8-6. *ng-inspector showing metadata values*

Robots Instructions

There are instructions you can give to the search engines via the index.html meta tags. Additionally, you can provide the search engines with two files: "robots.txt" and "sitemap.xml." In fact, it's highly recommended that you create these files in your root folder.

Robots Meta Tags

Google recommends that you place instructions on your index.html page via meta tags. Normally, if you wanted to include the page in the index and follow any links, you would say:

```
<meta name="robots" content="index, follow">
```

Here is a handy list of instructions you can give to the robots:

- NOINDEX: Don't index the page.
- NOFOLLOW: Don't follow any links on the page.
- NOARCHIVE: Don't cache a copy of this page.
- NOSNIPPET: Don't include a description of the page.

Robots Exclusion Protocol

Create a file called "robots.txt," place it on the root directory of your site, and tell the search engine any instructions you want to be followed. This process is called the "robots exclusion protocol." The default file content will look like this:

```
User-agent: *
Disallow: /
```

You can then give specific instructions to disallow the crawling of certain pages:

```
User-agent: *
Disallow: /some-folder/
```

You can also explicitly disallow specific pages:

```
User-agent: *
Disallow: /some-folder/some-page.html
```

Sitemap

Search engines require that you provide a "sitemap.xml" file that includes instructions on how often you change the content of the site and the priority and location of your home page. Take a look at the sample code to visit your site on a daily basis and point to the site "view1" as your home page:

```
<?xml version="1.0" encoding="UTF-8"?>
<urlset xmlns="http://www.sitemaps.org/schemas/sitemap/0.9">
<url>
```

```
    <loc>http://some-site.com/view1</loc>
    <changefreq>daily</changefreq>
    <priority>1.0</priority>
  </url>
</urlset>
```

Social Media Meta Tags

It's also good practice to leave instructions for popular social media robots. Listing 8-7 gives you an example of instructions for Google Plus, Facebook, and Twitter.

Listing 8-7. Meta tags for social media

```html
<!-- Schema.org markup for Google+ -->
<meta itemprop="name" content="Site-name.com">
<meta itemprop="description" content="{{ meta.description }}">
<meta itemprop="image" content="//images/favicons/apple-touch-icon-120x120.png">

<!-- Twitter Card data -->
<meta name="twitter:card" content="summary" />
<meta name="twitter:site" content="@TwitterAccountName" />
<meta name="twitter:title" content="{{ meta.title }}">
<meta name="twitter:description" content="{{ meta.description }}">
<meta name="twitter:image" content="//images/favicons/apple-touch-icon-120x120.png" />
<meta name="twitter:url" content="http://some-site.com" />

<!-- Facebook data -->
<meta property="og:title" content="Site-name.com" />
<meta property="og:type" content="website" />
<meta property="og:url" content=https://Site-name.com />
<meta property="og:image" content=http://[icon path]/some-icon.ico />
<meta property="og:site_name" content="Site-name"/>
<meta property="og:description" content="{{ meta.description }}">
```

Notice that the data is binding to Angular $rootscope, so you can tie it to the values you set in "ngMeta" or the service metadata example I provided you with.

Webmasters

Webmaster is responsible for the submission of pages to search engine robots. Google is the most notable search engine out there, so we will be focusing on Google for the submission of our pages. However, it's good practice to educate yourself on every single search engine you are targeting for optimal results. Luckily, Google is very transparent in regards to the submission of pages; you can use their webmaster tool dashboard to see how Google robots will crawl your site and then see if anything requires changes. You will first need to create an account or sign in to the webmasters section: https://www.google.com/webmasters/.

Next, you can add a "property," meaning an app or a site (Figure 8-7).

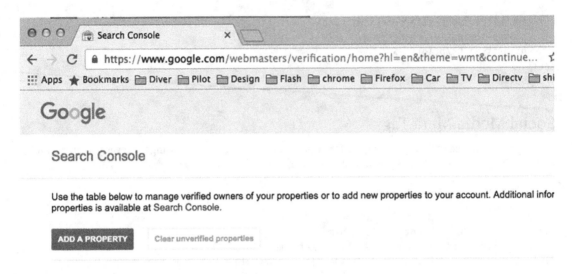

Figure 8-7. *Google Webmasters add a property*

A property can be a web site or an Android app. After verifying your properties, you can log back in and enter the following URL into the dashboard area:

https://www.google.com/webmasters/tools/dashboard

Submit Pages to Google

On the left menu, there is a link to "Crawl" and "Fetch as Google" (Figure 8-8).

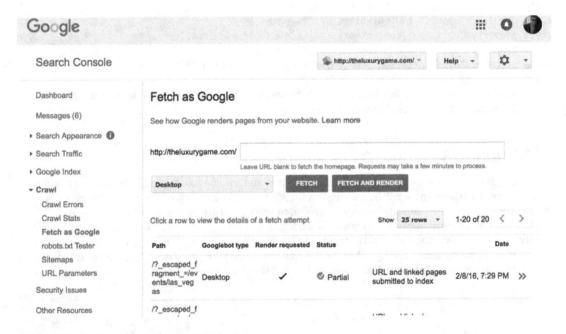

Figure 8-8. *Fetch as Google in Google Webmaster.*

In the "Fetch as Google" functionality, we are able to "Fetch and Render" the pages as a Google spider renders the page and displays any issues in reaching resources.

We would then submit the URL with the "escaped fragment" as the URL and our ".htaccess" will be redirected to the snapshots:

```
http://[somewebsite]/?_escaped_fragment_=/view1/1/08-05-2016/some_title
```

Ensure Successful Page Submission

After the submissions have been made, we can ensure that the page has been submitted to Google correctly and has been crawled by the search engine as expected, meaning you can check to see that your site's pages actually show up on Google. To do so, you'll use the following search:

```
https://www.google.com/#q=site:somesite.com
```

As a result, Google will return all pages that were crawled. Note that it may take Google few days to show the results.

Summary

In this chapter, we covered AngularJS SEO, configured AngularJS redirect settings, and began a new test AngularJS seed project. We covered the different options available in AngularJS to use HTML5 mode, as well as Hashbang mode. We learned how to create a snapshot of our pages by installing and configuring a "PhantomJS" server, applied "angular-seo" script and even applied a Grunt deployment script for each upload and snapshot of our pages. We also learned about how to set and redirect pages using the ".htaccess" file.

Additionally, we learned how to set AngularJS meta tags, update the meta tags using a service module, and update the meta tags with the "ngMeta" module. We studied the robot exclusion protocol and learned about setting specific instructions for search engines and social media robots.

Lastly, we learned about the Google Webmasters service, how to submit pages to Google robots, and how to ensure the pages' submissions were successful.

In the next chapter we will be covering build scripts.

CHAPTER 9

Build Scripts

When working on a JavaScript project, right from the beginning, we need to be mindful of the build scripts. However, with so many tools available, it is easy to get confused about what to use and when to use it.

As you may recall from Chapter 1, I introduced you to Grunt and Gulp, and we installed them via npm. Both Grunt and Gulp, while utilizing Node.js, help us to automate our tasks. These both require that we install plugins and create a build file, and both are command line packages that can enhance the capability of your local environment as well as the deployment servers, but what is the difference between these two tools? Additionally, what other tools can we utilize to do what is necessary in order to help us manage, automate, and deploy our project?

In this chapter, we will answer these questions and provide you with options for automating your build and getting it ready for deployment.

Browserify

As you have seen, there are tens of thousands of open source Node.js modules avaliable, and during previous chapters, we have used some of these examples and even created our own npm module. However, if we build a browser-based project such as AngularJS, we can't utilize these Node.js modules on the front-end code as is. Locating all of the modules in a project and bundling them into one file before we go to production is a common practice that reduces the end-user download time of loading large piles of JavaScript code to make our app work, as well as allowing us to prevent other developers from reverse engineering our code.

This is when Browserify can come in handy, solving our problem by bundling up all of these Node.js module dependencies, creating one bundle file that we can then use and include in all of the modules we need. Let's take a closer look to see how it works.

Create a New Node.js Module

First, let's create a New WebStorm Node Project. Open WebStorm and select "Create New Project" ➤ "Node. js Express App" ➤ "Create." You can name the project whatever you'd like, or simply leave the default name "untitled."

E. Elrom, *Pro MEAN Stack Development*, DOI 10.1007/978-1-4842-2044-3_9

The project is now created. Next, we'll create a Node.js module that will compute two numbers. To do so, create a folder named "compute" in the "node_modules" folder, and then create a file name: "index.js". The content of "node_modules/compute/index.js" will hold the following (see Listing 9-1):

Listing 9-1. "node_modules/compute/index.js" compute Node.js module

```
'use strict';
module.exports = function (x, y) { return x + y; }
```

Our node module computes two numbers and then returns the results. We can refactor the code by referencing a function for better readability, as shown in Listing 9-2.

Listing 9-2. "node_modules/compute/index.js" compute Node.js module refactored

```
'use strict';

function compute(x, y) {
    return x + y;
}
module.exports = compute
```

Additionally, add a "node_modules/compute/package.json" file and add the following minimum package.json code:

```
{
  "name": "my-compute-package",
  "version": "1.0.0"
}
```

Next, in the "app.js" entry file, add a reference to our Node.js compute module. At the end of the files, add two numbers and show the results:

```
var compute = require('compute');
console.log(compute(1, 2));
```

Now, to run the project, click the green "play" icon in the top right corner. The app is configured to run "bin/www," and you can see the results on the run console (see Figure 9-1).

Figure 9-1. *Compute module running in a Node.js project.*

Install Browserify

Now that we have our compute node module created, we can bundle it to be used in any JavaScript engine. Install Browserify globally via npm in the WebStorm command line window:

```
$ sudo npm install -g browserify
```

Compile a Browserify Bundle File

Next, to bundle our module, we will point to the compute module we created and tell Browserify to create a bundle file, which we'll name "bundle.js," like so:

```
$ browserify -r ./node_modules/compute/index.js > bundle.js
```

You can then confirm that a "bundle.js" was created in the root of the project. Given the way we instructed Browserify to compile the file, we will need to use the module file location in the AngularJS project we'll create shortly, add the bundle.js file as a reference in the index.html file, and then place the following statement in AngularJS:

```
var add = require('./node_modules/compute/index.js');
```

This does work, but to shorten the path and make the code align better with what we have in Node.js, we can also set the target name to "compute":

$ browserify -r ./node_modules/compute/index.js:compute ➤ bundle.js

---

■ **Note**   Browserify's "–r" option flag stands for "require." It requires that we place the module name. After doing so, we can then use the colon separator to set the target name.

Compiling with the target name will enable us to call "compute" in our AngularJS project instead of pointing to the file location:

```
var compute = require('compute');
```

Behind the scenes, Browserify compiled a "bundle.js" file for us that includes the code in Listing 9-3.

Listing 9-3. Portion content of "bundle.js"

```
require=(function e(t,n,r){function.............
'use strict';

function add(x, y) {
    return x + y;
}
module.exports = add
},{}]},{},[]);
```

Using a Node.js Module in an AngularJS Project

The end goal is to be able to use the "bundle.js" file we created in our AngularJS project. Let's go ahead and create an AngularJS project to use the bundle.js file we've just created. First, ensure you stop the Node.js app, since it will be holding up the same localhost port we need to use in our AngularJS project. You can stop the Node.js project from WebStorm by clicking the "Stop" icon on the Run console. See Figure 9-2.

Figure 9-2. *Stop "bin/www" icon in WebStorm*

I want to give you an additional handy tip to ensure that no Node.js projects are running in the background. If you have a project running and you run this command in the command line:

```
$ ps -ax | grep node
```

You will get a response showing any Node.js services running, such as:

```
59572 ?? 0:00.25 / WebStorm/untitled/bin/www
```

Now, to terminate the service, all you have to do is use the "kill" command with the service ID, which we received as a response:

```
$ kill -9 59572
```

That's it—now we are ready to create our AngularJS project.

1. In WebStorm, select "File" ➤ "New" ➤ "Project" ➤ "AngularJS" ➤ name the project "MyAngularProject" ➤ "Create." Select "New Window" so you can have both projects side by side.

2. Open the WebStorm Terminal window (bottom left corner) and run these two commands:

   a. $ npm install

   b. $ npm start

3. To view the project, open up a browser client:

   a. open http://localhost:8000

Now that we have an AngularJS project to work with, copy the "bundle.js" file we created in the Node.js project onto the AngularJS project "app/bundle.js." Next, reference the bundle file in our "index.html" file:

```
<script src="bundle.js"></script>
```

See Figure 9-3.

Figure 9-3. *Including bundle.js in index.html AngularJS project*

Now we can open "app/view1/view1.js" and add our script to the "view1.js" controller (Listing 9-4).

Listing 9-4. Using compute Node.js module in view1.js AngularJS project

```
.controller('View1Ctrl', [function() {
  var compute = require('compute');
  console.log(compute(3, 6));
}]);
```

All we're doing is adding a "require" to reference the module we're using and then sending the result of adding two numbers together to the console. Run the project or refresh the browser if you still have it open:

```
$ open http://localhost:8000
```

Inspect the element in the browser and look at the console messages. You should see the computed results of 9. See Figure 9-4.

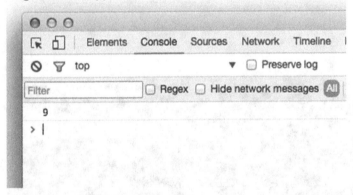

Figure 9-4. Console message in AngularJS project where compute module is used.

As you can see, this is powerful, considering Browserify not only allows us to bundle all of our modules together, but gives us the option to use tens of thousands of modules from Node.js.

Babelify

Many criticize JavaScript as second-class citizen due to its lack of object-oriented programming syntax and other deficiencies. JavaScript is evolving and, in fact, ECMAScript 2015 is the JavaScript standard that is also known as ES2015, or ES6. It holds the most significant update of the language since ES5, which was standardized back in 2009. However, many browser engines and other JavaScript runtimes such as Node.js have been implementing these features slowly, and not all the features from ES6 are available on all engines at the time of this writing. Babelify allows us to use ES2015 features today.

■ **Note**   ES6 transpiling is compiling code down to ECMAScript from 2009 (also known as ES5) so it can be backward compatible with JavaScript engines that don't yet support ES6.

Installing Babel

In the section below, we'll cover how to install Babel. In the same AngularJS project we created previously, install Babel CLI in the WebStorm command line and add a second window via "New Session" since we have "npm start" running, and install Babel via npm:

```
$ npm install babel-cli --save-dev
```

Next, we need to install "Babel 6 preset" for transpiling ECMAScript 6 locally, so that we can support all of the capabilities of ES2015:

```
$ npm install babel-preset-es2015 --save-dev
```

This download may take a while. Lastly, we will create ".babelrc" file in the root of the project that tells Babel that we are using ES2015:

```
{
  "presets": ["es2015"]
}
```

Setting Babel in WebStorm

Now that Babel is installed and configured, all we need to do is set a watcher so that the transpiling will happen automically via WebStorm and we won't need to compile the files every time. Click "command + ," to open the WebStorm preferences window and select "Tools" ➤ "File Watchers" ➤ "+" ➤ "Babel."

In the configuration window, set the Babel program location, which we have already installed: "node_modules/.bin/babel". See Figure 9-5.

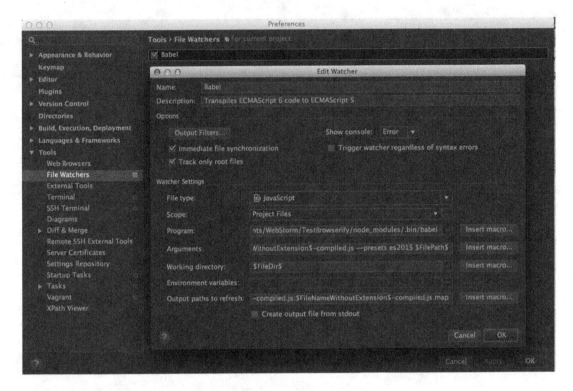

Figure 9-5. *Adding Babel File Watcher to WebStorm*

Notice that WebStorm, with its default settings, doesn't show ".bin" folders. You can navigate with the command line to view the contents of the folder, or check the "Show hidden files and directories" button in the "Select path" dialog box.

Writing ES6 Code

Now that we have Babel installed and configured and a watcher in place that will generate and compile files automatically for us, we are ready to do some coding; for example ES6 has a feature that will allow us to extend built-in JavaScript classes. Let's create a code that does just that. Add the code from Listing 9-5 into the " view1/view1.js" controller.

Listing 9-5. Extending Array JavaScript built in class

```
.controller('View1Ctrl', [function() {
    var compute = require('compute');
    console.log(compute(3, 6));

    class MyArray extends Array {
        constructor(args) {
            super(args);
        }
        speak() {
            console.log('I have ' + this.length + ' items');
```

```
    }
  }

var arr = new MyArray();
arr[1] = 12;
arr.length == 2;
arr.speak();
```

```
}]);
```

The code extends the built-in array and adds a method called "speak" that tells us how many items the array contains. We've created a basic example, but you can imagine how this feature will be useful in cases where you would want to create custom filtering and sorting of an array.

Once you save the file, you can see that WebStorm is executing the Babel task at the footer of WebStorm—see Figure 9-6.

Figure 9-6. *WebStorm executing Babel task*

We have extended the array's built-in class and added a method called "speak." Once we create a new instance of the class and use the new method, we can then open http://localhost:8000 and view the messages in the console to confirm that we're receiving the message "I have 2 items."

As you can see, this is a powerful tool, and will allow us to utilize ES6 today. There is a PDF document online that lists all of the features in ES6: http://www.ecma-international.org/ecma-262/6.0/ECMA-262.pdf., which is the ECMA-262 6th Edition, of the ECMAScript 2015.

Grunt

We have installed and run Grunt tasks before. As you may recall, back in Chapter 8 we used Grunt to create a task that would then create a static snapshot of our pages that we then deployed to our server. Grunt is often used to automate common tasks that we need to run in order to get our code ready for production. Common operations before deployment include renaming files, uglifying (obfuscating) files, minifying files, bundling together all of our assests, and uploading all of our files to a server.

Grunt with a Babel Task

We can create a Grunt task that can be used to run our code through Browserify and Babelify, either by calling the task directly or by placing a watcher on it, so when we make changes to our files, Grunt handles what is needed behind the scenes. This saves us the headache of dealing with all of that individually on our own.

To get started, create a Grunt build file in the root of your AngularJS project, "Gruntfile.js", and copy the code from Listing 9-6.

Listing 9-6. Gruntfile.js Babel task

```
module.exports = function(grunt) {

    require('load-grunt-tasks')(grunt);

    grunt.initConfig({
        babel: {
            options: {
                sourceMap: true,
                presets: ['es2015']
            },
            dist: {
                files: {
                    'dist/app/view1/view1.js': 'app/view1/view1.js'
                }
            }
        }
    });

    grunt.registerTask(run-babel', ['babel']);
};
```

As you may recall, the "Gruntfile.js" file consists of loading the plugins we'll be using, setting the project configurations, and creating tasks.

In the code above, we are setting a task to compile the "app/view1/view1.js" file into the "dist/app/view1/view1.js" location while using the "babel" plugin.

Install Grunt Babel Plugins

Next, we need to install Grunt locally, as well as the plugins we will be using:

```
$ npm install grunt load-grunt-tasks grunt-babel --save-dev
```

Note that, depending on your Internet connection, this may take a while to download. Additionally, you'll need the "present es-2015" plugin to be installed, which I covered previously.

Run Grunt Babel Task

Now that we have our Grunt file ready and we've installed all of the plugins we need, all we have to do is run the root of the project the task we want in the command line:

```
$ grunt run-babel
```

The task will compile our "view.js" file. If you open up "/dist/app/view1/view.js," you can see the following ES6 code we've created:

```
class MyArray extends Array {
  constructor(args) {
    super(args);
  }
  speak() {
    console.log('I have ' + this.length + ' items');
  }
}
```

...is replaced with the following code that will work on all ES5 JavaScript engines:

```
var MyArray = function (_Array) {
  _inherits(MyArray, _Array);

  function MyArray(args) {
    _classCallCheck(this, MyArray);

    return _possibleConstructorReturn(this, (MyArray.__proto__ || Object.
getPrototypeOf(MyArray)).call(this, args));
  }

  _createClass(MyArray, [{
    key: 'speak',
    value: function speak() {
      console.log('I have ' + this.length + ' items');
    }
  }]);

  return MyArray;
}(Array);
```

Grunt Babelify & Browserify Task

Similarly, we can run a task that will Babelify and Browserify our code and watch for changes in the file. This can be achieved by utiltizing the following Grunt plugins:

```
$ npm install babelify grunt-browserify grunt-contrib-watch --save-dev
```

These plugins include "grunt-browserify" to compile the Node.js modules, the "babelify" module to write our ES6 code, and "grunt-contrib-watch" so that Grunt can watch for changes, just as WebStorm is doing.

The task will replace the command line we've created in order to build the "bundle.js" file and will then compile the ES6 code so that we can actually code ES6 in our Node.js module. See Listing 9-7.

Listing 9-7. Browserify, babelify, and watch for changes Grunt task

```
browserify: {
    dist: {
        options: {
            transform: ["babelify"]
        },
        files: {
            "./dist/bundle.js": ["./node_modules/compute/index.js"]
        }
    }
},
watch: {
    scripts: {
        files: ["./modules/*.js"],
        tasks: ["browserify"]
    }
}
```

The complete Grunt file code is below (see Listing 9-8).

Listing 9-8. Complete GruntJS code to run babel, browserify, babelify, and watch for changes

```
module.exports = function(grunt) {

    require('load-grunt-tasks')(grunt);

    grunt.initConfig({
        babel: {
            options: {
                sourceMap: true,
                presets: ['es2015']
            },
            dist: {
                files: {
                    'dist/app/view1/view1.js': 'app/view1/view1.js'
                }
            }
        },
        browserify: {
            dist: {
                options: {
                    transform: ["babelify"]
                },
                files: {
                    "./dist/bundle.js": ["./node_modules/compute/index.js"]
                }
            }
        },
        watch: {
            scripts: {
```

```
            files: ["./modules/*.js"],
            tasks: ["browserify"]
        }
    }
});

grunt.loadNpmTasks("grunt-browserify");
grunt.loadNpmTasks("grunt-contrib-watch");

grunt.registerTask("default", ["watch"]);
grunt.registerTask("build", ["browserify"]);
grunt.registerTask('run-babel', ['babel']);
};
```

Before you run the task, add the following files we created in the Node.js project, inside of our AngularJS project: "/node_modules/compute/index.js." As you may recall, all the Node.js module does is include a code that computes two numbers:

```
'use strict';
module.exports = function (x, y) { return x + y; }
```

Now we can build the "bundle.js" file using the build task:

```
$ grunt build
```

We can see the results in the command line, confirming that the task has been completed successfully.

```
Running "browserify:dist" (browserify) task
>> Bundle ./dist/bundle.js created.

Done.
```

Grunt Watch

As you have seen previously, we've utilized a "grunt-contrib-watch" plugin in the Grunt file:

```
        watch: {
            scripts: {
                files: ["./modules/*.js"],
                tasks: ["browserify"]
            }
        }
```

This task is used to watch for changes. It can replace the action of WebStorm, or we can use the built-in feature in WebStorm when we develop locally and then use Grunt for deployment.

In the Grunt file, we set the default task to utilize the watcher:

```
grunt.registerTask("default", ["watch"]);
```

To see the code in action, run the default GruntJS task in the command line:

```
$ grunt
```

```
In the command line, we can confirm that the watcher is in progress:
Running "watch" task
Waiting...
```

To cancel the watch task, click "command + c". Additionally, you can open the "dist/bundle.js" file and see the code that has been generated by Grunt for us automatically.

Gulp

Gulp is a rival task runner of Grunt. Let's take a look at the differences between the two, as well as another choice for you to use while creating tasks.

Differences Between Grunt and Gulp

1. **Coding**: Grunt is similar to Ant or Maven (if you've ever used these tools). It is configuring tasks, while Gulp is writing a JavaScript code that utilize plugins.

2. **Streaming**: Gulp offers streaming, so you end up with one simple file instead of dealing with multiple folders and files. Remember that we created a watch task in Grunt—it's not needed in Gulp, since it's a core functionality.

3. **Plugins**: Plugins in Gulp are more loosely coupled and aimed at solving a single task, whereas Grunt connects plugins to create a shared functionality, making Grunt more like a composition.

■ **Note**   In a nutshell, Gulp is a better tool, but Grunt has about 6,000 plugins (at the time of this writing) while Gulp only has about 2,700. Grunt having been around longer gives it a big edge.

In the end, it's more about your own preferences. If you have not used other automating tasks such as Ant or Maven, Gulp is probably a better choice, since it's just programming as opposed to configuring tasks. However, if you are already using Grunt, it may not be worth your effort to move to Gulp.

Installing Gulp

Although we installed Gulp back in Chapter 1, we haven't used it in this book yet, so let's see how the same tasks of Browserify, Babelify, and watching the file for changes will look in Gulp.

Previously, we installed a version of Gulp globally, so you can run it at any time:

```
$ sudo npm rm --global gulp
```

To ensure the old version of Gulp doesn't collide with "gulp-cli," let's install the latest "gulp-cli":

```
$ sudo npm install --global gulp-cli
```

Next, install Gulp locally and add a reference in package.json, devDependencies:

```
$ npm install gulp --save-dev
```

Creating a Gulp Task

Now that we have Gulp installed, we can create "gulpfile.js" at the root of our project. Gulpfile is the equivalent to Gruntfile. Both are written in JavaScript, but rather than configuring tasks, Gulp prefers code over settings configuration. See Listing 9-9.

Listing 9-9. Gulpfile talks to Browserify, Babelify and watch for changes

```javascript
var gulp = require('gulp');
var browserify = require('browserify');
var watchify = require('watchify');
var babel = require('babelify');
var sourcemaps = require('gulp-sourcemaps');
var source = require('vinyl-source-stream');
var buffer = require('vinyl-buffer');

function compile(watch) {
    var bundler = watchify(browserify('./node_modules/compute/index.js', { debug: true
    }).transform(babel));

    function rebundle() {
        bundler.bundle()
            .on('error', function(err) { console.error(err); this.emit('end'); })
            .pipe(source('build.js'))
            .pipe(buffer())
            .pipe(sourcemaps.init({ loadMaps: true }))
            .pipe(sourcemaps.write('./'))
            .pipe(gulp.dest('./build'));
    }
    if (watch) {
        bundler.on('update', function() {
            console.log('bundling');
            rebundle();
        });
    }
    rebundle();
}

function watch() {
    return compile(true);
};

gulp.task('build', function() { return compile(); });
gulp.task('watch', function() { return watch(); });
gulp.task('default', ['watch']);
```

The Gulpfile consists of setting references to all of the plugins we will be using, compiling our scripts, streaming, and watching for changes. Lastly, we will create a Gulp task to build and watch.

Installing Gulp Plugins

We have referenced Gulp plugins, but we haven't yet installed them, so let's go ahead and install all of the Gulp plugins we will be using, via npm:

```
$ npm install browserify gulp-sourcemaps vinyl-source-stream vinyl-buffer watchify babelify
--save-dev
```

Running Gulp Tasks

Now that we have the Gulp file and all of the plugins created, we can run the Gulp task. We will be using the default task, which is set up to watch for changes:

```
$ gulp
```

We can then confirm that everything is working. Take a look at a typical output result:

```
[15:47:54] Using gulpfile ~/Documents/WebStorm/[project name]/gulpfile.js
[15:47:54] Starting 'watch'...
[15:47:54] Finished 'watch' after 19 ms
[15:47:54] Starting 'default'...
[15:47:54] Finished 'default' after 4.78 ms
```

As you can see, streaming and watching is much simpler than with Grunt, and the coding was simply that of JavaScript, rather than a clumsy configuration file.

■ **Note**   To conceptually understand streaming in Gulp, think of our files passing through a pipe. At one or more points along that pipe, a task is done—for example, renaming files.

Webpack

We took a look at Grunt and saw the simplicity of Gulp, and we configured these tools to bundle our modules and allow us to do other tasks such as writing ES6 JavaScript code, but there are additional tools worth mentioning. Webpack and Browserify do pretty much the same thing, which is bundling our JavaScript modules to be used in a browser environment. Webpack does this more easily, since it doesn't need Grunt and Gulp or knowelge of Node.js. In fact, Webpack was built taking into account the deficiencies of Grunt/Gulp and Browserify. It's more "set it and forget it" when it comes to watchers. Let's take a look.

Installing Webpack

First, we must install Webpak globally via npm, just as we've done with the other tools:

```
$ sudo npm install webpack -g
```

Then, in the command line, pack the bundle the same way we did with Browserify:

```
$ webpack ./node_modules/compute/index.js bundle.js
```

The syntax was entry and output. We should get an output in the command line that looks like this:

```
Hash: be87e8b8b39b72caef48
Version: webpack 1.13.2
Time: 53ms
    Asset      Size  Chunks             Chunk Names
./bundle.js  1.45 kB       0  [emitted]  main
    + 1 hidden modules
```

As you can see, although both tools do practically the same thing, Browserify uses Grunt and Gulp with the help of installed plugins to get the job done, while Webpack includes all that you need, straight out of the box. In the end, deciding to use Webpack or the Browserify Grunt/Gulp combo boils down to personal preference and team experience. Teams that are unfamiliar with Node.js may find that it's better and easier to use Webpack.

Creating Webpack Config File

As mentioned previously, Webpack offers out-of-the-box features without the need to install anything else. For instance, Webpack acknowledges that assets such as CSS and images are dependencies of your project and treats them as such. As the deployment script becomes more complex, we will need a config file and will need to add loaders. Loaders are the preprocess files as you require() or "load" them and can add a task, or as Webpack calls it, "transform" them to a different language, such as CoffeeScript to Javascript. You can even create a pipeline and pass the files through that pipeline as you apply multiple transformation. That is similar to the tasks we saw in Gulp.

The config file is somewhat similar to the Grunt and Gulp file and is configured similarly to Grunt. In the root directory of the project, create a "webpack.config.js" file.

A basic "webpack.config.js" file holds the entry and output destination. See Listing 9-10.

Listing 9-10. Webpack minimalist config file

```
module.exports = {
    entry: './node_modules/compute/index.js',
    output: {
        filename: './bundle.js'
    }
};
```

The minimalist config file includes an entry file location and an output to help build our bundle file. Now, run the Webpack command and you'll receive the same results as we did in the previous command, where we included the entry and output location.

```
$ webpack
```

Webpack Watcher

Next, remember how we set the config file in order to watch for changes in Browserify. In Webpack, it's built out of the box, so all we have to do is set the watch flag:

```
$ webpack --watch
```

Or, in short, "w":

```
$ webpack --w
```

To cancel, just type "command + c". Alternatively, we can set the watch flag "watch: true" in the "webpack.config.js" configuration file—see Listing 9-11:

Listing 9-11. Adding watch flag to webpack.config.js

```
module.exports = {
    entry: './node_modules/compute/index.js',
    output: {
        filename: './bundle.js'
    },
    watch: true
};
```

Webpack Transpiling ES6 Code

Just as we used the "Babelify" module to write ES6 in Grunt and Gulp, we can do the same in Webpack. All we have to do is create a loader that will let Webpack know how to handle the ES6 code.

As you may recall, in "app/view1/view1.js," we coded our ES6 code:

```
class MyArray extends Array {
  constructor(args) {
    super(args);
  }
  speak() {
    console.log('I have ' + this.length + ' items');
  }
}

var arr = new MyArray();
arr[1] = 12;
arr.length == 2;
arr.speak();
```

Next, we need to install the Webpack loader and Babel through npm:

```
$ npm install babel-loader babel-core --save-dev
```

You have to have Babel installed. As you recall, we installed it previously:

```
$ npm babel-preset-es2015 --save-dev
```

Lastly, we need to config Webpack's "webpack.config.js" file in the root of the project, which needs to be set to use the loader, and configure the entry and output file location. See Listing 9-12:

Listing 9-12. Configure webpack.config.js to compile ES6 code

```
module.exports = {
    module: {
        loaders: [
            {
                test: /\.js$/,
                exclude: /node_modules/,
                loader: 'babel',
                query: {
                    presets: ['es2015']
                }
            }
        ],
    },
    entry: './app/view1/view1.js',
    output: {
        filename: './dist/app/view1/view1.js'
    }
};
```

Run Webpack via the command line "$ webpack" and you will see the output of Webpack in the terminal (Figure 9-7):

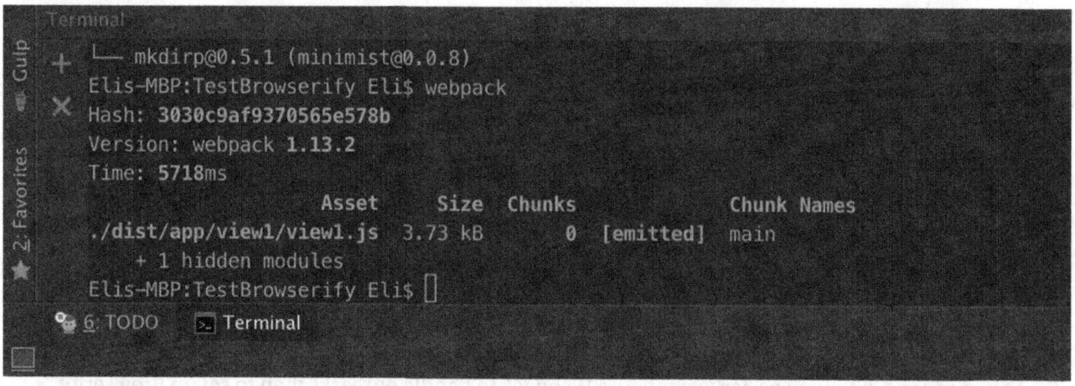

Figure 9-7. Webpack output transpiling ES6 code

Next, open the file in "/dist/app/view1/view1.js" to view the content. As you can see, it has compiled the file to ES5 code.

Webpack CSS Loader

Next, to allow Webpack to handle CSS, we will perform the same action as we did with Babel—we will add a CSS loader. We do so by installing a CSS loader and then a Style loader, via npm:

```
$ npm install css-loader style-loader --save-dev
```

Now all we have to do is add a reference in our "view1/view1.js" code to the CSS file at the top of the document:

```
require('../app.css');
```

Lastly, we need to add the loader to the Webpack config file. See Listing 9-13.

Listing 9-13. Configure webpack.config.js to compile ES6 code and CSS

```
module.exports = {
  module: {
    loaders: [
      {
        test: /\.js$/,
        exclude: /node_modules/,
        loader: 'babel',
        query: {
          presets: ['es2015']
        }
      },
      {
        test: /\.css$/,
        exclude: /node_modules/,
        loader: 'style!css'
      }
    ],
  },
  entry: './app/view1/view1.js',
  output: {
    filename: './dist/app/view1/view1.js'
  }
};
```

Now that we have the loader set up, all we have to do is run Webpack once again:

```
$ webpack
```

As you can see, it's much easier to configure Webpack to handle our tasks than to set up Browserify. Webpack's ease of use is especially significant in a team where the members are not familiar with Node.js, Grunt, and/or Gulp. In the next chapter, we'll have a more in-depth discussion as well as examples of Gulp, Grunt, Browserify, and Webpack so you can better understand the trade-offs.

Vagrant VM

In the previous sections of this chapter, we showed you how to bundle different tools in order to use the latest JavaScript ES6 today, as well as how to bundle modules, automate tasks, and watch for changes.

Once your environment is all set up, how neat would it be to be able to just fire up a script and the same environment is reproduced anywhere and for all the team members of the project? Vagrant VM does just that. We can fire up or, as Vagrant calls it, "Vagrant up" and everything will be installed and configured.

Installing Vagrant & Virtual Machine

At the time of writing, Vagrant 1.8.5 is the latest Vagrant version; download Vagrant from the following link:

```
https://www.vagrantup.com/downloads.html
```

Vagrant also requires a virtual machine. That could be VirtualBox, VMware, AWS, or others. We'll be using VirtualBox, since it's free at the time of writing. On a Mac OS X, the latest version is "VirtualBox 5.1.6 for OS X." It can be downloaded from the following link:

```
https://www.virtualbox.org/wiki/Downloads
```

Now that we have Vagrant and VirtualBox installed, all we have to do is initialize Vagrant. In your WebStorm command line, run this command:

```
$ vagrant init hashicorp/precise64
```

Notice that Vagrant has created a Vagrantfile in the root of the project. The Vagrantfile includes a description of machines and resources needed to run and the software to be installed. Next, fire up Vagrant:

```
$ vagrant up
```

A successful output looks like Figure 9-8.

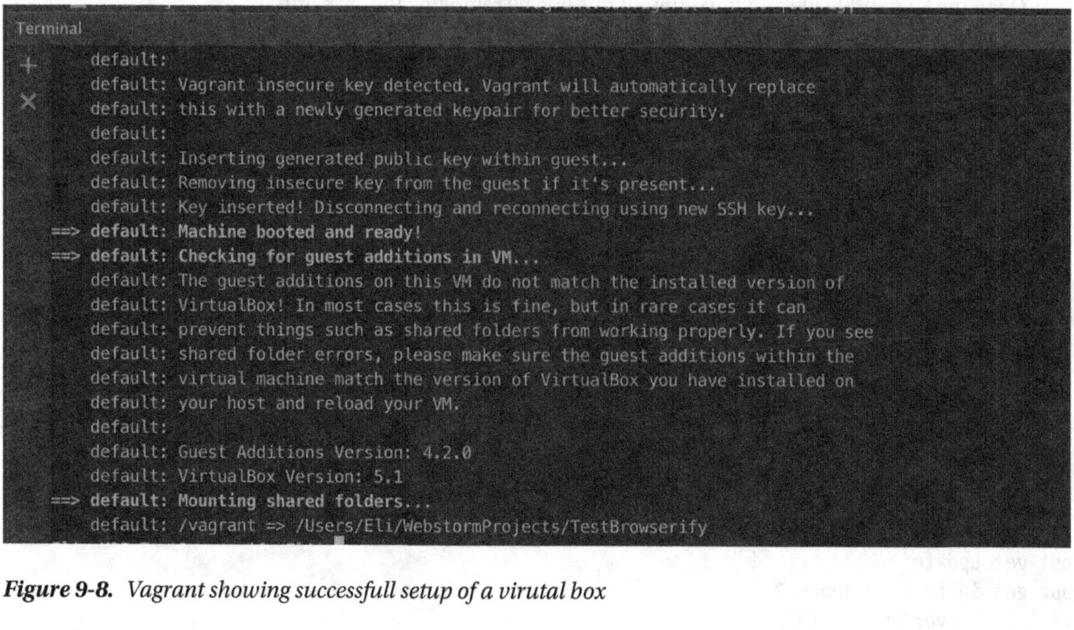

Figure 9-8. *Vagrant showing successfull setup of a virutal box*

Now we can SSH the virtual machine:

```
$ vagrant ssh
```

Once you SSH the virtual box, you can view all of the files we've downloaded by typing into the command line:

```
$ ls /vagrant
```

To exit the virtual box, simply type "exit":

```
$ exit
```

If at any time you make changes, type "reload":

```
$ vagrant reload
```

```
Or to reload and provision:
```

■ **Note "** Provision" in Vagrant means that you allow automatically installed software and its altered configuration of the virtual machine. When you first Vagrant up the machine, it is done automatically.

```
$ vagrant reload --provision
```

Networking Access

In this section, we will set up Vagrant networking so that other authorized guests can access the box. We do so by setting up an Apache web server.

Open the Vagrantfile file and uncomment this line by removing the "#" symbol:

```
# config.vm.network "forwarded_port", guest: 80, host: 8080
```

Before the end of the script, at the section "# Enable provisioning with a shell script. Additional provisioners such as", add the following line:

```
config.vm.provision :shell, path: "bootstrap.sh"
```

Save and close the file. Next, SSH the virtual box and install Apache:

```
$ vagrant ssh
$ sudo apt-get update
$ sudo apt-get install -y apache2
$ exit
```

Set a file named "bootstrap.sh" at the root of the project with the following content:

```
#!/usr/bin/env bash
apt-get update
apt-get install -y apache2
if ! [ -L /var/www ]; then
  rm -rf /var/www
  ln -fs /vagrant /var/www
fi
```

Then reload and provision:

```
$ vagrant reload --provision
```

Now you can navigate to the following URL and see all of the files we are setting up for sharing, since we have a web server up: http://127.0.0.1:8080/. See Figure 9-9:

Index of /

Name	Last modified	Size	Description
Gruntfile-compiled.js	16-Sep-2016 22:56	1.1K	
Gruntfile-compiled.js.map	16-Sep-2016 22:56	1.8K	
Gruntfile.js	16-Sep-2016 22:56	1.0K	
LICENSE	15-Sep-2016 21:24	1.1K	
README.md	15-Sep-2016 21:24	11K	
Vagrantfile	18-Sep-2016 16:48	3.0K	
app/	15-Sep-2016 21:25	-	
bootstrap.sh	18-Sep-2016 16:44	137	
bower.json	15-Sep-2016 21:24	377	
build/	16-Sep-2016 22:48	-	
bundle-compiled.js	17-Sep-2016 02:36	1.5K	
bundle-compiled.js.map	17-Sep-2016 02:36	2.6K	
bundle.js	17-Sep-2016 15:10	1.4K	

Figure 9-9. *Vagrant networking configured and web server up*

HTTP Sharing

In this section, we will share the Vagrant box. Share allow collaboration on your Vagrant environment. Vagrant currently provides three types of sharing—HTTP sharing, SSH sharing, and general sharing— through HashiCorp's Atlas account. Since the people you're sharing with don't need Vagrant installed, it's ideal to share with managers, clients, or just about anyone.

The first step of sharing is creating a free account at https://atlas.hashicorp.com/account/new.

Now that we have an account with Atlas, we need to log in to the account. In the WebStorm command line, type:

```
$ vagrant login
```

The command line will ask for your username and password and will then confirm that you are logged in correctly:

```
Username or Email: [your username]
Password (will be hidden): [your password]
You are now logged in!
```

Now we can share. Type into the WebStorm command line:

```
$ vagrant share
```

You will get a share of information via the command line output:

```
==> default: Creating Vagrant Share session...
    default: Share will be at: spoiled-crocodile-4501
==> default: Your Vagrant Share is running! Name: spoiled-crocodile-4501
==> default: URL: http://spoiled-crocodile-4501.vagrantshare.com
```

You can confirm that the share was successful by looking at your account on the Atlas website. See Figure 9-10.

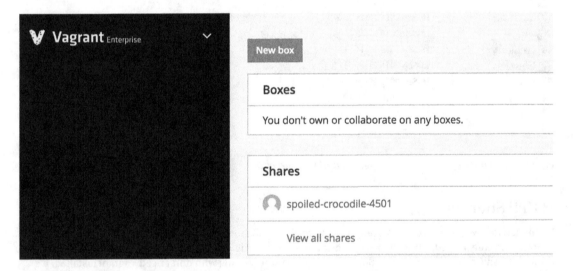

Figure 9-10. *Vagrant site show share*

To connect via the command line, type the following command into the Terminal:

```
$ vagrant connect spoiled-crocodile-4501
```

Note that this name "spoiled-crocodile-4501" will be different for you. Refer to the name in your share from Figure 9-10.

This is what a guest user will see when they connect. To end the session, just type "exit" and "ctrl+c" to stop the connection. You can also navigate to the URL provided when you share (see Figure 9-11):

Index of /

Name	Last modified	Size	Description
Gruntfile-compiled.js	16-Sep-2016 22:56	1.1K	
Gruntfile-compiled.js.map	16-Sep-2016 22:56	1.8K	
Gruntfile.js	16-Sep-2016 22:56	1.0K	
LICENSE	15-Sep-2016 21:24	1.1K	
README.md	15-Sep-2016 21:24	11K	
Vagrantfile	18-Sep-2016 16:48	3.0K	
app/	15-Sep-2016 21:25	-	
bootstrap.sh	18-Sep-2016 16:44	137	
bower.json	15-Sep-2016 21:24	377	
build/	16-Sep-2016 22:48	-	
bundle-compiled.js	17-Sep-2016 02:36	1.5K	
bundle-compiled.js.map	17-Sep-2016 02:36	2.6K	
bundle.js	17-Sep-2016 15:10	1.4K	

Figure 9-11. *Vagrant share via web browser*

Share with SSH Access

In this section, we will set our Vagrant box with SSH access for others to connect. This is useful for pair programming, debugging, and working with quality assurance.

Similar to the way we shared HTTP in the previous section, we can share and provide SSH access to guests. You do so by sharing with the SSH flag:

```
$ vagrant share --ssh
```

To connect, add the SSH flag:

```
$ vagrant connect spoiled-crocodile-4501 --ssh
```

When you share, Vagrant will ask you for a password that you will provide to the guest user for security reasons.

Vagrant can help you ensure that you share your whole project or only part of the project with other members of your team, and can help in the deployment process, which makes it a great tool to add to your arsenal of helpful built script tools.

You can read more about sharing from the Vagrant docs: https://www.vagrantup.com/docs/share/

Provision AngularJS Projects

We have created a basic "bootstrap.sh" file for setting up Apache and installing an entire project for learning purposes. However, for Node.js and AngularJS projects, we want to be able to set the project with the tools needed, such as Grunt, Gulp, npm, Node.js, and Git. We don't want all of our node modules and code downloaded, but we do want them to be installed on each machine. This is why we set a "package.json" file to begin with; it stores all of the modules that the project needs, so we don't need to upload all of them. To achieve this, we can use "Puppet" (not covered in this book), which Vagrant supports, or we can extend our "bootstrap.sh" file. Open the "bootstrap.sh" file we created and paste the following code:

```
#! /bin/bash
if [ ! -f /home/vagrant/isSettingInstalled ]
then
  echo "UPDATING APT-GET"
  apt-get -qq update
  echo "INSTALLING NODE.JS"
  apt-get -qq -y install Node.js
  echo "INSTALLING NPM"
  apt-get -qq -y install npm
  echo "INSTALLING GIT"
  apt-get -qq -y install git

  echo "CLONING CODE"
  cd /home/vagrant
  git clone https://github.com/angular/angular-seed
  cd angular-seed
  git checkout -f step-0

  echo "INSTALLING MODULES"
  sudo npm install
  echo "STARTING NPM"
  sudo npm start

  touch /home/vagrant/isSettingInstalled
  echo "COMPLETE"
else
  echo "SETTINGS ALREADY INSTALLED"
fi
```

With this code, we have created a flag to check whether the installation has already taken place or not. We have named the flag file "isSettingInstalled". We have installed all of the tools we will need via "apt-get," cloned the "angular-seed" project, installed the npm module, and run the npm start command. Instead of setting a box via the command line every time, we can simply connect to Vagrant and be up and running quickly. You can see how powerful Vagrant can be when used to set up environments quickly.

Summary

In this chapter, we focused on build scripts, created a new Node.js module, and installed Browserify and compiled a Browserify bundle file. Then, we used the bundle file, which included the Node.js module, and used that module in a new AngularJS project. We took a look at the new ES6 changes and learned how to utilize it today on any JavaScript engine using Babelify. We learned how to set up Babel in WebStorm and began writing ES6 code, then continued to learn more about Grunt and created a Grunt file with Babel task. Next, we installed Grunt plugs and ran a Babel task. We also created a Grunt task with the ability to Babelify, Browserify, and create a Grunt File Watcher.

We continued with installing Gulp and learned the differences between Grunt and Gulp. We created a Gulp task, installed Gulp plugins, and ran the Gulp tasks. We then looked at the installation of Webpack, created a Webpack config file, and learned how to use a watcher in Webpack. We learned how to use Webpack for transpiling ES6 code and also learned how to use the Webpack CSS loader.

Lastly, we reviewed how to set up a Vagrant VM, installed Vagrant, set a Virtual Machine for sharing access, and set up custom SSH scripts for AngularJS and Node.js projects. Selecting the right tools for the job is all about personal preference, as well as team knowledge and experience; it is an extremely important part of building any app.

In the next chapter we will be covering platform deployment.

CHAPTER 10

■ ■ ■

Platform Deployment

In this chapter, we will be deploying our Node.js and AngularJS applications on production. AngularJS is the front-end side, while Node.js is often used for building the service layer, which can be used by any device, as we have seen throughtout this book. In order to illustrate the process of deploying our app and the service layer to a server or to an application store such as Apple App Store, we would use the Node.js and AngularJS seed projects. We will be covering the same tools we have been covering throughout the book, such as Grunt, Gulp, Browserify, and Webpack, as well as deployment of the Cordova app through PhoneGap and Ionic. Lastly, we will cover the Travis Continuous Integration server to ensure that our code is tested and will continue to work once changes have been committed. Each deployment is different and has specific requirements, so there isn't one basic solution that would fit all projects. However, our goal is to give you the essential tools so you will be able to identify your options and decide for yourself which tools you'd like to use.

Node.js Deployment

To create a Node.js seed project in WebStorm, from the splashscreen, select: "Create New Project" ➤ "Node. js Express App." Name the app "node" in the location input box and complete by selecting "create."

To start the app, select the green "play" button at the top right corner. You should see it in the run that JavaScript used as an entry point: "bin/www." Once you run the project, the console will confirm that the app is running correctly with the following output message:

```
/usr/local/bin/node /Users/eli/Documents/WebStorm/service/bin/www
  service:server Listening on port 3000 +0ms
```

You can confirm that the app is indeed running by navigating to the following URL:

```
http://localhost:3000/.
```

You will see the "Welcome to Express" message (Figure 10-1).

© Elad Elrom 2016
E. Elrom, *Pro MEAN Stack Development*, DOI 10.1007/978-1-4842-2044-3_10

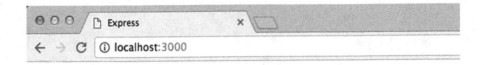

Express

Welcome to Express

Figure 10-1. *Node.js application deployed locally*

Connect to Node.js Ubuntu Server

As you may recall, in Chapter 2 we rolled out an Ubuntu server on AWS and set it up. You can log in here to ensure that the server is still running:

```
https://us-west-2.console.aws.amazon.com/ec2/v2
```

Visit Chapter 2 to set up the server if you have not already. You won't need to use AWS—you can use any Ubuntu server you would like. Just follow the steps listed below.

■ **Note** Remember to terminate the server and/or ensure Amazon is not billing you. The billing home page can be viewed here: `https://console.aws.amazon.com/billing/home`

Once an Ubuntu server is set through Amazon or any other provider, you can access the server using the following command:

```
$ sudo ssh -i key.pem ubuntu@[IP ADDRESS OR DNS]
```

The SSH command uses the user name with the IP address. The user name would be "ubuntu" on AWS and the IP address or public DNS can be found at the Instance description under "instances":

```
https://us-west-2.console.aws.amazon.com/ec2/v2/home#Instances
```

In Chapter 2, we set up easy access to help us connect to the server through an "SSH" command.

We also set up a shortcut to connect us to the server in the Terminal through the ~/.ssh/config. We used the following command:

```
$ ssh api
```

■ **Note** It may have been a while since you've worked on Chapter 2, and your IP address may have changed. Make sure you add the IP address to the security section in the EC2 console: https://us-west-2.console.aws. amazon.com/ec2/v2/home?region=us-west-2#SecurityGroups. For more information, refer back to Chapter 2.

Now that we can access the Ubuntu server again, we want to deploy our Node.js seed app.

Deployment with Grunt

We have already worked with Grunt in previous chapters. As you may recall, we need to first install Grunt locally and install the plugins we will be using:

```
$ npm install grunt --save-dev
$ npm install grunt-shell grunt-open --save-dev
```

The "grunt-shell" plugin provides the ability to run a command line so that "grunt-open" can read the files.

Each deployment is different and would need to be customized to your specific needs; there will not be just one universal solution to fit every single deployment. However, one easy way to deploy our app is to SSH the Ubuntu server, upload the files, and restart Node. A second option would be to check the files into version control and then pull them on the server. We can FTP the server as well, but SSH is a much more secure option.

We will create a task which will SSH into the server and copy the files to the server. We will also create a task that will be able to commit our changes more easily into a Git version control, so that we will have our changes backed up.

Place "Gruntfile.js" at the root of the project. Take a look at the following Grunt file that does just that (Listing 10-1):

Listing 10-1. Gruntfile.js publish Node.js app and commit changes to version control

```
module.exports = function (grunt) {

  grunt.loadNpmTasks('grunt-shell');
  grunt.loadNpmTasks('grunt-open');

  grunt.initConfig({

    /**
     * We read in our `package.json` file so we can access the package name and
     * version.
     */
    pkg: grunt.file.readJSON('package.json'),

    shell: {
      multiple: {
        command: [
          'git add .',
          'git add -u',
          "git commit -m '<%= pkg.version %> -> <%= pkg.commit %>'",
          'git push'
        ].join('&&')
      },
      server_upload: {
        command: 'scp -r -i /[PATH TO key.pem] /Users/[USER]/Documents/WebStormProjects/
        node/* ubuntu@[SERVER IP OR PUBLIC DNS]:/home/ubuntu/www'
      },
      stop_node: {
        command: "ssh -i /[PATH TO key.pem] ubuntu@[SERVER IP OR PUBLIC DNS]  'sudo forever
        stop 0'"
```

251

```
      },
      start_node: {
        command: "ssh -i /[PATH TO key.pem] ubuntu@[SERVER IP OR PUBLIC DNS] 'cd /home/
        ubuntu/www; sudo forever start bin/www'"
      }
    }
});

grunt.registerTask('default', ['shell:multiple', 'shell:server_upload', 'shell:stop_node',
'shell:start_node']);
grunt.registerTask('build', ['shell:server_upload', 'shell:stop_node', 'shell:start_
node']);
grunt.registerTask('node-restart', ['shell:stop_node', 'shell:start_node']);
};
```

■ **Note**   Add your own parameters in the commands in brackets.

Take a look at the code "grunt.loadNpmTasks". It is used to load our plugins. Next, look at our "package.json" file. You may notice that we are expecting the "package.json" file to have a node for version and commit. Version is already included in the "package.json" file, but we need to add an entry for the commit comment. In "package.json," we will add the "commit": "Update" commands as shown below:

```
{
  "name": "angular-seed",
  "commit": "Update",
  "private": true,
  "version": "0.0.0",
  "scripts": {
      "start": "node ./bin/www"
  },
  ...
}
```

"server_upload" is set up to use the "scp" command line, which allows us to do an SSH copy.

The location of the files is set with "/Users/[USER]/Documents/WebStormProjects/node," which is based on the latest WebStorm EAP (3). For this project, we're running the early access preview for WebStorm 2016.3, the upcoming major release of WebStorm at the time of this writing, and you can use these EAP builds with lots of new features for free.

```
https://blog.jetbrains.com/webstorm/2016/08/webstorm-2016-3-early-access-preview/
```

You will have to change the locations to the URLs and server IP or public DNS. We've also set two additional commands to stop and start the server using "forever".

Now, to upload the files, run this command:

```
$ grunt build
```

You will get an error ("scp: /home/ubuntu/www: No such file or directory") if you haven't followed all the steps in Chapter 2 to create the www folder. If you did, you should be able to view our Node.js application here:

```
http://[IP ADDRESS OR PUBLIC DNS]
```

Keep in mind that it may take a while to transfer all these files to the server. You can SSH the Ubuntu server "ssh api" and watch the files being uploaded (Figure 10-2).

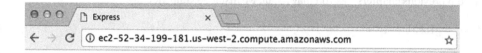

Express
ec2-52-34-199-181.us-west-2.compute.amazonaws.com
Express
Welcome to Express

Figure 10-2. *Node.js application deployed on Ubuntu server*

If you are experiencing any issues, you can SSH the server:

```
$ ssh api
```

Navigate to the Node.js public folder we created back in Chapter 2:

```
ubuntu:~$ cd /home/ubuntu/www
```

Ensure that all of the files are there:

```
ubuntu:~$ ls
```

Next, stop Forever if it's running:

```
ubuntu:~/www$ sudo forever stop 0
```

The server will reply with the following message if Forever is not running:

```
error:   Forever cannot find process with id: 0
```

To run JavaScript through Node.js, run:

```
ubuntu:~/www$ node bin/www
```

To cancel Node.js, run "ctrl + c". Then you can run Forever to keep the connection persistent:

```
ubuntu:~/www$ sudo forever start bin/www
```

Deployment with Gulp

Similar to Grunt, we can use Gulp to deploy our code to the Ubuntu server. Gulp should already be available on your computer from previous chapters—as you may recall, we installed Gulp globally:

```
$ sudo npm install --global gulp-cli
```

Next, we will need to install Gulp locally and add a reference in "package.json" devDependencies by using the save-dev flag:

```
$ npm install gulp gulp-shell --save-dev
```

Now we need to create a Gulp file ("Gulpfile.js") that will include the task of publishing our code. Take a look at the content of the Gulp file:

Listing 10-2. Gulpfile.js deployment of Node.js seed project to Ubuntu server

```
var gulp  = require('gulp');
var shell = require('gulp-shell');

gulp.task('server_upload', shell.task([
    'echo "CLEAN OLD"',
    'ssh -i /[PATH TO key.pem] buntu@[IP OR PUBLIC DNS] "rm -rf /home/ubuntu/www; mkdir /
    home/ubuntu/www"',
    'echo "START UPLOAD"',
    'scp -r -i /[PATH TO key.pem] /[PATH TO PROJECT]/bin ubuntu@[IP OR PUBLIC DNS]:/home/
    ubuntu/www/bin',
    'scp -r -i /[PATH TO key.pem] /[PATH TO PROJECT]/public ubuntu@[IP OR PUBLIC DNS]:/home/
    ubuntu/www/public',
    'scp -r -i /[PATH TO key.pem] /[PATH TO PROJECT]/routes ubuntu@[IP OR PUBLIC DNS]:/home/
    ubuntu/www/routes',
    'scp -r -i /[PATH TO key.pem] /[PATH TO PROJECT]/views ubuntu@[IP OR PUBLIC DNS]:/home/
    ubuntu/www/views',
    'scp -r -i /[PATH TO key.pem] /[PATH TO PROJECT]/*.js ubuntu@[IP OR PUBLIC DNS]:/home/
    ubuntu/www/',
    'scp -r -i /[PATH TO key.pem] /[PATH TO PROJECT]/package.json ubuntu@[IP OR PUBLIC
    DNS]:/home/ubuntu/www/package.json',
    'echo "COPY COMPLETE"',
    'ssh -i /[PATH TO key.pem] ubuntu@[IP OR PUBLIC DNS] "cd /home/ubuntu/www; npm
    install"',
    'echo "NPM INSTALL COMPLETE"',
    'ssh -i /[PATH TO key.pem] ubuntu@[IP OR PUBLIC DNS] "forever stopall; sudo killall
    node; ps axl | grep node; forever list"',
    'echo "KILL NODE"',
    'ssh -i /[PATH TO key.pem] ubuntu@[IP OR PUBLIC DNS] "forever start /home/ubuntu/www/
    bin/www"',
    'echo "START NODE"',
    'open http://[IP OR PUBLIC DNS]'
]));

gulp.task('default', ['server_upload']);
```

Gulp-shell provides us with a plugin so that we can type commands just as we've done in the Terminal; it is similar to the Grunt-shell plugin. We will delete the old code from the Ubuntu server, uploading all the files we need. Notice that we are not loading all of the files in this example. We purposely did not upload the "node_modules" folder, since it's not necessary. We keep the reference to the version and node modules we will be using in our package.json, and once we are done uploading all the files to the server, we will be using the "npm install" command, which will install all of the node modules on the Ubuntu server.

Next, we want to stop node from running. To do so, we need to use the following commands:

```
ubuntu$ forever stopall
ubuntu$ sudo killall node
ubuntu$ ps axl | grep node
ubuntu$ forever list
```

"Forever stop all" stops any "forever" service that may be running. "killall node" will ensure that all of the Node.js apps have stopped. We can then confirm all of the Node.js applications by running a "ps axl | grep node" command. "forever list" should not show sign of any forever tasks currently running.

We can now start Node.js again using this command:

```
ubuntu$ sudo forever start /home/ubuntu/www/bin/www
```

Lastly, we will open our browser with the Ubuntu server URL so we can ensure that it's up and running as expected.

```
$ open http://[IP OR PUBLIC DNS]
```

Notice that we are repeating all of these server and local definitions many times with these commands. We can refactor the code by adding an object "config" that will hold the variables we will be using, so we can simply change our config object to reflect the changes. See Listing 10-3.

Listing 10-3. Gulpfile.js

```
var gulp  = require('gulp');
var shell = require('gulp-shell');

var config = {
    key: '/[PATH TO KEY]/key.pem',
    server_user: 'ubuntu',
    ip_dns: '[IP OR PUBLIC DNS]',
    server_home: '/home/ubuntu/www',
    project_home: '/[LOCAL PROJECT]'
};

gulp.task('server_upload', shell.task([
    'echo "CLEAN OLD"' ,
    'ssh -i ' + config.key + ' ' + config.server_user + '@' + config.ip_dns + ' "rm -rf ' +
    config.server_home + '; mkdir ' + config.server_home + '"',
    'echo "START UPLOAD"',
    'scp -r -i ' + config.key + ' ' + config.project_home + '/bin ' + config.server_user +
    '@' + config.ip_dns + ':' + config.server_home + '/bin',
    'scp -r -i ' + config.key + ' ' + config.project_home + '/public ' + config.server_user
    + '@' + config.ip_dns + ':' + config.server_home + '/public',
```

```
        'scp -r -i ' + config.key + ' ' + config.project_home + '/routes ' + config.server_user
        + '@' + config.ip_dns + ':' + config.server_home + '/routes',
        'scp -r -i ' + config.key + ' ' + config.project_home + '/views ' + config.server_user +
        '@' + config.ip_dns + ':' + config.server_home + '/views',
        'scp -r -i ' + config.key + ' ' + config.project_home + '/*.js ' + config.server_user +
        '@' + config.ip_dns + ':' + config.server_home + '/',
        'scp -r -i ' + config.key + ' ' + config.project_home + '/package.json ' + config.
        server_user + '@' + config.ip_dns + ':' + config.server_home + '/package.json',
        'echo "COPY COMPLETE"',
        'ssh -i ' + config.key + ' ' + config.server_user + '@' + config.ip_dns + ' "cd ' +
        config.server_home + '; npm install"',
        'echo "NPM INSTALL COMPLETE"',
        'ssh -i ' + config.key + ' ' + config.server_user + '@' + config.ip_dns + ' "forever
        stopall; sudo killall node; ps axl | grep node; forever list"',
        'echo "KILL NODE"',
        'ssh -i ' + config.key + ' ' + config.server_user + '@' + config.ip_dns + ' "forever
        start ' + config.server_home + '/bin/www"',
        'echo "START NODE"',
        'open http://' + config.ip_dns + ''
]));
```

```
gulp.task('default', ['server_upload']);
```

Since we've set the task as the default task, all we'll have to do is run:

```
$ gulp
```

In our example, we are not utilizing the full functionality of Gulp, such as streaming and watching for changes, so the code is somewhat similar to Grunt. However, you may notice that placing variables in Gulp is really just writing JavaScript code. Instead of utilizing tokens as we have done with Grunt, we are using "<%= pkg.version %>". Even in a simplified example, you can see the advantages of using Gulp.

AngularJS Deployment

Just as we've done with Node.js, we will create a seed application in WebStorm and deploy the application with Grunt, Gulp, Browserify, and Webpack.

Close your "node" project and create an AngularJS seed project.

1. In the WebStorm splashpage, select "Create New Project" ➤ "AngularJS" and name the project "angular" ➤ "Create." Select "New Window" to view both projects side by side.

2. Open the WebStorm Terminal window (bottom left corner) and run these two commands:

    a. $ npm install

    b. $ npm start

3. To view the project, open up a browser client:

    a. open http://localhost:8000

The browser opens up with the seed application—see Figure 10-3.

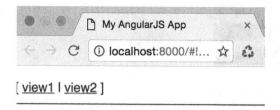

[view1 | view2]

This is the partial for view 1.

Angular seed app: v0.1

Figure 10-3. AngularJS seed project deployed locally

When it comes to deploying your AngularJS app, there are many options to choose from. You may deploy your application on different web servers that serve HTML content, such as nginx or Linux.

Heroku is a popular paid platform that offers a minimal Express and Node.js script to publish your AngularJS front-end code. Additionally, you can deploy your pages on Amazon S3 bucket (free for the first year) or even on GitHub Pages for free.

As you may recall from Chapter 2, we created a Linux server (see "Start a Linux server"). This server can be used to deploy our static front-end AngularJS pages, as well as for other purposes.

Log in to Amazon: https://us-west-2.console.aws.amazon.com/console/home

Once the Linux server is set up and we have configured an SSH shortcut by adding our host information inside the "~/.ssh/config" file, all we have to do to connect is call:

$ ssh app

Next, to install LAMP, type the following commands on the Linux server:

```
[ec2-user@ip] $ sudo yum update -y
[ec2-user@ip] $ sudo yum install -y httpd24 php56 mysql55-server php56-mysqlnd
[ec2-user@ip] $ sudo service httpd start
[ec2-user@ip] $ sudo chkconfig httpd on
```

And you can confirm Linux is running correctly by visiting your IP address or public DNS (see figure 10-4):

```
[ec2-user@ip] $ cd /var/www/html
```

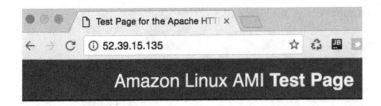

Figure 10-4. *Linux server running on Apache*

If you recall from Chapter 2, we previously edited the Linux " ~/.bashrc" file with shortcuts, so we can type "$ cdr" to navigate to the public root directory where we will deploy our application: "/var/www/html"

```
[ec2-user@ip] $ sudo vim index.html
```

Type "i" in vim to insert content, and then type:

```
hello world
```

To close and save vim, type "Escape + : + wq + Enter" (as you may recall from previous chapters). You can confirm your changes by refreshing your browser (see Figure 10-5).

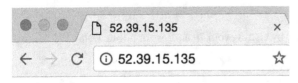

hello world

Figure 10-5. *Linux server running on Apache with "hello world"*

Web Deployment with Grunt

Now that we have a Linux server running and a seed AngularJS application added locally, we can upload the app with a Grunt deployment script. Create a Grunt file:

```
$ npm install --save-dev grunt
$ npm install grunt-shell --save-dev

$ touch Gruntfile.js
```

Add the following to Gruntfile.js in the project's root directory:

```
module.exports = function (grunt) {

    grunt.loadNpmTasks('grunt-shell');

    grunt.initConfig({

        shell: {
            cleanup: {
                command: "ssh -i /[PATH TO KEY]]/key.pem ec2-user@[IP OR PUBLIC DNS] 'sudo
                rm -rf /var/www/html; sudo mkdir /var/www/html; sudo chown ec2-user /var/
                www/html'"
            },
            server_upload: {
                command: 'scp -r -i /[PATH TO KEY]/key.pem /[PROJECT LOCATION]/angular/app/*
                ec2-user@[IP OR PUBLIC DNS]:/var/www/html/'
            }

        }
    });

    grunt.registerTask('default', ['shell:cleanup', 'shell:server_upload']);
};
```

Run the default Grunt command:

```
$ grunt
```

259

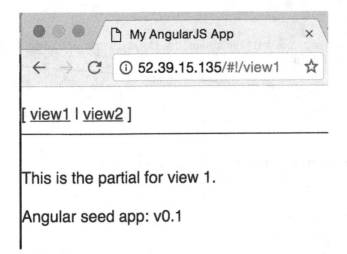

Figure 10-6. *AngularJS seed deployed on Linux server*

Web Deployment with Gulp

Deploying our AngularJS app with Gulp can be done in the same way as our Node.js application. In Gulp, we can SSH to the Linux server to clear up and then "scp" our files over to the Linux server (see Listing 10-4).

Listing 10-4. Gulpfile.js

```
var gulp  = require('gulp');
var shell = require('gulp-shell');

gulp.task('server_upload', shell.task([
    "ssh -i key.pem ec2-user@[IP ADDRESS] 'sudo rm -rf /var/www/html; sudo mkdir /var/www/
    html; sudo chown ec2-user /var/www/html'",
    'scp -r -i key.pem /[PROJECT]/angular/app/* ec2-user@[IP ADDRESS]:/var/www/html/'
]));

gulp.task('default', ['server_upload']);
```

However, in a more realistic application, we will want to do more than simply move our files. A full working application often includes the following:

1. **Minification and Uglified:** removing unnecessary characters from your code without changing the functionality of your code; compressing your code and mangling (obfuscating) names

2. **JSHint / ESLint**: Think of a code review. Running your code through JSHint / ESLint can help identify potential errors.

3. **Browserify**: As we saw in Chapter 9, using Browserify will allow us to bundle our modules together so we can "require" modules.

4. **Watch**: We often want to watch for changes and update our local instance. I covered this in Chapter 9, when we used Babel. The watch can be used to automatically deploy if we want it to.

5. **LESS / SASS Support**: give CSS superpowers, preprocessing & compatible with CSS, it adds features such as variables, partials, and Mixins.

There is so much more—indeed, Grunt has plugins for all of these tasks. You can also add each task, but utilizing Gulp can help streamline this process. Let's take a closer look.

We need Browserify locally:

```
$ npm install browserify --save-dev
```

Next, we need to install all of the Gulp plugins that we will be using:

```
$ npm install gulp-browserify gulp-concat gulp-jshint gulp-uglify pump jshint --save-dev
```

Now, we need to create a "Gulpfile.js" and parse. See Listing 10-5.

Listing 10-5. Gulpfile.js to boundle with Gulp

```
var gulp  = require('gulp'),
    shell = require('gulp-shell'),
    jshint = require('gulp-jshint'),
    browserify = require('gulp-browserify'),
    concat = require('gulp-concat'),
    uglify = require('gulp-uglify'),
    pump = require('pump');

gulp.task('jshint', function() {
    gulp.src('./app/*.js')
        .pipe(jshint())
        .pipe(jshint.reporter('default'));
});

gulp.task('browserify', function() {
    gulp.src(['app/entry.js'])
        .pipe(browserify({
            insertGlobals: true,
            debug: true
        }))
        .pipe(concat('bundle.js'))
        .pipe(gulp.dest('app'));
});

gulp.task('compress', function (cb) {
    pump([
            gulp.src('app/bundle.js'),
            uglify(),
            gulp.dest('app')
```

```
        ],
        cb
    );
});

gulp.task('watch', ['jshint'], function() {
    gulp.watch(['app/*.js', 'app/*/*.js'],[
        'jshint',
        'browserify'
    ]);
});

gulp.task('server_upload', shell.task([
    "ssh -i key.pem ec2-user@[ip] 'sudo rm -rf /var/www/html; sudo mkdir /var/www/html; sudo
    chown ec2-user /var/www/html'",
    'scp -r -i key.pem [project location]/angular/app/* ec2-user@[IP]:/var/www/html/'
]));

gulp.task('default', ['jshint', 'browserify', 'compress']);
gulp.task('deploy', ['browserify', 'compress', 'server_upload']);
```

'jshint' will report and lint suggestions in our code to ensure that it's written according to our specs. "Browserify" will browse through our entry.js file, which we will create. In our entry.js file, we want to reference the AngularJS files we will be using, and then Browserify will take over and extract any scripts needed.

Create the following file ("app/entry.js") and reference all of the AngularJS files:

```
'use strict';

var angular = require('./bower_components/angular/angular.js');
require('./bower_components/angular-route/angular-route.js');
require('./view1/view1.js');
require('./view2/view2.js');
require('./components/version/interpolate-filter.js');
require('./components/version/version-directive.js');
require('./components/version/version.js');
require('./app.js');
```

The "compress" task will uglify our files to reduce our file size and remove any extra code. We can utilize Gulp with the default task:

```
$ gulp
```

Gulp builds our bundle file. Remember to update the "index.html" file and comment out all references to the AngularJS JavaScript, since Browserify will bundle all of them for us. We only need: " <script src="bundle.js"></script>" (see below).

```
<!-- <script src="app.js"></script>
<script src="view1/view1.js"></script>
<script src="view2/view2.js"></script>
<script src="components/version/version.js"></script>
```

```
<script src="components/version/version-directive.js"></script>
<script src="components/version/interpolate-filter.js"></script> -->

<script src="bundle.js"></script>
```

We can also use the "watch" task to have jshint watch for any changes and build our bundle file:

```
$ gulp watch
```

Lastly, we can deploy the code to our Linux server:

```
$ gulp deploy
```

Confirm that the code is present by refreshing the browser and checking that the bundle file is in fact still there (see Figure 10-7).

Figure 10-7. *bundle.js file deployed on Linux server*

We have deployed "bundle.js" to the app folder, but when things start to get complex, it's wise to deploy it to a distribution folder so we can know what's on the server and what is local.

■ **Note**   You can create your own directory structure or deploy anywhere you want final files, but many times you will see the final build in a folder called: "dist." This is considered best practice by many developers.

Web Deployment with Webpack

As you recall, in Chapter 9, we covered Webpack and installed Webpack globally via npm:

```
$ sudo npm install webpack -g
```

We used Webpack to watch for changes and transpile ES6 Code, and we used the Webpack CSS Loader, all without using Grunt or Gulp.

To bundle using Webpack, we will install two plugins: "webpack" to get out-of-the-box functionality such as optimization and "webpack-shell-plugin" to allow us to upload files to the server.

```
$ npm install --save-dev webpack webpack-shell-plugin
```

Now that we have our plugins installed, we must create a "webpack.config.js" file and write the code below—see Listing 10-6.

Listing 10-6. webpack.config.js to bundle and optimize AngularJS code

```
var WebpackShellPlugin = require('webpack-shell-plugin'),
    webpack = require('webpack');

module.exports = {
    entry: './app/entry.js',
    output: {
        filename: './app/bundle.js'
    },
    plugins: [
        new WebpackShellPlugin({
            onBuildStart:[
                "ssh -i /[PATH TO key.pem] ec2-user@[IP ADDRESS] 'sudo rm -rf /var/www/html;
                sudo mkdir /var/www/html; sudo chown ec2-user /var/www/html'"
            ],
            onBuildEnd:[
                'scp -r -i /[PATH TO key.pem] /[LOCATION OF APP]/app/* ec2-user@[IP ADDRESS
                OR PUBLIC DNS]:/var/www/html/',
                'open localhost:8000',
                'open http://[IP OR PUBLIC DNS]'
            ]}),
        new webpack.optimize.UglifyJsPlugin({
            compress: {
                warnings: false
            },
            include: /\.min\.js$/,
            minimize: true
        })
    ]
};
```

We set the entry file "app/entry.js," which is the same file as before. It includes all of the required libraries for the AngularJS project. We also set the output folder; in our test application, it will be "app/bundle.js." WebpackShellPlugin is set to run SSH script "onBuildStart," which we are cleaning and removing from the HTML folder on the server and "onBuildStart", which we will be using with "scp" to SSH copy our files to the server, just as we've done in Gulp:

```
scp -r -i /[PATH TO key.pem] /[LOCATION OF APP]/app/* ec2-user@[IP ADDRESS OR PUBLIC DNS]:/
var/www/html/'
```

264

Lastly, we're utilizing the UglifyJsPlugin built-in plugin to optimize the bode. What's neat about Webpack implementation is that, as you may recall, we needed six plugins in Gulp to get the job done, and in Webpack we only need to use a single shell plugin; you can see the appeal.

AngularJS App Deployment

We installed XCode in Chapter 1 from here: `https://developer.apple.com/xcode/download/`

Additionally, in Chapter 4, we covered iOS deployment on a browser and an emulator to simulate usage on an actual device. In this section, we will provide you with the necessary tools to submit your application to the iOS store.

Note that, to deploy your application on iOS, you will need to purchase a Development Certificate from Apple through their Apple Developer Program: `https://developer.apple.com/account`.

In Chapter 4, we covered Cordova, PhoneGap, and Ionic Cordova distributions. Go ahead and download the Android SDK if you have not done so already: `https://developer.android.com/studio/index.html`.

The Android SDK is a JetBrain custom installation of IntelliJ (same as WebStorm) that gives Android developers an IDE. We won't need to use this, since we won't be building our app natively.

Be sure to export the path of the SDK folder:

```
$ export ANDROID_HOME="[PATH TO ANDROID SDK]/sdk/"
```

Ours looks like this:

```
$ export ANDROID_HOME=/Users/Eli/Library/Android/sdk
```

You will also need to have Java SDK installed. To make sure it's installed, type:

```
$ java -version
```

If you don't have Java SDK installed, you can download it from here: `http://www.oracle.com/technetwork/java/javase/downloads/index.html`

Cordova Distribution makes it extremely easy to deploy your app onto different devices. In the following section, we will deploy our app to iOS, Android, and Windows mobile.

PhoneGap Deployment

PhoneGap is a popular Cordova Distribution that allows deployment of our JavaScript code without installing native code or actually opening our application in any third-party environment, as opposed to Cordova or Ionic, where we would need XCode and Android SDK. We covered this information in Chapter 4.

As you may also recall from Chapter 4, we installed the PhoneGap desktop app from: `https://github.com/PhoneGap/PhoneGap-app-desktop/releases`

As well as the CLI via npm: "sudo npm install -g PhoneGap@latest". Additionally, in Chapter 4, we installed the PhoneGap mobile app, available for each device. We want to take the app we've created for development and actually be able to submit the file to application stores.

We will be creating a seed project to work with. In WebStorm, create a new project by going to "File" ➤ "New" ➤ "Project..." and selecting "PhoneGap/Cordova app." Name your app "myapp" and hit "create."

Deployment with PhoneGap

To view the developer's build in a browser, type in the WebStorm Terminal:

```
$ PhoneGap serve
```

You should receive the following message from the Terminal output:

```
Phone gap sets a server and reply with the ip address and port number such as:
[PhoneGap] listening on 192.168.1.65:3000
```

The PhoneGap seed project comes with an out-of-the-box browser platform deployment. You can see a browser folder under Platforms ➤ "myapp/platforms/browser." To see the app deployed, open your browser in the IP address and port provided to you in the Terminal output—see Figure 10-8.

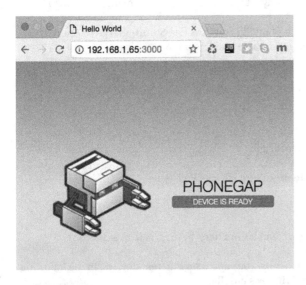

Figure 10-8. *PhoneGap deployed on a web browser.*

To shut down the server, hit "control + c" in the WebStorm Terminal.

To view the developer built on your device, such as Android, iOS, or Blackberry, you will need to have the "PhoneGap developer" app. As you may recall from Chapter 4, you can download the app directly onto your devices from your device's app store. You can find the app under the keywords "PhoneGap Developer." The app will use socket connection on your network to download the files and deploy them.

Build Your App on Different Platforms

To install our app on other platforms, rather than the browser, all we have to do is add a platform and Cordova will compile the code through Cordova. Then, we can deploy the code on our devices. Here is a handy command to use to find out what platforms are supported by PhoneGap:

```
$ PhoneGap platform list
```

This command will output the installed and available platforms in the Terminal. See what we are receiving at the time of writing:

```
Installed platforms:
  browser 4.1.0
Available platforms:
  amazon-fireos ~3.6.3 (deprecated)
  android ~5.1.1
  blackberry10 ~3.8.0
  firefoxos ~3.6.3
  ios ~4.1.0
  osx ~4.0.1
  webos ~3.7.0
```

To install iOS or any other platform, all we have to do is add the platform we want. For example, we will add iOS and Android:

```
$ PhoneGap platform add ios
$ PhoneGap platform add android
```

We can confirm that the platforms were added by checking to see if they were added to the platform folder: "myapp/platforms/ ." See Figure 10-9.

Figure 10-9. *iOS and Android platforms added in PhoneGap*

To serve the app again on different platforms, just type again:

```
$ PhoneGap serve
```

Open up the "PhoneGap Developer" app on your device to view the app. You will have an option to connect to the application via socket and view the app on your device. See Figure 10-10.

Figure 10-10. *Connect to PhoneGap deployed application on device*

You can also use the PhoneGap desktop app we installed in Chapter 4, downloaded from here: `http://docs.phonegap.com/getting-started/1-install-phonegap/desktop/`

To start and stop the server anytime you want, instead of using the command line, all you have to do is drop your PhoneGap folder into the PhoneGap desktop application—see Figure 10-11.

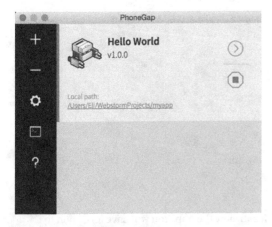

Figure 10-11. *Starting PhoneGap server through PhoneGap desktop app*

So far, we have deployed our app to our devices as testing/developer built. When you are ready to deploy your app to any of the PhoneGap available device stores, PhoneGap offers free deployment for up to one app on a private repo, or unlimited deployment for open source apps. Visit Adobe's page to find out more about their pricing policy:

```
https://build.PhoneGap.com/plans/free-adobeid
```

The deployment process is where PhoneGap really shines, since it allows production deployment without the hassle of actually dealing with native code, installing SDKs, or maintaining compatibility. Create a profile to take a look:

```
https://build.PhoneGap.com/
```

Once you create an account and log in, you can upload your PhoneGap project and generate IPA (iOS), APK (Android) or an XAP (Windows Mobile) files, which can be deployed to device stores. See Figure 10-12.

Figure 10-12. *Building application on multiple devices using PhoneGap*

You will need to create a key and have certification on devices, but once you create a key, you will be able to easily build and download files that you can submit to be deployed on multiple platforms. This process is easy and will make the deployment process painless.

Ionic Deployment

Similar to PhoneGap, Ionic provides tools to build and deploy your application, which is easier than using the out-of-the-box Cordova platform. Close the PhoneGap project we've created ("myapp" project), since we will now be creating an Ionic project.

Creating an Ionic Project

Keep in mind that you will need to have Ionic and Cordova installed. If you haven't done so already, install these tools globally via npm:

```
$ sudo npm install -g cordova ionic
$ npm install -g cordova
```

Next, navigate to the location of your WebStorm projects:

```
$ cd /[LOCATION OF WEBSTORM PROJECTS]
```

Ionic provides three types of seed projects: "blank," "tabs," or "sidemenu. For our example, we'll pick the sidemenu seed and, as the name suggests, the app will have sidemenu built in.

```
$ ionic start myIonicApp sidemenu
```

During the command line installation, you will be asked if you want to "Create an Ionic Platform account to add features like User Authentication, Push Notifications, Live Updating, iOS builds, and more?"

Select "Y" if you don't already have an account and want to create one. This will redirect you to the Ionic signup page:

```
https://apps.ionic.io/signup
```

Set Up Ionic Project in WebStorm

To import the project we've created, in WebStorm, select "Open" and navigate to the location of "myIonicApp" and select "open."

Add Platforms

Just as with PhoneGap, you can see the list of supported platforms and install platforms for iOS, Android, and browser:

```
$ ionic platform list
$ ionic platform add browser
$ ionic platform add ios
$ ionic platform add android
```

Just as with PhoneGap, you can confirm that these platforms were added by checking the "myIonicApp/platforms/" folder.

Deploy Development Build

Also, as with PhoneGap deployment, we simply need to type the serve command:

```
$ ionic serve
```

This creates a server and will deploy our app. The browser opens up automatically for us with our app (see Figure 10-13).

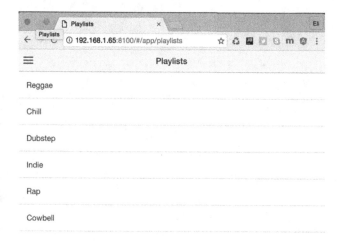

Figure 10-13. *Ionic deployed on a browser*

Build and Emulate on iOS

As we've mentioned, you will need to have Xcode installed for the build and emulators to work. To build for iOS, run the following commands in the Terminal:

```
$ ionic build ios
$ ionic emulate ios
```

Or simply type:

```
$ ionic run ios
```

Note that the first time you run this command, it may take a few minutes, but eventually the Xcode emulator will open up with our app. See Figure 10-14.

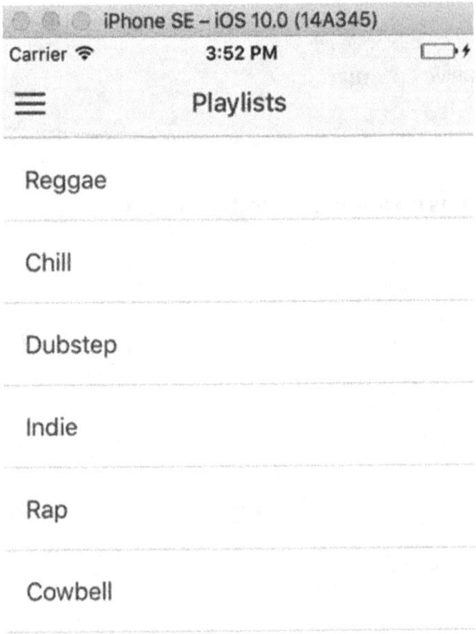

Figure 10-14. Ionic app running on iOS 10.0 emulator

You need to install additional tools to generate a build and target the SDK you have installed. To find out what's installed on your box, open the Android SDK Manager. This depends on your installation, the default settings should install the Android SDK Manager here(see Figure 10-15):

```
$/Users/[USER]/Library/Android/sdk/tools/android
```

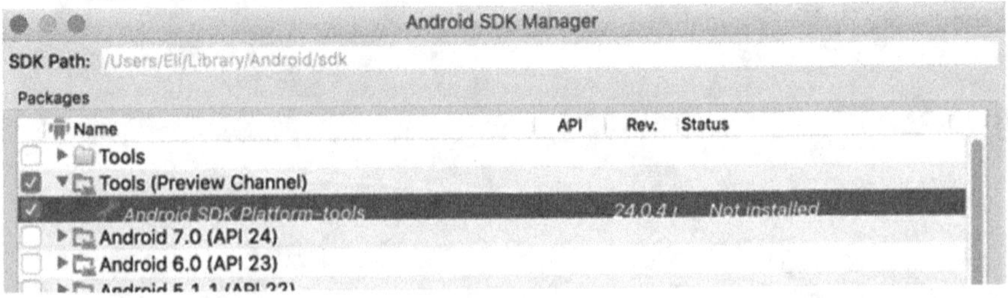

Figure 10-15. Android SDK Manager

Make sure that you have the latest "Android SDK Platform-tools" and "Android SDK Build-tools." Also, you should check out which SDK platforms are already installed (see Figure 10-15).

These two files need to point to a target you have installed:

```
platforms/Android/CordovaLib/project.properties
platforms/Android/project.properties
```

On our machine, the Android SDK was set to 23, but we did not have SDK 23 installed (only 24), so we changed the files to the following:

```
target=android-24
```

Failure to have the latest SDKs build tools and SDK platform and tools will output the following error code in the Terminal:

```
Hint: Open the SDK manager by running: /Users/[USER]/Library/Android/sdk/tools/android
```

You will require:

```
1. "SDK Platform" for android-23
2. "Android SDK Platform-tools (latest)
3. "Android SDK Build-tools" (latest)
```

Now you can run the following command:

```
$ ionic build android
```

You can connect an Android device and deploy your app directly onto the device. Additionally, to emulate Android, you need to install an emulator on your computer. Otherwise, you will receive the following error message in the Terminal:

```
Error: No emulator images (avds) found.
```

To open the Android virtual device emulator menu, type in the command line:

```
$ /Users/[USER]/Library/Android/sdk/tools/android avd
```

At the Android Virtual Device (AVD) menu, you can select an emulator to run your application on. See Figure 10-16.

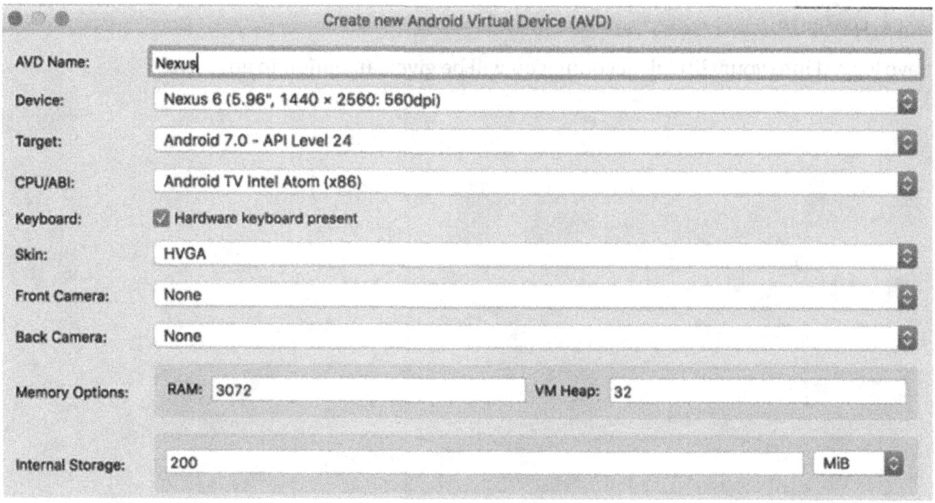

Figure 10-16. *Android Virtual Device (AVD*

Once the emulator is installed and running correctly, you can run the application on the emulator:

```
$ ionic run android
```

From here, you can now easily deploy on Android and iOS.
Use the release commands to create APK and IPA files:

```
$ ionic build --release android
$ ionic build ios --release
```

You will need to have certificates for both the Apple App Store and Google Play; visit the Ionic publishing page for instructions:

```
http://ionicframework.com/docs/guide/publishing.html
```

As you can see, deploying and publishing an app is similar in PhoneGap and Ionic, since they are both based on Cordova. Both will provide out-of-the-box deployment tools, so you won't need to create your own.

Continuous Integration with Travis CI

If you have ever dealt with Continuous Integration (CI), you know that it can be very time consuming and frustrating at times. It's an essential part of the deployment process to be able to recognize if the changes committed broke the build.

An easy way to test and deploy open source code is by using Travis CI. Travis offers free continuous integration for open source projects as well as inexpensive paid options for private repositories.

Authenticate Travis CI

To utilized Travis CI, you need to have an account with GitHub, and the account must authorize Travis. To do so, visit Travis' authorization page:

```
https://travis-ci.com/auth
```

Once you have logged into your GitHub account, you will be given an option to authorize (see Figure 10-17).

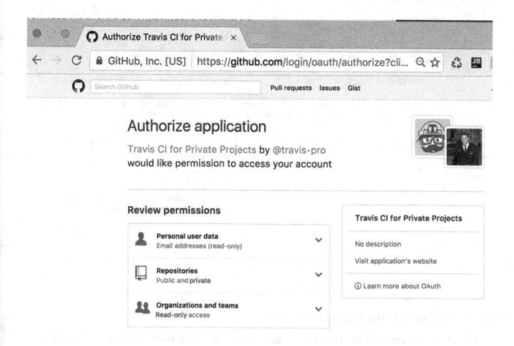

Figure 10-17. Travis CI GitHub authorization

Integration of Travis CI and GitHub Projects

Next, you want to install an integration between Travis and the GitHub repo. This can be done by navigating to the settings page on GitHub:

```
https://github.com/[USER]/[REPO NAME]/settings/installations
```

If you don't have a repo, you can just create a new repo on GitHub to experiment. Log in to GitHub, and under the GitHub home page, you will see a link called "new repository."

Once you are on the settings page, select "Integrations & services" and add "Travis CI" as a service. See Figure 10-18:

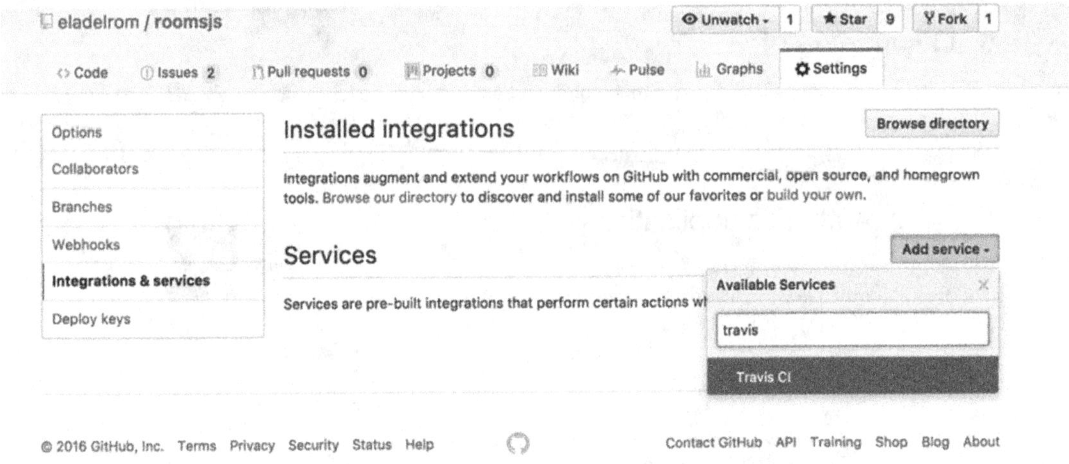

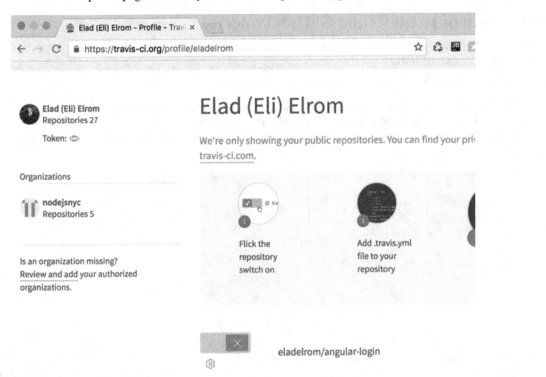

Figure 10-18. *Service integration of Travis and GitHub repo*

Next, you will be redirected on GitHub to set the "Automatic configuration from Travis CI" in "Services"
➤ "Add Travis CI" page or redirect to your profile page on Travis: https://travis-ci.org/profile/[USER]
The Travis profile page will allow you to activate repos—see Figure 10-19.

Figure 10-19. *Activate repos on Travis profile page*

Customize and Configure Travis CI

You can create a ".travis.yml" file where you can configure and customize the build. For instance, you can set the language of your repo so that Travis will know what to expect:

```
language: node_js
node_js:
  - 4.4.7
```

More options regarding customizing your build can be found on Travis' website: https://docs. travis-ci.com/user/customizing-the-build.

We can now watch the build and ensure that it passes on Travis: https://travis-ci.org/[USER]/ [REPO]/settings

See Figure 10-20.

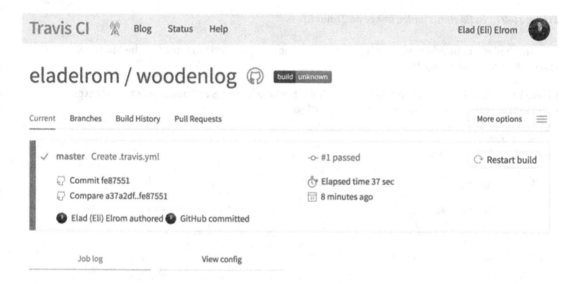

Figure 10-20. *Travis CI repo status page*

Generating a Status Badge on Travis CI

On the Travis page, you can find a status badge image, which you can use to display the status of your repo. Just click the "build" badge and you will receive an option to get a status image URL. See Figure 10-21.

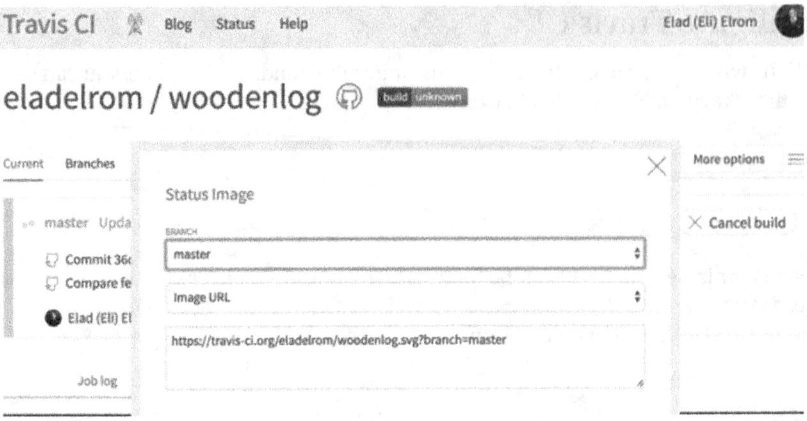

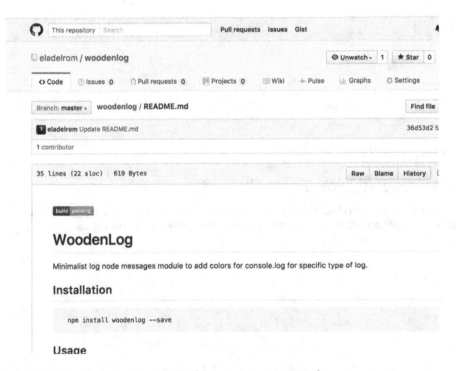

Figure 10-21. *Build status badge image on Travis CI*

This badge can be added to your "README.md" page on your GitHub repo. Use the Markdown language to create an image tag:

```
[![Build Status](https://travis-ci.org/eladelrom/woodenlog.svg?branch=master)](https://
travis-ci.org/eladelrom/woodenlog.svg?branch=master)
```

See Figure 10-22.

Figure 10-22. *Displaying Travis CI build status image on GitHub repo*

As you can see, we have set a continuous integration to test our code automatically upon change to ensure that it's still working as expected.

Summary

In this chapter, we covered platform deployment and extended our knowledge of working with previously used tools. We created and deployed a Node.js app on the Ubuntu server with Grunt and Gulp, and we learned how to restart the app with Forever and automate the process. Additionally, we created an AngularJS project and deployed the project to the Web using Grunt and Gulp on a Linux server. We learned more about the different deployment techniques used to streamline the process and create one bundle file. We also deployed using Webpack, eliminating the Grunt and Gulp plugins, for easy bundling and deployment of our AngularJS app.

We then moved to mobile deployment. We set up a PhoneGap mobile app in WebStorm and took a look at PhoneGap and the process of deploying our app to iOS, Android, and Windows Mobile, without the need for native SDKs installed on our box.

We created an Ionic seed project and looked into the Ionic deployment of the mobile app process. Lastly, we covered Continuous Integration with Travis CI and were able to test our app and create a status badge on GitHub.

"Congratulations!! You have completed the entire book and should be proud of yourself, because you have acquired much knowledge and improved yourself. I would love to hear your feedback about your experience and any projects you may be working on. You can reach out to me at http://www.linkedin.com/in/eladelrom or http://twitter.com/EliScripts, looking forward hearing from you!"

Index

■ W

Webmasters, 217–219
Webpack
  Config file creation, 237
  CSS loader, 239–240
  ES6 code, 238–239
  installation, 236–237
  watcher, 237
WebStorm Run Terminal results, 73

Woodenlog API, 72
Woodenlog error message, WebStorm, 63
Woodenlog module, mocha, 65–66
Workbench MySQL connection, 46

■ X, Y, Z

Xcode, 1, 24–25, 80, 81, 86, 89, 99, 265, 271
XMLHttpRequest (XHR) services, 129

Get the eBook for only $4.99!

Why limit yourself?

Now you can take the weightless companion with you wherever you go and access your content on your PC, phone, tablet, or reader.

Since you've purchased this print book, we are happy to offer you the eBook for just $4.99.

Convenient and fully searchable, the PDF version enables you to easily find and copy code—or perform examples by quickly toggling between instructions and applications.

To learn more, go to http://www.apress.com/us/shop/companion or contact support@apress.com.

Printed in the United States
By Bookmasters